CURRENCY 6.0

The Essence, Principles and Reconstruction of Money

Hailin Zhou

DEDICATION

All the qualities needed to build a perfect world are just common sense and conscience of humanity. I regard this book as my gift to humanity.

CONTENTS

Definition

Currency: The most widely accepted products in the market. The transaction value is its core value, including all the media used for commodity transactions.

Material Currency: Goods that are widely accepted based on their natural attributes.

Receipt Currency: A storage credential for Material Currency, which is obtained by depositing Material Currency in a store.

Promise Currency: The holder does not have actual storage of Material Currency, and the storage credential is lent to the borrower by a recognized Material Currency storage depositor. The storage provider promises that the holder of the storage credential can claim payment of Material Currency at any time.

Contract Currency: Similarly, a storage credential lent by a recognized Material Currency depositor to a borrower. However, the original Material Currency depositor explicitly informs the holder that they will no longer pay any Material Currency to the holder. It can be understood as a " Empty Storage Credential ". Usually, the current legal currency in various countries is Contract Currency, which is commonly used in this book with cash or cash notes to represent the same currency.

Deposit Currency: A deposit certificate for Contract Currency, which is obtained by depositing Contract Currency in a commercial bank.

Loan Currency: The holder does not have actual storage of the contracted currency, and the deposit certificate is lent to the borrower by a commercial bank. The commercial bank promises that the holder of the deposit certificate can claim payment of the Contract Currency at any time.

Credit Currency: The general commodity manufactured by Currency Issuer using the borrower credit, which is a general term for Contract Currency, Deposit Currency, and Loan Currency.

Initial Currency: Refers to the currency issued by Currency Issuer based on the credit of the borrower, and the currency borrowed by the borrower from Currency Issuer.

Wealth: All things that can meet human needs. In a broad sense, wealth includes money, goods, or services. In a narrow sense, wealth refers to all goods or service excluding money.

Commodities: Wealth available for market circulation. In a broad sense, commodities include money, goods, or services. In a narrow sense, commodities refer to goods or service excluding money.

Production Capacity: The ability to produce and supply goods or service.

Government: Specifically refers to the government in a narrow sense, namely, the administrative and law enforcement agencies other than Issuer of Currency, legislative organ, and judicial organ.

Currency Issuer: A department or unit which is qualified to examine the credit of borrowers and lend money to them, synonymous with the coiner. In a broad sense, the Currency Issuer includes the central bank under the current monetary system and commercial banks that issue loans based on partial reserve requirements. In a narrow sense, the Currency Issuer excludes commercial banks that do not have the right to issue currency as deemed in this book, and only refers to the central bank.

Currency Issuance: Currency Issuer, relying on the borrower credit, issues loans to the borrower by obtaining the borrower creditor's rights. The currency therefore leaves Currency Issuer system and enters the market circulation. If Currency Issuer exports currency by purchasing foreign exchange or gold, it is considered that Currency Issuer also acts as a borrower to complete the loan application to itself, and then acts as a currency user to bring the currency into the market circulation. legal coinage and Currency Issuance are synonymous.

Preface

In 2017, When I was studying at Shanghai Advanced Institute of Finance, Shanghai Jiaotong University, a classmate who had done a lot of research on central banks shared the topic of "the balance sheet of the central bank" in our class. He said, "Every dollar we have in our hands is a liability of the US central bank (the Federal Reserve System) to us." As a lawyer, I am used to analyzing everything in the world into specific and achievable rights and obligations. I can't help but ask, "If I take a hundred dollars to the door of the Federal Reserve System and demand repayment, how will they settle the debt?" This classmate was obviously stumped by the question. "The balance sheets of central banks around the world are all recorded in this way. If the holder of US dollars demands repayment, the Federal Reserve System will give you equivalent small-denomination US dollars," he replied. I was instantly filled with righteous indignation. This is equivalent to the judge's ruling in the loan dispute case I represented: "The debtor only needs to replace the original large-denomination IOU with several small-denomination IOU, and it wound be considered as having paid off the debt", which obviously doesn't convince me. I will immediately decide to appeal. Later, as the course of "Monetary Finance" progressed, I learned that the most authoritative financial textbooks and the most prestigious finance professors in the world are making the same statement, and I began to feel confused, like I was holding a first-instance judgment and wanted to appeal but couldn't fully argue my case, and knew that the second-instance court would uphold the original judgment. I realized that there must be a huge mistake in this, but I couldn't solve this problem. I searched many books and papers, I didn't find the answer I wanted. So, I began to explore the reasons myself and rewrite the authority.

I was born in Chaohu City, Anhui Province, which is economically backward. Later, I studied in Ningbo City, Zhejiang Province, where the modern business is prosperous. Then I served as an officer in the Navy. After my retirement from the military, I entered a commercial bank to take charge of credit work. Later, I later resigned to pursue a career as a lawyer, and subsequently became a senior partner at a law firm. Along the way, I have witnessed migrant workers working hard like cormorants but earning little, businessmen living a leisurely life but making a lot of money, company employees unable to obtain housing loans due to insufficient or unstable bank flow, and Large real estate companies often get approved for bank credits of several billion dollars, the futures market investor around me claimed to have made so much money that his hands shook, the successful lawyer team charged hundreds of millions for a single case, and there were even corrupt officials who were able to enrich themselves without being punished. I began to think that although the money in people's hands has the same purchasing power, the ways and amounts of money obtained by different groups of people are vastly different. As a legal practitioner who pursues fairness and justice, I examine the unfairness brought by money to people and naturally believe that people should have equal opportunities to obtain money. The prices of assets such as futures, stocks, and even real estate should not fluctuate greatly, and people should obtain money through honest labor. At the same time, I also realized that the general public knows very little about important money issues, and should pay more attention to understanding money and improving their skills to earn money. However, I have been unable to articulate where exactly the injustice and unfairness of money lies, what causes it, and how reforms and improvements should be made in the system and mechanisms.

Over the centuries, there have been many insightful and renowned economists in human history, whose theories are clear and firm, and whose ideas are like lights in the darkness, illuminating the human consciousness space and making outstanding contributions to human progress. At the same time, their views are often contradictory, forming many economic schools. Careful study of their views reveals that these economists generally have limitations of the times and one-sided perspectives. Some emphasize the self-regulation of the market, some emphasize government intervention, and Some people believe that humans are rational economic agents, while others think of humans as blind and disorganized masses. Faced with real economic phenomena, the most authoritative economists often display embarrassment in observing inaccuracies, interpreting inappropriately, applying ineffective strategies, and making inaccurate predictions. Up to this day, Economics, which should be rigorous, scientific, and accurate, still presents a vague and rough situation and gropes in the dark, just likes a blind man touching an elephant. Many economic theories and views only stay on the surface of economic phenomena and discuss things in a superficial way, failed to analyze by delving into the essence of things. "Knowing the phenomenon but not understanding its underlying reasons", "By being vague oneself, one cannot enlighten others". There are few specialized discussions on currency, and most of the time, they Grasp the thing superficially and give up.

It is the unfairness, uncertainty, and confusion in my mind about the monetary system that drives me to explore money. As a professional lawyer, I do not have sufficient practical experience and industry data in the financial industry. Leveraging my professional expertise and eschewing inductive reasoning, I adopted methods of deductive, analogical, hypothetical, and causal reasoning to meticulously explore and attain insights through the construction of a small island trading model, gradually developing my own monetary theory system. Over the years, whether driving, jogging, waking from dreams, before sleeping, during chores, during conversations, I have often been suddenly enlightened during my constant thinking. and I often rushed to pull out my phone or picked up a pen and paper to record these flashes of inspiration, which I later revisited at my desk to to enrich and improve. I have not majored in finance or economics, I am just an ordinary currency pursuer, currency user, and currency researcher. With compassion for the people, concern for society, exploration of truth, and pursuit of ideals, I am groping forward on the road to revealing the essence of money. Every insight brings me great joy. I am glad that I can think deeply and reason rigorously, and I am grateful to God for bestowing upon me the wisdom and insight to develop a logically consistent and unique monetary theory system.

I originally thought that my non-financial background would hinder my exploration of currency. Upon looking back, I realized that the modern monetary system, as well as the modern economic system centered around it, are actually constructed from a series of agreements on rights and obligations. It is no exaggeration to say that the modern monetary and economic systems are built on contracts. And isn't analyzing contracts, deconstructing rights and obligations, and ascertaining the truth of facts exactly what a professional lawyer like myself excels at? As a lawyer, I also have an advantage, which is my innate instinct for pursuing fairness and justice. I always pay attention to equality, and the balance and unity of rights, obligations, and interests. It is this legal ideal that makes me more sensitive and indignant about the unfairness between countries, the unfairness between the government and the private sector, the unfairness between banks and other non-banking entities, and the inequality between people under the current monetary system. This further drives me to explore a just, equitable, and scientific monetary ideal world. After discovering my legal professional advantages, I am even more grateful for my non-financial professional background, which allows me to think and explore monetary and financial issues without bias and prejudice, without being constrained by academic authority, and to think freely, which has led to many novel perspectives. In the process of writing this book, I

8

distinctly felt that I had undergone a journey from shallow to deep, with the topics discussed ranged from currency to wealth, then to price, economy, and further to national monetary strategy and world monetary ideals. Some of my thoughts may seem too profound or even obscure, but I believe they are all closely related to the interests of the country and the people, and are necessary and valuable content. I have tried to express them in simple words.

After the completion of this book, in order to verify my own views and to identify gaps and avoid making assumptions without thorough research, I supplemented the purchase and reading of a large number of books and papers related to currency, finance, and economics, and also consulted with many experts and professors in related fields. The thoughts of those prophets in the fields of currency, finance, economics, sociology, and political science have greatly inspired and encouraged me. I am delighted to find that many existing theoretical perspectives have confirmed the correctness of my research results. I was pleasantly surprised to find that many of my views and propositions based on logic have been shared by economists in history. The sense of kinship and pride that comes from sharing similar ideas arises spontaneously. At the same time, I also fully feel that after I grasp the essence and principles of money and economy, I can clearly examine the relevant economic theories of the past and confidently evaluate the views of economists. Comparing my own theoretical system, I can clearly point out which of the money-related books and papers I read are superficial appearances, which are clear fallacies, which are one-sided cognitions, which are obvious omissions, and which are the evasive responses with unclear words. Faced with the complex economic phenomena and views from self-media, I can also dispel the previous confusion, blind belief and echo what others say, Confucius said: " A gentleman puts basic principles first, which will illuminate the way forward ", I am confident that I have grasped the essence, logic, and code of money. As the saying goes, " Learn the Way in the morning, be content with death at night", I am happy with my exploration of truth.

The analytical perspective, classification method, and reasoning conclusions of this book are unique in many ways, and I believe that these studies and reflections are extremely valuable. I am not satisfied with using this book as a general accumulation of financial knowledge, but strive to complete the construction of an original and new monetary theory system in this book. I can't wait to share my research process and ideological achievements with ordinary people who love money, pursue money, store money, and use money like me, especially those scholars who study money, care about the economy, and seek the truth. I believe that this book, being the research outcome of an ordinary individual without formal education in finance or economics, will surely be easier for the general public to understand, accept, and apply. I hope this book can bring inspiration and harvest to readers, bring new policies and advancements to the country, and bring equality and justice to society. I regard this book as my gift to the public.

Prologue

" Those who are beguiled by the study of the nature of money, are even more numerous than those who are beguiled by love." sighed William Ewart Gladstone, a British liberal thinker in the 19th century who served as the Prime Minister of the United Kingdom for four times. Money is a complete man-made creation, humans have fashioned money with their own hands, yet it puzzles humans themselves. This is truly the greatest joke humans have played on themselves. Money and monetary theory are the core of economics, and monetary science is regarded as the most complex and difficult part of economics. It can be said that monetary issues are the biggest problems that humans have set for themselves. At the same time, only by truly understanding money can we truly understand economics and economic operation. Economics without money and monetary theory can only be a "theory-defective economics". Therefore, compared to other issues we can choose to avoid, the issue of money is also a "required question" that humanity must answer well.

"People die for wealth, birds die for food"; from ancient to modern times, both in the East and West, regardless of the degree, no one does not love wealth, and the most direct form of wealth is money. "With money, one can make the devil turn the mill." People can use money to maximize their needs and solve the problems they face. It can be said that money is the best thing in the world. At the same time, The Bible's Gospel of Matthew states: "to everyone who has, more will be given, and he will have abundance; but from him who does not have, even what he has will be taken away". There are also some proverbs that say: "The rich get richer, and the poor get poorer." "The poor must serve the rich." It can be said that money is the most unfair thing in the world.

There is no doubt that money is the greatest, most mysterious and complex man-made object. Money is closely related to human interests, and we often directly use money as a synonym for wealth and benefits. We all love money, use money every day, and cannot live without money. It can be said that money is the thing we know best. However, do we truly understand money? It can be asserted that the vast majority of us lack an understanding, or even contemplation, of money. If we seek something that is intimately linked to people's direct interests, relentlessly pursued, used throughout life, and taken for granted. Yet, at the same time, it remains distant from people's understanding, with little knowledge sought, explanations not delved into deeply, opinions swayed by others, and even an indifference towards its essence and principles. Money is the only thing that fits this peculiar description and this special category, so to speak, money is our "most familiar stranger."

This is a very unreasonable and dangerous state. Is there any rationality and inevitability in the cruel reality of "the laggards are beaten and the ignorant are harvested"? If so, should we all focus on and understand money instead of blindly pursuing it?

What is money? A gold ingot, a piece of paper with a pattern, a string of numbers on the mobile banking app or computer screen, a commercial bank deposit certificate, or a check, people use these to trade, and they all think that the money in their hands is wealth, but they rarely care about what the money actually is and what rights it represents. Is money a right of property domination, a claim of creditor's rights, or a right of formation and a right of defense? How does the central bank release water? How does interest rate increase and decrease play a role? Why is inflation a common phenomenon in various countries? How do Americans play with finance? These topics that we are familiar with are almost confusing. The economic phenomenon with money as the core is even more confusing and elusive. The economic schools are complex and diverse, and the regulation and prediction of the economy often go against people's wishes, which makes people feel surprised. Money, which is a common thing in most people's eyes, is full of mystery.

For more than 200 years, economists have been trying hard to provide a rigorous theoretical framework for money, but most of their efforts have failed. The most surprising reality is that as economic research becomes more refined, economic theories have less and less discussion on the nature of money. The 18th-century economist David Hume argued that money is a commodity that can be used to buy goods and service, David Hume summarized a seemingly obvious truth that the price level reflects the balance between money supply and demand, while Nobel Prize winner in economics Christopher Sims believes that this view has become "outdated". Even for some economic theorists, the existence of money itself has become a mystery. The renowned Cambridge University economist and late professor Frank Hahn once wrote: "The existence of money poses the greatest challenge to theoretical researchers: there is no place for money in the most perfect economic models."[1]

By understanding the essential attributes and operating rules of money, we can better grasp money, manage wealth, benefit society, and enjoy life. The development of money has accompanied the evolution of human history, and modern money has gradually evolved through human life practices. Looking at the current status of monetary theory and monetary practice, we cannot help but sigh: "Human beings create, manage, use, and interpret money based on practicality rather than scientific and impartiality, relying on instinct rather

---

[1] Mervyn King. The End Of ALCHEMY: MONEY, BANKING AND THE FUTURE OF THE GLOBAL ECONOMY[M]. Beijing: China CITIC Press, 2016.

than rationality." Money, which is the most relevant thing for human interests, lacks rational support in basic theories and fundamental systems, resulting in logical confusion and loopholes. Building monetary theory and systems based on human reason and ideals rather than experience and instinct is crucial for the common well-being of humanity and the progress of human civilization.

This book clearly analyzes the transformation process of money from version 1.0 to version 6.0 based on the evolution of monetary forms and the inherent legal relationships contained in various forms of money. Through the construction of a small Island Z model, it elucidates the origin and essence of 1.0 Material Currency, 2.0 Receipt Currency, 3.0 Promise Currency, 4.0 Contract Currency, 5.0 Deposit Currency, and 6.0 Loan Currency from the interrelationships between a farmer, a blacksmith, a masseuse, a coiner, a banker in depth yet concisely. Based on the grasp of the essence of money, it boldly looks forward to the birth path of the future international common currency of mankind, helping readers to fully understand the past, present, and future of money. This book completely solves the major issues of what money is, where it comes from, and where it goes.

With the exploration of the nature of money, this book further discusses the nature of wealth, the measurement of wealth, and the relationship between money and other forms of wealth, namely the formation of commodity prices, helping people to look beyond the appearance of money to see the nature of wealth itself and people's own needs.

Through logical reasoning and meticulous analysis, this book profoundly unveils that the core value of Credit Currency lies in its inherent "borrower credit". The "gold content" of money has evolved into "credit content", and this credit is not the credit of the central bank, nor the credit of the government, nor the credit of the country, but the credit of the borrower. The role of the central bank, government, and country is only to ensure the authenticity and reliability of the borrower credit and its smooth operation. The book firmly grasps the core of "borrower credit" and analyzes the essence of money, interest classification, types of borrowers, root causes of inflation, principles of Currency Issuance, equality of Monetary Powers, government debt limit and other major issues, and has constructed a complete, unique and scientific monetary theory system.

This book argues that understanding money is to better meet human needs, and the essence of economics is to understand and meet human needs. To discuss money, we must discuss the relationship between money and the entire economy. This book deeply explores important economic themes such as how money drives economic growth, the root causes of inflation, and the types of debtors of Currency Issuers. It lists the "market Transaction Equation" and conducts a total factor analysis of inflation and deflation. This book pioneers three laws of monetary economics, creates many new economic concepts such as "basic unit of wealth value", "objective wealth value", "value perception", "subjective wealth value", "issuance interest", "rental interest", "transaction ratio", and "Monetary Power", and leads to new economic topics such as "classification and regulation of interest", "how to define and measure human needs", and "conversion, measurement, and management of various currencies under new classification". In order to express specifically and visually, this book also takes the United States as a case study, analyzing the path to financial dominance of the United States, its systemic vulnerabilities, and the coping strategies of other countries. Unlike other monetary books that delve into various economic topics with little relevance to currency, this book focuses solely on the core subject of money, discussing only economic phenomena directly related to currency. It not only clarifies the relationship between money and the economy, but also successfully avoids topic generalization and focus dispersion.

This book employs legal reasoning and promotes a critical spirit, boldly revealing many traditional cognitive misconceptions in the field of economics from the perspective of the rights and obligations of various participants in the currency operation process. For example, the misunderstandings about the nature of money and wealth, errors in the recording of items on the balance sheet of central banks, and misinterpretations of various economic phenomena. It proposes that modern currency is not a liability of the central bank but an exercise of legal coinage power, the credit core of modern currency lies not in the central bank but in the borrower, the measurement standard of wealth should not be currencies of various countries but the needs of all mankind, the driving force of economic growth is not in currency but in education, the root cause of inflation is not in the amount of currency issued but in the degree of borrower default, monetary authority should not belong to any currency user but should become an independent fourth political power, the legal coinage power should not spill over to commercial banks but should be monopolized by the central bank, Currency Issuance should not target specific subjects but should benefit all economies, and the default of the Currency Issuer's borrowers should not be directly written off but should be uniformly compensated. These challenges even subvert the existing monetary theory and monetary practice.

On this basis, the book proposes ten bold reform suggestions for the current monetary system, and strongly advocates that monetary authorities break through the barriers and shackles of practicalism and empiricism, and recognize, design, establish and operate a new and adaptive "Equal Rights Monetary Theory" and "equal rights monetary system" based on rationality and idealism, and practice a new and people-oriented "Egalitarian Economics", so as to truly enable financial services real economy and truly realize people's finance.

The entire purpose of this book is to construct and promulgate a new "Equal Rights Monetary Theory" and "Egalitarian Economics", which mean

13

that supporting or following the idea all people are equal and should have the same rights and opportunities in monetary system and Economic System, aiming to promote a rational, efficient, and fair monetary system in human society. It seeks to enhance the role of currency as a means to the greatest welfare for all people, rather than a tool for mutual plunder among different classes and nations.

Chapter 1: Currency 1.0 to Currency 4.0

Money is a tool for measuring prices, a medium for purchasing commodities, and a means of preserving wealth. Money is also a special commodity. If we can only define money in one sentence, it should be "the most universally used commodity in society". It can be said that the great and magical power of money lies in the hearts of people, in their widest recognition and acceptance. As human history progresses, the ways and means of capturing people's hearts and minds are constantly evolving and changing, and money itself is constantly being transformed. Now, we will unveil the mysterious veil of money through a simple Island model, fully understanding the appearance and essence of money.

I. Currency in 1.0 Version, Material Currency

On an isolated island called Z Island, three people drifted over from three different ethnic groups, a farmer, a blacksmith, and a masseuse, representing the agricultural, industrial, and service industries of modern society. The farmer produced grain and needed spades, the blacksmith made spades and needed massage, and the masseuse provided massage and needed grain. The farmer produced 100 kilograms of grain a year and needed to use 1 spade, The blacksmith produced 1 spade a year and required 10 hours of massage, and the masseuse provided 10 hours of massage a year and needed 100 kilograms of grain. Life on the island could be self-sufficient in theory, but the three individuals could not communicate due to the language barrier, making it impossible to understand each other's needs or complete a triangular trade. The three people could only live a hard, hungry, and tired life.

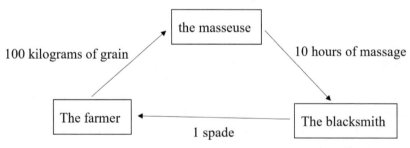

In their spare time, they would go to the beach alone to relax. Occasionally, they found a kind of shell on the beach that was unique in shape, brightly colored, and hard in texture, they all liked it very much. Each time they found one, they would bring it back for collection. These tiny shells brought great solace to the people living in the barren material and spiritual life on the island.

As life went on, the masseur found the farmer playing with his collection of shells at his own doorstep, guessing that the farmer also shared the same hobby. The next day, the masseuse came to the farmer's house with 10 shells and pointed to the 100 kilograms of grain stacked in the corner of the wall, signaling that she would hand over the shells in his hand to the farmer. The farmer took the shell, very pleased, for he had only eight shells in his house, and they were hard won over the past three years, and he didn't need the 100 kilograms of grain himself. The masseur reluctantly gave up what he loved but pulled back the 100 kilograms of grain he had longed for, greatly improving his quality of life. The farmer was fond of the newly acquired shells and was also deeply inspired. He wondered if he could use shells to exchange for the long-awaited spade since the masseuse could exchange my grain for shells. The next day, the exchange was successful, and the farmer exchanged 10 shells from the blacksmith for a spade. On the third day, the blacksmith did the same thing, using one shell to enjoy a one-hour massage at the masseuse's place. The economic activities on the island began to flourish, and everyone got great satisfaction.

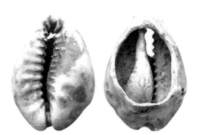 

Ancient Coins, 3,500 years ago

The simple story reflects the origin of the most primitive currency in human history. Natural seashells are the ancestor of currency. The seashells in the picture were unearthed from sites such as the Fuhao Tomb at Yinxu, Henan Province, China, dating back to about 3,500 years ago. In various parts of the world, different forms of physical objects are used as currency for circulation in the trading market within a specific range. the white deer skin in the era of Emperor Wu of Han in China, squirrel pelts in ancient Russia, cloth in the Tang Dynasty in China, salt in the Sahara Desert region during the Middle Ages, pig's teeth among the people of Vanuatu, amber-gold coins in ancient Greece, and cigarettes in Germany after World War II are all different forms of currency, but they all have a common feature: "widely needed by people". This universal demand among specific groups of people comes from people's physiological needs for food and clothing, spiritual aesthetic needs, or other hobbies for specific items.

Squirrel skin in ancient Russia   Pig teeth among the people of Vanuatu

Amber gold coins in ancient Greece   Cigarettes in German after World War II

Before World War II, there was a currency that circulated in most parts of Europe like the euro is now, which was the legal currency of Germany, the Reichsmark. After World War II, Germany, as one of the initiators of the war, faced the defeat of unconditional surrender and a chaotic situation in the country. The Nazi forces in Germany were eliminated, and the territory was divided into two parts by the Berlin Wall, which was built up, becoming an occupied area by the Soviet Union and the United States.

Under such circumstances, the Reichsmark was naturally not recognized by everyone, and almost lost its original function. In most transactions, merchants refused to accept the Reichsmark, preferring to return to the primitive society of barter.

The smart Germans soon found that cigarettes have monetary attributes in the market. Firstly, the standard of cigarettes is easy to verify. Secondly, they are easy to carry and not prone to deterioration, especially the Camel cigarettes produced in the United States, which are made with high-quality tobacco leaves and traditional craftsmanship. Each cigarette has a striking trademark, making it more resistant to counterfeiting. Camel cigarettes quickly became a commonly accepted currency.

Since then, cigarettes have become the only stable currency on the black market in the post-war Allied occupation zone, and everything on the market can be bought with cigarettes. In the black market at that time, a pack of ordinary cigarettes cost around $30, while American cigarettes could be worth up to $80. One cigarette can cover a family's daily expenses, and two cigarettes can be exchanged for a beautiful night with a young girl.

As early as World War II, cigarettes had become popular among the general population as a form of currency. Not only that, in Nazi concentration camps, prisoners of war also chose to exchange cigarettes for things they wanted. In the classic movie "The Shawshank Redemption", there were scenes of exchanging cigarettes for goods, which were based on real-life scenes from World War II.

Exchange is an innate nature of human beings. Cross-multiple exchange behavior naturally forms the trading market. Some goods are universally needed, loved and accepted by people in the trading market due to their universally applicable practical value, aesthetic value and other natural attributes. They are widely used in transactions between people because they are universally accepted. In long-term life practice and extensive market transactions, the transaction attributes of these specific goods have been fully demonstrated and played out, and they begin to stand out among many goods and become unique. Eventually, they are selected and named as "money". The transaction attributes are the core characteristics of money. The transaction attributes of these goods are based on their inherent natural attributes, and they have their own value even if they are not used as currency for transactions. When the transaction attributes of specific items are discovered in practice, people begin to use these items as raw materials to create more artistic and easily recognizable crafts, which are then put into a broader market for trading. These special goods commonly used in the general commodity market trading process, such as shells, cloth, cigarettes, silver coins, etc., are the most primitive currencies in human history, which we call the 1.0 version of money "Material Currency". In the era of Material Currency, money is naturally a commodity, and only specific commodities with "transaction attributes" have the opportunity to be selected as currency in the trading market. Throughout history, various exquisitely crafted metal coins in the world are merely artistic representations of tangible objects.

Silver Penny from the time of Ethelstan in England

Among the numerous physical materials, gold is widely loved and used by humans due to its natural characteristics such as exquisite appearance, chemical stability, safe use, convenient shaping, appropriate availability, and easy carrying. The transaction attributes of gold shine among many Materials, and this universal love of humans has made gold known as the "king of metals". The monetary attributes of gold are highlighted, and it has gradually become the most accepted Material Currency among people around the world.

Kai yuan Tong bao Gold Coin of Tang Dynasty in China

Macedonian gold coin in ancient Greek

Small gold ingot coins of the Qing Dynasty in China

II. Currency in 2.0 Version, Receipt Currency

Life on Island Z continued, and the number of shells on the island was increasing. People have always loved shells for their natural characteristics such as texture, shape, and color. Now, shells were still widely used in the market transactions on the island. The three people on the island had formed a rigid need for shells, and shells were cherished by everyone. On this day, a man who knew the languages of the other three people and worked as a warehouse administrator drifted in from the sea. After landing, he discovered the fact that shells were commonly loved by the three people on the island. He learnt that there had been incidents of shells being forgotten or even stolen at home and lost during transactions on the island. Therefore, he leveraged his linguistic and professional advantages to hang a sign in front of his residence, displaying a name in three languages used by the masseuse, the farmer, and the blacksmith: "Z Island Shell Warehouse". He also went to the homes of the masseuse, the farmer, and the blacksmith to persuade them: "You all store your shells in my warehouse, and I will issue you with vouchers indicating the quantity of shells. When you need to trade with each other, you only need to deliver the voucher indicating the corresponding quantity to the other party. In this way, your transactions can proceed smoothly, and shells can be retrieved and played with at any time. In case of vouchers loss, I also have an account book here, and you can come and report the loss and apply for a replacement. This can also avoid possible losses and wear and tear caused by the use of physical shells." The three people thought that the warehouse administrator's words is reasonable, so they gladly agreed with him. Since then, shells no longer appeared on the trading scene, replaced by warehouse administrator's shell deposit receipts.

The story of the small island is truly reflected in human history. In the early years of the Northern Song Dynasty in China, people used iron, copper, gold, and silver as currency. Among them, iron coins were heavy in weight

22

and small in value. 1000 iron coins weighed 12.5 kilograms, and it took 1000 iron coins to buy 1 bolt of silk. There was a need for 45 to 50 kilograms of iron coins, which was inconvenient to carry. Therefore, In Chengdu, Sichuan, there emerged "silver note shops" specifically operating cash custody services for merchants carrying large amounts of money. The depositor delivered the metal currency to the shopkeeper, who filled in the amount of metal currency deposited by the depositor on a scroll made of a special type of paper made from paper mulberry bark, and then returned it to the depositor. When the depositor withdrew metal currency, 30 wen of interest was paid to the shopkeeper for each string, which was equivalent to a 3% custody fee. This kind of paper coupon with the deposit amount filled in temporarily was called " Silver Note ". With the development of the commodity economy, the use of " Silver Note " became more and more widespread. Around 1008 AD, 16 officials and merchants in Chengdu jointly used paper made from the bark of the paper mulberry tree for printing vouchers, which are adorned with patterns, codes, signatures, and seals, The denomination depends on the recipient. The denomination is temporarily filled in according to the cash paid by the recipient, serving as a payment voucher for circulation. The world's earliest use of paper money, "Jiaozi," emerged in response to people's needs.

Jiaozi of the Northern Song Dynasty   Official Silver Note of Jiangxi Province, China in 1907

When Material Currency was stored in the warehouse of the custodian, the owner of the tangible assets received a storage voucher issued by the shop and used it for market transactions. At that point, the transactional attribute of Material Currency had been extracted from its practical functions. This transactional attribute was printed on the storage certificates of Material Currency. Material Currency in version 1.0 was put into the warehouse, and the currency circulating in the market was upgraded into the storage voucher of Material Currency, which we call "Receipt Currency" in version 2.0. Behind Receipt Currency was still the physical object universally accepted by humans, and people could retrieve the physical item from the physical custodian at any time. Receipt Currency had two functions: one was to redeem the physical item from the issuer of Receipt Currency, and the other was to conduct extensive transactions with other market entities.

III. Currency in 3.0 Version, Promise Currency

Life on the island continued. With the improvement of material conditions and labor skills, the production capacity on Island Z had significantly increased, and demand had also expanded. The farmer produced 1000 kilograms of grain a year, requiring the use of 10 spades. The blacksmith produced 10 spades a year, requiring 100 hours of massage. The masseuse provided 100 hours of massage a year, requiring 1000 kilograms of grain. It could be said that both supply and demand were booming.

Although the masseuse, the farmer, and the blacksmith still collected shells in their spare time, the number of shells on the island was still very limited. The warehouse administrator counted the inventory and found only 150 shells, including 40 stored by the masseuse, 20 by the farmer, 60 by the blacksmith, and 30 collected by the warehouse administrator himself. If the original standard of 10 shells for 100 kilograms of grain or 10 hours of massage or 1 spade was used for trading, the masseuse, farmer, and blacksmith all needed a deposit certificate for 100 shells. The number of shells on their hands was not enough. The transactions between them either could not be carried out or could only be completed after multiple turnovers. Currency shortage occurred on Z Island, making transactions extremely difficult and the economy fell into a contraction.

The intelligent warehouse manager had learnt about the plight of the small Island and found them to lobby. He said to the masseuse, "In addition to helping you keep the shells, I have spent my free time going to the seaside to find shells over the years. The three people on the Island also store a large amount of shells in my warehouse. Now I have a sufficient number of shells, but I can't disclose the exact number. However, I can guarantee that the number is surprising to you. I understand that you need 100 shells a year to buy food, but you only store 40 shells here. What do you think about the following suggestions? I will write a deposit receipt indicating 100 shells for you, and give you an extra 60, these 60 shells are lent to you. You can use this deposit receipt to trade with the farmer. The farmer doesn't need to know

24

where your shells come from, and you can take a note for me to tell him, If he needs these 100 shells, he can come to my warehouse at any time to collect them with this deposit receipt. Of course, it doesn't matter if you don't pass on the note of promise. The farmer and I have known each other for many years, and we have used this kind of deposit receipt for many years. This deposit receipt itself is my promise, and you all know it already. If you agree, just sign your name on my account book. The loan term is one year, upon the expiration of one year, you need to return me 63 shells or return the deposit receipt marked with 63 shells. The extra 3 shells are considered as the rental fee for borrowing 60 shells for you to use for one year. Is this reasonable? " The masseuse was deeply moved by the kindness and wisdom of the warehouse manager and happily signed as per his request. She took away the deposit receipt for 100 shells.

The warehouse administrator separately met the farmer and the blacksmith and said the same things to them, and issued them both with a deposit certificate for 100 shells. The transactions on the island became smooth again. At this time, the total number of shells displayed on the deposit certificate on Island Z was 300, while the actual number of shells stored in the warehouse was only 150, including 40 belonging to the masseuse, 20 belonging to the farmer, 60 belonging to the blacksmith, and 30 belonging to the warehouse administrator. The warehouse administrator lent out 180 shells by creating a false deposit certificate, of which 60 were borrowed by the masseuse, 80 by the farmer, and 40 by the blacksmith. One year later, the warehouse administrator received a "rental fee" of 9 shells for issuing a total of 180 deposit certificates to the three people, which was deducted from the deposit certificates of the masseuse, farmer, and blacksmith by 3, 4, and 2 respectively. The masseuse's shell inventory decreased from 40 to 37, the farmer's shell inventory decreased from 20 to 16, and the blacksmith's shell inventory decreased from 60 to 58. During this year, although there were actually only 150 shells on the island, there were a total of 300 shells displayed on the deposit certificate in the market, which fully guaranteed the transactions of 1000 kilograms of grain, 100 hours, and 10 spades on the island. The economy of the island flourished again.

When the warehouse administrator not only issued physical storage vouchers to physical depositors, but also issued them to those who did not have physical deposits by means of virtual lending, while claiming that the physical storage voucher could be exchanged for physical goods from the issuer, Receipt Currency in version 2.0 was upgraded again, and the "Promise Currency" in version 3.0 was created by warehouse administrators with specific credit. Individuals acquired Promise Currency based on their promise to "return the same amount to the issuer," which they used for broader market transactions. Those who were willing to accept Promise Currency in exchange for their goods or service do so because of the issuer's promise that it could be "exchanged for the same amount of Material Currency" They believed that holding this voucher allowed them to exchange it with the issuer for tangible assets at any time. Since then, Promise Currency had been born under multilateral commitments, and the value of Promise Currency itself came from the credit of Currency Issuer.

In the latter stages of World War II, in order to facilitate the post-war world economy, the major Western countries began to conceive and design the post-war international monetary system. At this time, the United States had three-quarters of the world's gold reserves. In July 1944, the United States invited representatives of 44 governments participating in the establishment of the United Nations to hold a meeting in Bretton Woods, USA. After intense debate, all parties signed the "Bretton Woods Agreement" at the financial conference, in this agreement, the US government promised to "link the dollar to gold" and the Federal Reserve System issued US dollars, anyone holding 35 US dollars could exchange it for an ounce of gold at the commercial bank window in the United States. This is to tell the world that the dollar is the storage credential of gold and the value of the dollar is the value of gold. Based on the commitment of the US government, people have no doubt about the "gold content" of the dollar, and the embryonic form of the international monetary system centered on the dollar, the Bretton Woods system, had been established. People's love and acceptance of gold had been transferred to the dollar, and people began to call the dollar "US gold". However, whether the US dollars can really exchange for gold depends not only on the commitment of the US government, but also on the willingness of the US government to fulfill its commitment, and even more on whether the US government has the ability to hand over enough gold.

If the US government were to ask the world at that time, "Is it important for the US dollar to be convertible into gold?" We believe that most people would answer, "It is very important, the US dollar is just a piece of paper, without the ability to exchange it for gold, it holds no intrinsic value, it has no value in itself." At that time, whether the US dollar can be exchanged for gold was a decisive factor in its ability to be widely used in transactions. The new US dollar needed the endorsement of the "king of metals" gold to establish its universal acceptance among people. At that time, the US dollar is essentially a commitment letter from the Federal Reserve System, 3.0 version of "committed currency".

At that time, people were attracted by the half function of the specific item, that was, the dollar could be exchanged for gold. People did not realize that the dollar had become an internationally recognized currency at that time, and the other half of its function was its greatest value. The fundamental function of the dollar is not to be exchanged for physical goods for practical use, but to be widely accepted for international commodity trading. As long as people continue to believe in the dollar and use it, even if they cannot exchange it for gold as promised, it will not affect the fundamental function of the dollar as an international currency.

IV. Currency in 4.0 Version, Contract Currency

Life on Island Z continued, and the thoughts of the warehouse manager continued. He was thinking, "I keep issuing shell deposit receipts, and their transactions are all conducted through deposit receipts. As for the shells in the warehouse, except for occasional withdrawals of a small amount for a few days, the three people basically don't care. If the shells themselves have nothing to do with the transaction, why don't I invent a new type of paper that can also allow them to complete the transaction as long as they all agree? I can also avoid the risk of losing credibility by not being able to exchange sufficient amounts of shells.".

After making up his mind, the warehouse manager called the masseuse, farmer, and blacksmith to his residence at the same time. At this time, the signboard of "Z Island Shell Warehouse" at his gate had disappeared, replaced by a more eye-catching signboard with three different languages written in large letters: "Central Bank of Island Z". The warehouse manager said in the languages that the three people could understand: "For many years, I have lent you shells so that you can trade with each other. The shells you originally stored in my warehouse have basically become mine because you pay me a 5% interest every year. Of course, you may say that I didn't hand over the real shells to you, I just issued a shell deposit certificate to you. This is true, but does it affect your use? No. Your fundamental goal is not to possess a large number of shells, but to use the deposit certificate for trading. Isn't it? I put myself in your shoes and think that it is not easy for you to collect a little shell in your spare time. Since the transaction between you only requires a deposit certificate and does not require shells, why should we be bound by shells?"

Upon hearing the warehouse administrator's analysis, the masseuse, farmer, and blacksmith all had a moment of realization and then nodded repeatedly in agreement.

"After careful consideration, I have decided to no longer work as a warehouse manager, but to switch to making a unique type of paper. I have also chosen a name for this paper, which is called 'Z coin'. In fact, 'Z coin' is not mysterious, it is a slight change from the previous deposit receipts, where the number of shells was indicated, to the number of 'worth' now. By the way, 'worth' is a unit of measurement invented by me, which is equivalent to the number of shells in the 'Z coin'. Of course, in order to distinguish from the previous deposit receipts, I plan to use 'Z coin' marked as '10 worth' instead of the original deposit receipt marked as '1 shell'. You can understand it this way, '100 worth ' is equivalent to 10 shells, '1000 worth ' is equivalent to 100 shells, and so on. In the future, you can use this 'Z coin' for transactions. Shells and deposit receipts are no longer used for transactions. The shells currently stored in my warehouse are available for everyone to take home and appreciate. The issuance of shell deposit certificates will no longer be carried out in the future." The warehouse administrator spoke eloquently. No! He could no longer be called a warehouse administrator, as he had become Z coinage maker for the central bank!

The three of them felled into deep thought upon hearing this, and the masseuse suddenly realized and took the lead to speak: "What you said does make sense. We originally collected shells out of love, without thinking of using them specifically for trade, let alone expecting such a large volume of transactions. Even if the 'Z coin' you invented can allow us to trade as well, we have no reason to refuse.".

The farmer continued, "However, I have a question. Even if we all agree to accept your 'Z coin' as a means of payment, when I hand over 1000 kilograms of grain to the masseuse, he will pay me 100 'Z coin' for it. If the blacksmith cannot produce spades, will 'Z coin' become worthless in my hands?"

The warehouse manager, no, the central bank coiner heard this and confidently replied: "I have already thought about this question. Now that you are willing to accept 'Z coin', it is already half the success of our currency reform on Island Z! What you are worried about now is whether 'Z coin' can always be exchanged for the items you need. This is a very reasonable question. After all, in the past, you could exchange your deposit receipts for the shells you needed. That was my promise to you before. Now that I have no promise, I fully understand your concerns ".

The central bank coiner took a sip of water and continues, "But this question is really unnecessary. Mr. Farmer, think about it, based on your past experience over the years, can the blacksmith make spades?" The farmer smiled and said, "Yes, in recent years, he has been able to produce 10 spades every year.".

" Mr. Blacksmith, I'm asking you now. I'll lend you 100 'Z coins' and you can exchange them for 100 hours of massage from a masseuse. Can you promise to produce 10 spades in the next year?" The central bank coiner faced the blacksmith and asked solemnly.

"Of course! I have always been able to do it, as everyone knows, and I am still improving my methods. The output will only increase, not decrease," the blacksmith replied loudly.

The central bank coiner faithfully translated the blacksmith's words to the farmer, and said firmly, "With the blacksmith's promise, I can assert that the blacksmith will provide 10 spades as always. The currency reform on Island Z has been completely successful! "."Mr. Farmer, you can rest assured, in addition to the blacksmith's promise just now, I will also be responsible for you. Just think about it, the deadline for the blacksmith to use 'Z coin' is the same as that for you and the masseuse, both of which are one year. When the

28

deadline arrives, the blacksmith must return 'Z coin' to me in full. If he cannot produce the spades you need, you will not pay him 'Z coin', and the blacksmith's 'Z coin' has already been paid to the masseuse, so he cannot obtain 'Z coin' to return to me. So, in the coming year, I will not lend 'Z coin' to him again. What will he use to buy massages? If you are a blacksmith, will you try to complete these 10 spades? Please think about this again! ". "In addition, I've also thought of the issues you haven't considered. In case of the blacksmith's accidental death, I promise you that I will try to contact people outside this island, either by bringing in another blacksmith or by establishing trade with a blacksmith outside this island. You can use your 'Z coin' to purchase spades from the new blacksmith. "The coiner spoke eloquently and patiently, doing the ideological work for the three people.

The farmer felt relieved and said happily, "With the blacksmith's statement and your fairness, I'm at ease. I don't have to look for shells to protect my transactions in the future!".

The people on the island reached a consensus to use the "Z coin" of the coiner as the tool for trading with each other. The "Z coin" was only used for trading and no longer exchanged for shells from the warehouse administrator. This day was a major day in the history of the island's currency. The people on the island created a man-made object that had no connection with natural objects. This was a new type of currency, a currency based on the spirit of mutual contract between people. It was different from the three types of currencies that had appeared before. The credit of this currency did not depend on natural objects or the Currency Issuer. Its credit connotation will be analyzed in detail in the third section of Chapter 4, "The Essence of Credit Currency and Three Layers of Credit".

The fable reflects the reality that the Nixon administration of the United States under the Bretton Woods Agreement also completed the transformation from a "warehouse keeper" to a "central bank coiner". In July 1971, the seventh dollar crisis broke out. On August 15, the Nixon administration announced the implementation of the "New Economic Policy", which stopped fulfilling the obligation of foreign governments or central banks to exchange gold for dollars in the United States. The Bretton Woods system was officially disintegrated. When the dollar can only be used for transactions and cannot be exchanged for gold from the Federal Reserve System, The US dollar is no longer the promise of gold convertibility by the U.S. government and the Federal Reserve System. The dollar is only used for transactions, and it is no longer a 3.0 version of "Promise Currency".

Under the Bretton Woods system, The US dollar bore the promise of the US government to redeem gold, but as more dollars were printed, the US government's gold reserves did not increase accordingly.

Just as the governor of the Bank of France, Emil Moreau, demanded the Bank of England to exchange 3 million pounds of gold every week in May 1927, in the 1960s, the clever European strategist and the first president of the Fifth Republic of France, Charles de Gaulle, saw the problem with the United States. The French once again took the lead and resolutely decided to exchange all their dollars for gold and bring the gold home. Charles de Gaulle even threatened that he would personally drive a warship to transport dollars to the United States and exchange them for the gold that should have belonged to France. After that, France drove planes, ships, and submarines to transport gold from the United States and stored it in the Paris vault. By 1971, France had exchanged 3,000 tons of gold.

Germany, Italy and other Western European countries felt uneasy and followed the steps, and there was an endless stream of gold being shipped back from the United States. The loss of gold in the United States was increasing, and by 1970, the remaining gold in the U.S. Treasury was less than 10,000 tons. Finally, the United States could not hold on any longer.

On August 15, 1971, Nixon officially announced the suspension of the convertibility of the US dollar into gold! The Bretton Woods system, which had been in operation for 27 years, collapsed, and the world entered the era of credit currencies.

The Bank of England, the originator of modern banking, issued banknotes that could be exchanged for gold at any time in 1694. Karl Marx once commented on the Bank of England notes: "As long as banknotes can be exchanged for currency at any time, banks must not arbitrarily increase the number of banknotes in circulation." In 1720, when the historical "South Sea Bubble" burst, people flocked to the Bank of England, causing the Bank of England to face a severe run on Material Currency, forcing it to adopt deliberate slow payment actions and pay in small-denomination coins to cope with the situation. As time went on, at the end of the 18th century, London merchants finally accepted the Bank of England notes that could not be exchanged for gold without discount. The famous "gold debate" in the British Parliament was triggered around whether banknotes should be cashed in gold unconditionally. The debate ended with the enactment of the "Restoration of Cash Regulations" in 1819, but it was later hit by two economic crises in 1825 and 1836-1839, causing repeated Bank Run Incidents and ending he gold standard monetary system. Paper money eventually broke away from the backing of physical commodity money by the issuer.

Today, no country's Currency Issuer continues to fulfill the promise that currency holders can claim gold and silver from them, but the sample of the 3.0 version of "Promise Currency" is still intact and preserved on the British banknotes. Take out a recent version of the 50 pounds British banknote at random, and it is written on the face of the bill that "I PROMISE TO THE BEARER ON DEMAND THE SUM OF FIFTY POUNDS", which was the original promise of the Bank of England. The bearer can exchange the banknote for gold, and this solemn promise had been faithfully and diligently fulfilled. Now, it can only be seen as the best memorial to the old era of "Promise Currency". At the same time, Isn't this a sharp irony? this promise also warns us in the most significant way that currency has changed, and our understanding of it should also keep pace with the times! Unfortunately, we don't feel irony, and our understanding of currency still lags far behind the times. We will discuss this in detail in Chapter 5, "Current Misconceptions of Money".

Isaac Newton is a well-known British physicist, mathematician, and philosopher. But few people know that he also began to serve as the director of the Royal Coiner in 1699 and remained in office until his death in 1727.

In 1717, Newton fixed the price of gold per ounce at 3 pounds, 17 shillings, and 10.5 pence. One pound was equivalent to 20 shillings, one shilling was equivalent to 12 pence, and one ounce was equivalent to 28.350 grams. After conversion, it can be seen that one pound is equivalent to 7.28090 grams of pure gold.

In 1816, Britain passed the Gold Standard Act, which legally recognized gold as the standard for issuing paper currency. In 1821, Britain officially adopted the gold standard, and the pound sterling became the standard monetary unit in Britain, with a fixed value of 7.32238 grams of pure gold per pound sterling. Citizens could exchange their paper currency for gold coins based on the gold content of the currency.

Until 1931, the British gold reserves were in a critical situation, and the stability of the pound sterling was severely impacted. In fact, it was unable to continue to fulfill its commitments. On September 20, 1931, Britain officially announced the abolition of the gold standard for the pound sterling.

When Promise Currency can no longer be withdrawn from the warehouse of Currency Issuer in any physical form, the transaction attribute of Promise Currency is further refined. At this point, there is only a purely transactional attribute on the currency. We call this new type of currency that loses the promise of Material Currency exchange as the "Contract Currency" in version 4.0. Under the current monetary system, the central bank paper cashes used by people in various countries are this type of Contract Currency, We so name them because the issue of these notes is by loan contract. Some people may question: "At present, central banks in various countries issue currencies not entirely through lending, but also through purchasing gold or other countries' currencies." Yes, these two methods do exist, and perhaps in the future central banks may also purchase other assets, but this book first believes that this method still belongs to lending, and can be seen as the central bank as a Currency Issuer first lending money to itself, and then using itself as a currency user to buy and sell externally. Secondly, this book opposes the central bank's behavior of issuing currency on its own, and believes that the central bank should focus on its role as a Currency Issuer, only conducting external lending and recycling of currency. It is not necessary for it to act as a currency user by buying and selling goods to regulate the currency, this task can be assigned to the government. We will discuss this in detail in the relevant chapters of this book.

Unlike Promise Currency, whose value is based on the credit of the central role of Currency Issuer, Contract Currency can no longer Promise specific physical goods from Currency Issuer. People are willing to accept Contract Currency for another reason: "believing that the currency in hand can be exchanged for other people's goods in the market". Why can they believe this? Because ordinary rational people can make such a speculation: "The source of money is in Currency Issuer. When Currency Issuer lends money, the borrower has promised to Currency Issuer that he will repay the loan within a certain period of time, and the repayment currency can only be obtained by exchanging it in the market. This means that the borrower must provide sufficient value commodities to the market, otherwise he cannot repay the debt.". According to this logic, the value of Contract Currency is actually based on the credit of the borrower who borrows money from Currency Issuer, that is, the borrower will provide sufficient value to society as agreed. We will further elaborate on what is value and the value basis of Contract Currency in Chapter 6 " The Nature of Wealth and the Measurement of Wealth Value" and Section 3 of Chapter 4 " The Essence of Credit Currency and Three Layers of Credit ".

The borrower will provide sufficient commodities is an ought-to event, not a must-be event. A legally valid loan contract can certainly receive legal support, but the law cannot guarantee the creditor's realization of every debt claim, nor can anyone ensure that the borrower will definitely provide enough commodities for the market. So why are people still willing to accept Contract Currency? This is because people still believe that even if the borrower does not provide, there will be new market participants who can provide goods or service of comparable value and are willing to accept their own currency.

Therefore, the value of Contract Currency is based on the following two contracts and one confidence. Contract one refers to the common agreement of market participants to use this currency. Contract two refers to the borrower of Currency Issuer providing goods and repaying loans as agreed. Confidence refers to the assurance that even if debtors are unable to repay, other entities in society still have sufficient goods to supplement and provide trading targets for the market.

Law is the common contract of society, and market innovation and people's hard work are the sources of supplementing production capacity. Therefore, Contract Currency often relies on legislation and is often referred to as legal currency. People have always advocated development, and only development can compensate for the problem of insufficient production capacity of defaulting borrowers.

So far, the development of currency has gone through four forms.

The 1.0 version of Material Currency possesses universal practical attributes carrying transactional attributes. The 2.0 version of Receipt Currency uses its universal practical attributes to enhance transactional attributes. The 3.0 version of Promise Currency is endorsed by the issuer's own credit for transactional attributes. In contrast, the 4.0 version of Contract Currency undergoes a complete transformation; its credit endorsement comes from the users themselves rather than the issuers, granting it more independent transactional attributes.

The earliest form of currency was tangible goods, which naturally emerged from human social activities.

The Currency Issuer created Receipt Currency based on people's recognition of the natural value of Material Currency, and the credit of Receipt Currency comes from Material Currency.

After widespread use, the credit of Receipt Currency was strengthened, and Receipt Currency used its own credit to help the issuer establish the issuer's credit. The issuer then used the issuer's credit to create Promise Currency. Promise Currency also strengthened its own credit in transactions, and then utilized its own credit to break away from the dependence on the issuer's credit. With the assistance of the issuer, Promise Currency evolved into a Contract Currency with independent credit. Currency and Currency Issuers work together and support each other. Through thousands of years of effort, they gradually extracted the essence of currency, namely the transaction function, from goods, establishing human recognition of the purely transactional attributes of currency.

Chapter 2: The Operation of Contract Currency

Contract Currency is the mainstream currency type issued by central banks around the world. Deposit Currency and Loan Currency we will introduce later are also based on the credit of Contract Currency, so that people do not realize the essential differences between them. As a core element of finance and economy, Contract Currency is widely discussed and is highly expected by governments to promote economic development. Understanding its operating mechanism is a basic requirement for a comprehensive understanding of monetary phenomena.

I. Contract Currency Ensures the Smooth Progress of Market Transactions

Let's review the creation process of "Central Bank of Island Z" and "Z coin" in the fourth section of Chapter 1. After the coiner persuaded and educated the farmer, the blacksmith, and the masseur on Island Z, combined with the past experience of production and trade exchange on Island Z, the people of Island Z reached a consensus through consultation: "The coiner will make a green banknote marked with '100 worth', called 'Z coin', and replace the original deposit certificate marked with '10 shells' with one such 'Z coin'. The original deposit certificate of '10 shells' can be exchanged for 1 spade, 10 hours of massage, and 100 kilograms of grain. Now, 1 'Z coin' which is 100 worth can be used to purchase 1 spade, 10 hours of massage, and 100 kilograms of grain respectively. The new 'Z coin' will be used starting on the arrival of the New Year.".

$$100 \text{ shells} = \begin{matrix} 1000 \text{ kilograms of grain} \\ 100 \text{ hours of massage} \\ 10 \text{ spades} \end{matrix} = 10 \text{ "Z coin"}$$

At this time, a miser came to Island Z again, who produced nothing and consumed nothing, but he had a special fondness for the green paper currency "Z coin" issued by the coiner. He focused on collecting "Z coin" and was extremely concerned about its purchasing power. He wound witness the changes in the purchasing power of "Z coin".

As the sun rose on New Year's Day, the currency reform on the island was officially implemented, and "Z coin" began to circulate. Four people, a farmer, a masseuse, a blacksmith, and a miser, respectively came to the residence of the coinage maker and wrote the mark of "-1000 worth" on the white wallboard of coiner's residence and pressed their handprints. Then they took away 10 pieces of "Z coin". So, the farmer took 10 pieces of "Z coin" to the blacksmith and exchanged it for 10 spades. The blacksmith took 10 pieces of "Z coin" to the masseuse and exchanged it for 100 hours of massage. The masseuse took 10 pieces of "Z coin" to the farmer and exchanged it for 1000 kilograms of grain. The miser took back 10 pieces of "Z coin" and put them under his pillow, falling asleep and feeling comfortable.

At this time, 1 kilogram of grain was equal to 1 worth, 1 hour of massage was equal to 10 worth, and 1 spade was equal to 100 worth. Although the miser did not need to trade, he knew it well. According to the rules of using "Z coin" that they were familiar with, the farmer, blacksmith, and masseuse borrowed "Z coin" from the coiner on January 1 every year and returned it all on December 31 every year. However, the miser did not need to repay regularly, only when the coiner required it to return. If the coiner did not require repayment, it could not be returned.

The "Z coin" successfully replaced the shell deposit certificate, ensuring the transaction of 1000 kilograms of grain, 100 hours of massage, and 10 spades on the island. The livelihood of the farmer, blacksmith, masseuse, and miser was maintained year after year, and the four people lived happily on the Z Island.

At this point, the physical value of Contract Currency was reduced to the value of a piece of paper (if information is displayed on the paper), which was almost negligible. However, it had no impact on the transactions on the island. People had established a consensus that this piece of paper guaranteed the market transactions and economic operations on Island Z. We call the story of the perfect assurance of transactions by Contract Currency Story 1.

II. The Excess of Output over Consumption Leads to the Generation of Savings

The farmer's luck came, this year, the weather was favorable and rainfall was timely, coupled with the farmer's hard work, the grain harvest increased by half, with an annual output of 1500 kilograms. The masseuse loved the grain and decided to buy it all. On January 1st of the new year, the masseuse came to the coiner to explain the situation and expresses his desire to borrow an additional "500 worth". The coiner readily agreed. Therefore, the masseuse wrote the words "-1500 worth " on the white wallboard of the coiner and took away 15 "Z coins", then payed them all to the farmer. However, this year, the masseuse did not provide more massage services. As in previous years, the masseuse only exchanged 10 "Z coins" from the blacksmith by providing massage services. The blacksmith also sold 10 spades to the farmer as usual and obtained 10 "Z coins". On December 31st of that year, the farmer paid off the loan and had 5 "Z coins" left in his home. However, the masseuse still owed the coiner 5 "Z coins" that he had not repaid. For the first time on the island, someone owned "Z coins" without his own debt, which increased his wealth and generated savings. The 5 "Z coins" was deposited in the drawer of the farmer. We call the story of generating savings Story 2.

III. The Economy will Grow Every Time the Currency is Used

The fundamental purpose of economic activities is to meet people's needs. The diverse needs of human beings can only be fulfilled through transactions, and the medium of transactions is money. Therefore, the use of one cent by people increases the economy by one cent, and increasing the transaction volume of money in the market can directly improve the economy. We call this specific relationship between the use of money and economic growth the first law of monetary economics. There are several ways to increase the use of

37

money.

1. Increase Credit

The coiner was still thinking about how to increase the satisfaction of the four people on the Island Z, so that they could live a happier life. Inspired by the farmer's harvest and the masseuse's increased borrowing, on January 1st of the new year, the coiner said to the masseuse, "Last year, the farmer had a good harvest and there was still a deposit of 500 'Z coins' at the end of the year. He was very happy. This year, I will lend you an additional 1000 'A' coins. Please tell the farmer to work harder and produce more food. At the same time, you will also eat more, and I heard that there is still food in your house, so you should also work harder and improve the time of massage services. You can't keep delaying my 500 Z coins!". The masseuse was very excited and thanked him repeatedly. He took away 20 "Z coins" from the coiner, and the white wallboard read 'Massage: -2500'.

As expected, after receiving 20 "Z coins" from the masseuse, the farmer worked day and night. Although the weather was not enough good this year, through hard work, the farmer's annual output actually reached 2000 kilograms. At the same time, due to the increased workload and increased consumption of tools, he ordered 18 spades from the blacksmith this year, and the blacksmith also worked overtime to complete the delivery and received 1800 worth from the farmer. In order to completed the task, he needed more relaxation and therefore enjoyed 170 hours of massage services from the masseuse, for which he paid 1700 worth.

At the end of the year, the farmer received 2000 worth and paid 1800 worth, with a surplus of 200 worth. In addition to the cash retained in Story 2 , after paying off the loan from the coiner, his drawer had a savings of 700 worth. This year, the blacksmith received 1800 worth and paid 1700 worth. After paying off the loan from the coiner, he also had a cash savings of 100 worth for the first time. This year, the masseuse received 1700 worth, borrowed 2000 at the beginning of the year, and paid off the loan at the end of the year. His debt to the coiner increased by 300 worth, reaching 800 worth.

This year, the amount of the "Z coin" issued by the coiner increased from the original 3500 worth to 4500 worth, while the three people on Island Z created 2000 kilograms of grain, 18 spades, and 170 hours of massage services, with a total output 5500 worth. The wealth produced on Island Z increased, and the needs of the three people were mostly met. By issuing additional currency, the economy of the island was promoted. We can clearly see that the release of currency is a positive incentive to promote economic growth. We call the story of using loans to promote economic growth Story 3.

2. Reduce Savings

The story continued. It was another year. The masseuse borrowed 2000 worth "Z coins" from the coin-caster and bought 2000 kilograms of grain produced by the farmer. In order to further expanded production, the farmer used his savings of 300 wroth "Z coins" in his drawer and bought 23 spades. The blacksmith received 2300 worth "Z coins" and enjoyed himself by buying 220 hours of massage, paying 2200 worth "Z coins" for it. The blacksmith saved an additional 100 worth "Z coins". The masseuse paid 2000 worth "Z coins" and received 2200 worth "Z coins", which were returned to the coin-caster at the end of the year, reducing the original debt of 800 worth "Z coins" by 200. This year, the three people on Island Z created 2000 kilograms of grain, 23 spades, and 220 hours of massage, with a total output value of 6500 worth "Z coins". The wealth produced on Island Z has increased significantly compared to Story 3, and the needs of the three people had also been maximally met. Through the monetary savers putting money into consumption, the economy has achieved further growth. This story is what we call Story 4.

3. Private Lending

We have discussed two ways to increase the use of money and thus boost the total economic output: one is for the Currency Issuer to issue loans to people without money deposits, and the other is for the money depositors to put the money into use. We have deduced these two situations through stories 3 and 4. We will now tell another story. In story 2, the farmer overproduced 500 kilograms of grain through labor, and the masseuse exchanged the grain for 500 worth "Z coins" borrowed from the farmer. At the end of the year, the farmer's drawer remained with 500 "Z coins". In the new year after story 2, the coiner as in previous years, distributed 1000 worth "Z Coins" to each of the three individuals. The farmer learnt that the masseuse was willing and able to provide more massages, but the blacksmith was unable to produce more spades. In this situation, the farmer proposed to the blacksmith that his white wallboard could also be used for accounting purposes, and he was willing to lend the blacksmith 500 worth "Z coins", so the blacksmith wrote a mark of "Blacksmith: -500 worth " on the farmer's white wallboard, borrowed 500 worth "Z coins" from the farmer, and then paid the masseuse for 50 hours of massage services. At the end of the year, all three people had no remaining debts to pay to the coiner, but the 500 worth "Z coins" transferred from the farmer's drawer to the masseuse's drawer, and the blacksmith had a debt of 500 worth "Z coins" that could not be repaid to the farmer. This year, the retention of 500 worth "Z coins" was put into use to promote the output value of Z Island by 500 based on the borrowing and lending between the farmer and the blacksmith. In this new story, private lending has emerged, and a third way to increase the use of money and thus promote economic growth has emerged. We call this story story5.

IV. The Emergence of Contract Currency is a Historical Inevitability and Progress

Money was invented to ensure the multilateral exchange of various commodities, which requires that the supply of money match and adapt to the transaction volume of all commodities. Money has emerged and developed from human life practices. The primary money is either a single specific item or a certificate and promise of this specific item, which fundamentally determines that the supply of Material Currency in version 1.0, Receipt Currency in version 2.0, and Promise Currency in version 3.0 cannot meet the increasing transaction volume of human commodities, and will inevitably be eliminated by history. The emergence of Contract Currency in version 4.0 breaks the binding and restrictions of specific items on the transaction medium. Money is no longer a representative of a single item, but a representative of all items, not only the representative of existing items, but also the representative of future possible produced commodities. Only in this way can the supply of money adapt to the transaction volume of commodities, and money can better serve the transaction of all items. The emergence of Contract Currency is a historical inevitability and progress.

The dollar under the Bretton Woods system was essentially a promise by the US government to holders to exchange gold. It was a Promise Currency. If the Federal Reserve System wanted to ensure that all dollars have gold available for exchange, it could only issue dollars at a ratio of 35 dollars per ounce of gold, limiting the total amount issued to the amount of gold reserves it has. Outside of this range, if it wanted to issue more dollars, the Federal Reserve System could only complete the issuance of dollars by purchasing gold from gold holders. Only in this way can it ensured that it had sufficient gold reserves and thus had the ability to fully fulfill its exchange commitment.

The US dollar was mainly issued to domestic entities in the United States, No matter how abundant the total gold reserves in the United States government and within the country were, they were inevitably finite. However, with the development of globalization, the volume of international trade was increasing, and more and more US dollars were needed for transaction payments. The supply of US dollars linked to gold wound eventually be unable to adapt.

In the context of global free trade, domestic entities that had obtained US dollar issuance could use US dollars to trade with foreign entities. When the United States had a trade surplus, US goods flowed abroad and foreign dollars flowed back to the US, which meant that there was a shortage of foreign dollars. In this case, domestic entities could exchange their US dollars for gold held by foreign entities. The Federal Reserve System could continue to collect gold from domestic entities and kept the US dollars in their hands. If this continued, foreign gold wound continue to flow into the US in exchange for

US dollars as the US trade surplus increases. However, the amount of gold held by foreign entities was limited. Although the "dollar-gold pegging" system under a trade surplus can be sustained by the inflow of global gold reserves, it wound inevitably collapse in the end. Because the global gold reserves wound eventually be limited and could not support the massive supply of US dollars needed for global trades, the system wound inevitably collapse.

When the US had an overall trade deficit, it means that the US dollar would stay abroad. At this time, the demand for the US dollar outside the US was met, and the US could only rely on the gold owned by domestic entities to issue currency. The amount of gold that the Federal Reserve System can exchanged in and the amount of dollar that the Federal Reserve System can issued out were both even more limited, "dollar-gold pegging" system was set to accelerate towards collapse.

In summary, if the Federal Reserve System wanted to meet the domestic and international transaction payment demands and let the US dollar bear the burden of international payment, it needed to issue a large amount of US dollar. For every 35 US dollars issued, the Federal Reserve System's gold inventory would have a possibility of being exchanged for one ounce. At the same time, whether in the United States or around the world, the stock of gold was inevitably limited, and the increase in gold could not match the increase in goods that need to be traded. This wound only lead to two situations for the US dollar: either people did not require gold exchange at all, or they could not exchange gold at all. In either case, the "pegging of the US dollar to gold" could not be maintained for a long time.

The United States established the status of the US dollar as a world currency through the credit endorsement of gold. As a world currency, the US dollar needed to have a Currency Issuance volume that matched the volume of international trade. However, the issuance volume of the US dollar was limited by the gold reserves of the US government. The work that the US government tried to carry out in that year was actually trying to "use a currency with limited issuance volume to achieve unlimited Currency Issuance volume". This sounds quite ridiculous and funny, but it was indeed an impossible problem that the US government once set for itself. This problem was later detected by American economist Robert Triffin.

V. Decoding the Triffin Dilemma

One way to expressed the dilemma faced by Americans is the "Triffin Dilemma". Robert Triffin pointed out that the monetary strategy of the United States requires the country to achieve both trade surpluses and trade deficits, which is contradictory.

Why did the Triffin Dilemma happen? Let's imagine that if the amount of gold held outside the United States was infinite, then the dollars needed for international settlement could be exchanged for gold with the United States, eliminating the need for a long-term U.S. balance of payments deficit. Even if the United States maintained a long-term trade surplus, it could rely on the inflow of foreign gold to continuously export dollars. Correspondingly, if the amount of gold in the United States was unlimited, even if there was a long-term deficit, it could rely on domestic gold to continuously issue dollars for international purchases. In other words, Under the commitment of "pegging the dollar to gold", it is precisely because of the limited gold outside the United States that the dollar must be in long-term trade deficit as a world currency; it is precisely because of the limited gold reserves in the United States that the dollar must be in long-term trade surplus as a world currency. The root cause of the "Triffin Dilemma" was that the amount and growth of gold reserves in the United States and abroad could not match the volume of international trade. The commitment of pegging the dollar to gold and the requirement of matching the dollar with world trade are a natural contradiction that cannot be achieved simultaneously.

Under the Bretton Woods system, to internationalize the US dollar, it was necessary for the US to have a long-term trade deficit, because the US dollar could only be issued to its own country, while it needed to be continuously deposited overseas. With a long-term trade deficit, the US dollar could not be linked to gold, because a large amount of US dollar needed to be issued to maintained the long-term trade deficit, while the domestic gold reserves in the United States were always limited. The above derivation shows that the internationalization of the US dollar determines that the US dollar cannot be linked to gold. Under the Bretton Woods system, the complete dollar dilemma is that "to internationalized the US dollar, it was impossible to have a trade surplus and 'dollar-gold pegging'. To had a gold link, it was impossible to have a trade deficit and internationalize the US dollar. To had a trade surplus, it was impossible to internationalize the US dollar. To had a trade deficit, it was impossible to have 'dollar-gold pegging'".

In fact, the massive increase in trade volume requires a massive supply of US dollar, but the limited stock and limited increase of gold cannot be resolved. Whether the United States maintains a trade surplus or a trade deficit, as long as the US dollar is issued in large quantities (as a domestic currency or a world currency), the pegging of the US dollar to gold cannot be maintained for a long time. The trade surplus can only delay the decline in the gold content of the US dollar, but cannot fundamentally solve the problem because of limited foreign gold. Because, the decline in the gold content of the US dollar is only partially affected by the US trade deficit, and the trade deficit is not the fundamental reason for the decline in the gold content of the US dollar.

The Triffin Dilemma originates from the 1960 book "Gold and the Dollar Crisis: The Future of Convertibility" by American economist Robert Triffin. It refers to the situation:

Because the US dollar is pegged to gold and other countries' currencies are pegged to the dollar, the dollar has achieved the status of an international core currency. However, for countries to develop international trade, they must use the dollar as a settlement and reserve currency. This leads to a continuous accumulation of dollars overseas, resulting in a long-term deficit in the US balance of payments. Yet, the premise of the dollar being the core of the international monetary system requires maintaining the stability of the dollar's value, which in turn demands that the United States be a country with a long-term surplus in its balance of international trade.

These two requirements contradict each other, thus forming a paradox known as the "Triffin Dilemma."

The "pegging of the US dollar to gold" was not the purpose of the United States, but its means. The goal of the Americans was to ensure the credibility of the dollar so that it became the world currency. Therefore, only a dollar with sufficient credit could be accepted by people around the world. Under the objective limitation of limited gold, how to achieve the two goals of sufficient credit and sufficient issuance of the US dollar at the same time? Let's make an assumption. The Federal Reserve System can directly issue currency to foreign entities, that is, foreign entities can directly borrow US dollars from the Federal Reserve System. In this case, the US dollars needed for international settlement and international reserves can be obtained from the Federal Reserve System through the credit of foreign entities, without the need for the United States to have a long-term deficit in its balance of payments. Even if the United States maintains a long-term trade surplus, it can continue to export dollars by relying on the credit of foreign entities. The issue of declining dollar credibility and the rise in dollar supply, which are inextricably linked, will be solved readily and perfectly. Thus, we have found another reason for the "Triffin Dilemma": "The dollar can only be issued to domestic entities in the United States", which has not changed so far, resulting in the dollar dilemma not being completely resolved. We will elaborate on this in Chapter 13 "The Road to Financial Power and Its Weaknesses in the United States" Section VI " New Dilemma and solutions of the US dollar ".

The core issue of the Bretton Woods system was that the massive demand for money was artificially limited to a limited amount of gold. To solve this problem, we must break this unreasonable restriction. The disintegration of the Bretton Woods system was an overt breach of contract and collective default by the issuer of the US dollar and the US government. However, this stemmed from humanity's misunderstanding of currency, making it an inevitable breach, a progressive breach, and an inevitable outcome as monetary progress keeps pace with the overall advancement of human society. Contract Currency meets the needs of humans for extensive and massive transactions, promotes human communication, and enhances human welfare.

The progress of science and technology, the improvement of productivity, and the circulation of goods worldwide have determined that no physical object can support the huge demand for transactions. As a unique item that meets the needs of transactions, money does not need any other functions, nor does it need the endorsement of any other items with actual value. Contract Currency is the true money used only for transactions, it is pure money, advanced money.

Chapter 3: Commercial Banks Actually Own the Right to Issue Currency

People usually believe that there is only one legal currency in a country and it is issued by the central bank. People with financial knowledge also know that commercial banks have created a monetary multiplier on the currency issued by the central bank through disbursement of loans. However, no one points out that commercial banks have actually owned the right to issue currency, what's more, commercial banks have quietly become the main and direct Currency Issuer in various countries, and the currency created by commercial banks is completely different in nature with that created by the central bank. No one cares whether commercial banks, as profit-oriented corporate organizations, should be given the right to issue currency that is crucial to the country's destiny.

I. Commercial Banks Emerged as Warehouse Managers

The farmer had been keeping the 500 worth "Z coins" earned in Story 2 in his drawer for a long time. The farmer only produced grain and bought spades, and did not know how to manage "Z coins". At the same time, he is also worried that "Z coins" will mold and damage if left for too long.

On this day, another man drifted over to Island Z. He was a commercial banker. After familiarizing himself with the situation on the island, he followed the practice of the "Central Bank of Island Z" and set up two signs on his doorstep, one called "Commercial Bank of Island Z" and one called "Z Coin Warehouse". He found the farmer and told him about his rich experience in money management outside the island, gaining the farmer's trust. He gave the farmer a red paper with the words "Farmer has deposited 500 worth 'Z Coin' in my place" written on it. The paper's header showed a striking "Commercial Bank Deposit Certificate". The commercial banker signed his name on the red paper, and the farmer took away the "Commercial

Bank Deposit Certificate" while leaving the 500 worth "Z Coins" at the commercial bank.

II. Currency in 5.0 Version, Deposit Currency

The farmer has exchanged his 5 "Z coins" for a 500 worth "commercial bank deposit certificate". When the farmer purchased 23 spades from the blacksmith in story 4, in addition to directly paying the blacksmith the 1000 worth "Z coins" borrowed from the coinage maker and the 1000 worth "Z coins" received from the masseuse, he also took the blacksmith to the commercial bank and changed the "commercial bank deposit certificate" in his hand that read "The farmer has deposited 500 worth 'Z coins' in my place" to "The farmer has deposited 200 worth 'Z coins in my place" on the spot. At the same time, the commercial bank issued a "commercial bank deposit certificate" to the blacksmith that read "The blacksmith has deposited 300 worth 'Z coins' in my place".

The farmer, the masseuse, and the blacksmith found that it was more convenient and faster to directly go to commercial banks to change their "deposit certificates" than to exchange multiple 100 worth "Z coins" with each other, and it was also safer to leave the "Z coins" at commercial banks.

So, in the new year, the three of them kept all the "Z coin" borrowed from the coiner at the commercial bank. For future transactions, regardless of the amount, the three of them could simply change the amount on the "commercial bank deposit certificate" at the commercial bank. From then on, the three of them rarely touched "Z coin" again.

When commercial banks issued "deposit certificates" and provided "deposit certificate information changes" or "deposit certificate ownership transfers" as a common payment method in the Z Island Market transaction, the commercial bank's deposit certificates of currencies became a new type of currency. The commercial bank had changed from the original currency borrower and retainer to Currency Issuer of the new currency. At this time, the currency changed from green "Z coins" to red "deposit certificates".

Commercial banks seemed to be a professional and novel institution, but we feel familiar with them. The warehouse manager who first came to Island Z, then the central bank coinage maker, originally kept people's shells. Correspondingly, the commercial banker kept people's "Z coin". Both issue deposit certificates, and the stored shells and "Z coin" are both used for transactions. So it seems that there was no essential difference between the current commercial banker and the former shell warehouse manager. Just like the original shell deposit certificate, the current "Z coins" deposit certificate has the essence of 2.0 version of Receipt Currency again. As Mark Twain said, "History does not repeat itself, but it rhymes". The history of human currency has progressed and reappeared at this moment.

The 2.0 version of the Receipt Currency is deposit certificate of Material

Currency in the 1.0 version, and the current commercial bank's "currency deposit certificate" is the deposit certificate of "Contract Currency" in the 4.0 version. Thus, the 5.0 version of currency has been created my modern humans, it is the "currency deposit certificates" of commercial banks, which we call "Deposit Currency".

Every amount on the "Deposit Currency" has a corresponding "Z coin" existing. The "deposit certificate" is only a substitute for the "Z coin". The total amount of currency available for trading on the Z Island has not changed, and the total amount of currency issued was still firmly in the hands of the coiner. The deposit certificate of commercial banks only changed the means of retention and payment of currency. Commercial banks had transformed a new type of Receipt Currency based on Contract Currency because of their widely accepted "currency deposit certificate". So far, the function of commercial banks was still limited to storage and the accompanying change of storage information, and its essence was still a warehouse. Nowadays, the commercial bank was not fundamentally different from the former shell warehouse manager. The former stored shells, while the latter stored currency. However, their similarities do not end here. Next, the commercial banker wound also undergo a complete transformation. It wound issue empty "currency deposit certificates" like the former shell warehouse manager issued empty "shells deposit certificates".

III. Currency in 6.0 Version, Loan Currency

Following the previous narrative, the farmer deposited the 500 "Z coins" he had saved in Story 2 with a commercial bank, which issued a "deposit certificate".

The commercial bank found the masseuse and said to her, "As far as I know, the coiner is not willing to lend you more money. I have 500 worth here that I can lend to you, but you don't have to take it. You can keep it here with me, and I will issue you my commercial bank deposit certificate. This 500 worth bank deposit certificate can be used for trading and circulation as usual." The masseuse gladly agreed, and wrote a mark on the white wallboard of the commercial bank: "Masseuse: -500 worth". The masseuse took the commercial bank deposit certificate with the content of "The masseuse has deposited 500 worth 'Z coins' in my place" and went home, feeling the same joy as when her first borrowed the shell deposit certificate from the shell warehouse administrator.

The commercial bank found the blacksmith again and conducted a similar operation with him. At this time, the commercial bank only had 500 "Z coins" in stock, while there were already three 500 worth "Z coins" deposit certificates on the Z Island. However, behind the deposit certificates in the hands of the masseuse and the blacksmith were not real deposits, but two loans of 500 worth "Z coins" written on the white wall board of the commercial bank.

In the second year, the three individuals each borrowed 1000 worth from the coiner, but all three had the ability to pay 1500 worth. At the same time, the "Z coins" that the three individuals borrowed from the coiner were all deposited in the commercial bank, the payment of 1500 worth by each individual was no longer made directly through "Z coins", but through changing the deposit information at the commercial bank. At this point, because the masseuse and the blacksmith each had a 500 worth "empty" currency deposit certificate, the money supply on Island Z increased by 1000 worth. The commercial bank promised that this 1000 worth "Z coin" could be withdrawn from its warehouse at any time, but in fact, how this 1000 worth "Z coin" deposit certificate was generated is clear to us. It was issued by the farmer's actual retention and lent to the masseuse and the blacksmith in succession. The key issue was that the farmer already had a 500 worth deposit certificate, which was already in circulation in the market for trading. The issuance of an additional 1000 worth deposit certificate to the masseuse and the blacksmith completely formed a new increase in supply of currency. The "commercial bank deposit certificate" obtained through borrowing is a new increase in Currency Issuance, the liabilities corresponding to Currency Issuance have simply shifted from the white wallboards of the coiner to the white wallboards of the commercial bank.

At this time, the deposit receipts were not issued based on the retentions of cash, but on the basis of liabilities, this could also be seen as the borrower lending out money based on debt, and then depositing the money with the lender to obtain a deposit certificate. The effect of both is the same. Essentially, this was a "commercial bank deposit receipt" that was lent out, not a "commercial bank deposit receipt" that was deposited. It can be completely considered as a commercial bank issuing a deposit receipt out of thin air based on the borrower credit.

So far, the currency of the island not only was the green "Z coin" made by the coiners, but also the red "commercial bank deposit certificate" made by the commercial bankers to replace the "Z coin". In addition, there are also "empty" "commercial bank deposit certificates" borrowed by the masseuse and the blacksmith from commercial banks based on their own credit.

When the commercial bank could increase the money supply on Island Z by recording claims on his white wallboard based on his assessment of borrower credit, it had the function of a coiner. The history of human currency had once again evolved and advanced, and a version 6.0 of currency has been created. We refer to this "empty" "commercial bank deposit receipt" as "Loan Currency".

The appearance of "Loan Currency" is still a deposit certificate, but behind it is the corresponding liability of the holder to the commercial bank. To put it simply, "Deposit Currency" is based on deposits with commercial banks, while "Loan Currency" is based on loans from commercial banks. "Deposit Currency" is a replacement for the "Contract Currency" issued by the central bank, while "Loan Currency" is a new type of currency issued by the commercial bank.

Now, let's take a look at the changes in the balance sheet of commercial banks when deposit and loan occur, in order to deepen our understanding of the abstract new currency of "Loan Currency":

When someone deposits 1 million yuan with a commercial bank, the assets and liabilities of the commercial bank increase simultaneously.

asset	liabilities
Cash 1 million yuan (from depositors)	Deposit 1 million yuan (depositor holds deposit certificate)

Under the current monetary system, most countries require commercial banks to meet certain reserve requirements when issuing loans to the public. That is, after each deposit enters a commercial bank, the bank must retain a portion of the deposit for depositors to withdraw or transfer out, and only the remaining portion can be used to issue loans to the public. The retained portion is the reserve requirement, and the proportion of the reserve requirement is the reserve requirement ratio.

Based on the 7% deposit reserve ratio, commercial banks can issue 930,000 loans based on this 1million yuan deposit. When someone applies for 930,000 yuan loan and is approved, the commercial bank transfers the 930,000 yuan to the borrower's account opened at the bank. The borrower has a "commercial bank deposit certificate" that is Loan Currency, and the commercial bank has the borrower's loan contract. The balance sheet of the commercial bank further expands.

asset	liabilities
Cash 1 million yuan (from depositors)	Deposit 1 million yuan (depositor holds deposit certificate)
Loan of 930,000 yuan (credit to the borrower)	Deposit 930,000 yuan (the borrower holds the deposit certificate)

When the borrower pays out, withdraws or transfers the 930,000 yuan deposit to an account opened by others in other commercial banks, the assets and liabilities of the commercial bank decrease simultaneously.

asset	liabilities
Cash 70,000 yuan (from depositors)	Deposit 1 million yuan (depositor holds deposit certificate)
Loan of 930,000 yuan (credit to the borrower)	

Take a closer look at what happened! The depositor's 1 million yuan of cash in the bank's inventory has only been reduced to 70,000 yuan, and in fact, the depositor's 1 million yuan bank deposit certificate cannot be withdrawn completely from the commercial bank. Even if the depositor wants to transfer the 1 million yuan to another commercial bank account, the commercial bank that originally issued the deposit certificate cannot complete the transaction. 930,000 yuan was "misappropriated" by the commercial bank, and the depositor's 930,000 yuan deposit was "emptied" by the borrower, replaced by a loan contract issued by the borrower in the commercial bank's inventory.

In reality, commercial banks do not have only one 1 million yuan cash inventory. Each deposit will retain a certain proportion of reserves, and it is unlikely that each deposit will require the withdrawal of cash or transfer to other commercial banks at the same time. Commercial banks rely on the retention of reserves for all depositors and the retention of deposit certificates for some depositors to maintain the withdrawal and interbank transfer of a small number of people. Many copies of "70,000 yuan" reserve retention guarantee the withdrawal and transfer of a small number of "1 million yuan". Therefore, under normal circumstances, the bank deposit certificate held by the depositor with 1 million yuan can still be paid externally through transfer, which means that the loan of 930,000 yuan is a newly created currency by commercial banks.

The current popular modern monetary theory holds that "it is not deposits that create loans, but loans that create deposits". The first half of the sentence "it is not deposits that create loans" is correct. When lenders issue loans externally, they do not need the support of deposits. They can do so solely based on creditworthiness of borrowers. Even though some countries have implemented a partial deposit reserve system, this margin reserve is only for maintaining cash flow. Under the deposit reserve system, deposits can only be considered as a constraint of loans, not as a source of loans, and the deposit reserve system does not fundamentally constrain loans. and does not fundamentally constrain loans. As long as the money lent by the borrower does not flow out of the borrower's system, that is, the borrower does not withdraw cash from the deposit certificate or transfer it to other commercial banks, loans can be made without restrictions. Moreover, many countries require a reserve requirement ratio of zero.

The latter part of the sentence, "It is the loan that creates the deposit," is incorrect. The loan only creates a deposit certificate, not a deposit. The borrower only obtains the deposit certificate issued by the lender, which can be used in the market for commodity trading and as currency. Therefore, we regard it as a new type of currency. When the lender issues a deposit certificate, it also does not obtain a deposit, but only obtain the borrower's loan contract.

Deposits and deposit certificates are fundamentally different. In the classification of currencies in this book, the former is the cash notes issued by the central bank, which are Contract Currency, while the latter is a new type of currency issued by commercial banks, which can be classified as deposit certificates or loan deposit certificates, depending on their sources. When a borrower withdraws cash from a deposit certificate, the cash deposit flows from the lender's warehouse into the borrower's hands. The borrower uses the cash to trade in the market, rather than using the previous deposit certificate for transactions. In this process, the deposit is also not created, but only transferred from the lending commercial bank's warehouse to the market. Even if the borrower chooses to withdraw cash and deposit it in other commercial bank, or transfer the amount shown on the deposit certificate to any account opened in other commercial bank, or if the borrower purchases goods from others and the seller deposits the cash obtained into another commercial bank, it seems that the deposit of other commercial bank has increased, but the deposit of lending commercial bank has also decreased accordingly. The new deposit generated by another commercial bank can only be seen as a transfer of the original deposit of lending commercial banks. Loans still do not create deposits, nor can they create deposits, there is no deposit be created also. Because deposits come from cash notes, which are Contract Currency that can only be created by the central bank.

The supply of "Loan Currency" is the sum of N times of loan amounts. Due to the provisions of the deposit reserve ratio, each loan is a discount of the previous deposit. Even if the borrower does not withdraw cash from the bank after obtaining the loan, the amount of each loan issued by commercial banks will decrease progressively. Assuming that the initial cash deposit is A and the deposit reserve ratio is a, the amount withdrawn in the Contract Currency (paper cash) after the nth Loan Currency Issuance is B_n (transferring from one commercial bank to another commercial bank, can be regarded as deposit after withdrawal, since the operations of commercial banks are consistent, overall, it is not considered as a withdrawal.). Assuming that commercial banks can use all the amount other than the deposit reserve for loans each time, then the first Loan Currency A_1 generated by this part of Deposit Currency is:

$$A_1 = A * (1-\alpha) ,$$

Loan Currency A_n produced by the nth loan is:

$A_n = (A_{n-1} - B_{n-1}) * (1-\alpha)$

The total amount of Loan Currency X_n generated by the cash deposit A is:

$$Xn = \sum_{k=1}^{n}(A_{k-1} - B_{k-1}) * (1-a)$$

Assuming that all Loan Currency will not be withdrawn and will leave commercial banks in the form of Contract Currency (paper cash), then the nth Loan Currency A_n is:

$A_n = A * (1-\alpha)^n$

The total amount of Loan Currency X_n generated by the cash deposit A is:

$$Xn = \sum_{k=1}^{n} A * (1-\alpha)^k$$

In practice, commercial banks are unlikely to exhaust the deposit reserve ratio system, which means they are unlikely to exhaust the amount of loans they can lend to others. Therefore, the above formula is the maximum amount of Loan Currency that commercial banks can create based on cash deposits. The specific amount of Loan Currency issued by each commercial bank is the amount shown in the "Loans and Advance payment" account in its balance sheet.

IV. The Evolution of Currency

Material Currency in version 1.0 is based on the general acceptance of specific items by people. Receipt Currency in version 2.0 is a voucher that stores Material Currency. Promise Currency in version 3.0 claims to be able to exchange physical goods like Receipt Currency, but in fact it is issued by Currency Issuer through lending, and there are actually no sufficient physical goods for exchange in the issuer's warehouse. Contract Currency in version 4.0 directly breaks the legal obligation to exchange physical goods, telling people that there are no physical goods and that they are lent out completely out of thin air, but they can still be used for market transactions. Deposit Currency in version 5.0 is a storage voucher for Contract Currency in version 4.0. Loan Currency in version 6.0 claims to be able to exchange Contract Currency like Deposit Currency, just like Promise Currency in version 3.0 once promised, but in fact there is no corresponding Contract Currency, that is, cash notes, to retain.

The development and evolution of money follow its own characteristics and follow a simple and clear logic. The 4.0 version of Contract Currency is a new type of 1.0 version of Material Currency, the 5.0 version of Deposit Currency is a new type of 2.0 version of Receipt Currency, and the 6.0 version of Loan Currency is a new type of 3.0 version of Promise Currency. Through thousands of years of history, humans have slowly extracted the transaction function from natural objects for their own use, and money has evolved from a tangible physical object to a symbol that exists only in human consensus.

Imagine if the promise of Loan Currency is broken again, or more accurately, is discovered. At this time, commercial banks will experience a run on deposits, and people will no longer store Contract Currency in commercial banks. Then Deposit Currency in version 5.0 will disappear, and commercial banks will no longer have the function of issuing loans. Loan Currency in version 6.0 will disappear, and the right to issue currency will once again be completely controlled by the central bank. Human currency will return to the era of Contract Currency in version 4.0. When the credit of the central bank's Contract Currency collapses, humans can only regain Material Currency.

On December 30, 2023, the state of New Hampshire in the United States officially announced monetary independence, allowing employers to pay employees in gold and silver. On January 7, 2024, a proposal (HB1043) submitted by the Indiana House of Representatives announced that the state would take important steps in financial currency, considering gold and silver as currency that can be used to repay debts and taxes. On January 10, 2024, the Kentucky House of Representatives passed a bill (HB101), officially declaring that gold is considered legal currency in the state, and also exempting gold and silver transactions from capital gains tax. As of March 25, 2024, Wisconsin is the 44th state in the United States to abolish sales tax on gold and silver, which is a key step in considering gold and silver as currency rather than commodities.

V. Chinese Philosophical Speculation on Currency

In the Chinese book "Tao Te Ching", there is the saying "Tao gives birth to one, one gives birth to two, two gives birth to three, and three gives birth to all things". The Book of "Changes" narrates the universe as "three lines form a single hexagram, six lines form a composite hexagram, and composite hexagrams determine the universe". Dose the composite hexagram also fit the historical evolution of the six stages of currency? In a broad sense, currency is also a commodity, and both currency and the other commodities are human wealth. In a narrow sense, currency and commodity are a pair of contradictory and dialectical relationships that correspond to each other. They are yin and yang to each other, interact with each other and jointly maintain the operation of human wealth. We may use the speculative method of the Book of Changes to conduct a simple and interesting analysis of currency. Now, let's "eight diagrams" the currency together.

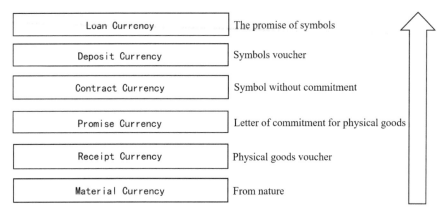

From the perspective of the philosophy of the Book "the I Ching" in China, yin means stability, pliancy, and nourishment, while yang means robustness, prosperity, and creativity. We believe that the natural attributes of money are more in line with the characteristics of yang, while the natural attributes of commodities are more in line with the characteristics of yin. Therefore, commodities should be yin wealth, and money should be yang wealth. Wealth is the source of human happiness, and we believe that money is the father of human happiness, while goods are the mother of human happiness. Therefore, the overall state of money should correspond to the Qian hexagram in the Book of Changes. The Qian hexagram symbolizes pure yang, indicating prosperity and robustness. The hexagram's words are "beginning, mogul, benefit, chaste", presenting auspiciousness and good fortune.

Qian Hexagram

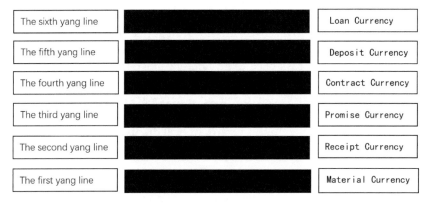

As for the specific meaning of each line of the hexagram, the statement of the first yang line is " Do not use the hidden dragon. ", which means "hidden dragon, do not show your power". Material Currency is in this position, which means that Material Currency should not be widely used in the market, but should be hidden more and need to be nurtured for the right time. We should not frequently use precious physical objects such as gold and jewelry or so-called "hard currency" for transactions, nor should we display these physical objects too much to the public, which is easy to lose and damage.

The second yang line reads, "Seeing the dragon in the field, it is beneficial to see the great man." This means that "the dragon has emerged from its hiding place and appeared on the ground, and it is time to play its role and show its power. This great man of great virtue has already appeared in the world, Its benefits will surely reach all under heaven, and people everywhere will be pleased to see it ". Receipt Currency is in this position, implying that Receipt Currency should be vigorously promoted for widespread awareness. Only then can more people store tangible goods, and more people will recognize this voucher, which will greatly benefit market transactions.

The commentary of the third yang line is "The gentleman is working diligently all day long, and is vigilant at night, originally in danger, but now there is no harm." It means "to be cautious and fearful all day long, and to strive constantly to improve oneself. Even at night, one should still be vigilant and not relax. In a dangerous place, there may be harm, but because it is vigorous and upright, it can achieve ' working diligently all day long, and is vigilant at night', and the harm is transformed into no harm. " Promise Currency is in this position, which means that Promise Currency should always be cautious and strive to improve itself, and there should be no relaxation. After all, there is no real physical storage behind Promise Currency, which is a clear mistake. If we cannot maintain sufficient hard work and diligence, it will cause doubts and lead to a run on Material Currency. This position is dangerous, but it can be effectively resolved and turned into safety.

The oracle of the fourth yang line is "either soar to the sky or dive into the abyss, no blame". It means "the dragon either leaps to the sky or dives into the dragon pool in accordance with the situation at that time, without any harm". Contract Currency is in this position, which implies that the issuance and use of central bank cash need to be carefully judged, assessing the situation and taking action accordingly. When it is necessary to strictly control, it should be strictly controlled, and when it is necessary to release, it should be released. How to grasp this degree depends on whether the borrower has future production capacity. In this regard, we will discuss in detail in the following chapters about the principles of Currency Issuance and the selection criteria of borrowers.

The phrase of the fifth yang line is "A flying dragon soars in the sky, benefiting those of greatness." This means "a soaring dragon, flying freely in the sky," and "a sage is the most brilliant and greatest among gentlemen and adults. His cultivation, wisdom, ability, and status are able to cope with any difficulties, just like a dragon flying in the sky, holy and noble, soaring freely, so that even the clouds, thunder, and rain can fall together and benefit the whole world. Such an adult is beneficial to all people in the world." [2] Deposit Currency is in this position, which means that Deposit Currency can be widely used, fully demonstrate its strength, fully play its role, and fully carry forward. Because Deposit Currency has real cash inventory, it can withstand any test. In the later chapters of this book, we strongly advocate confiscating the Currency Issuance rights of commercial banks and implementing a 100% deposit reserve system, allowing commercial banks to return to their original duty of currency management. This is also in line with the spirit of the book "the I Ching". In daily life, Chinese people emphasize that "cash is the king," while in the book "the I Ching", it is clearly stated that "deposits are Noble." Because Deposit Currency is just in the position of " Supreme Emperor ", " Noble " is supreme. In the ancient Chinese ruling class hierarchy, " Noble " represents the emperor, while "King" represents the vassals. "Noble " is obviously higher than "King." It is obvious that in Chinese philosophy, both deposits and cash have noble and distinguished status, and the status of deposits is higher than cash.

The formula of the sixth yang line is " The dragon that is too excited will regret it. ", which means: "People in high positions should guard against arrogance, otherwise they will regret their failure and later fall into decline." Loan Currency is in this position, which fully demonstrates that we should maintain a humble and cautious attitude when using loans. If the leverage is used too much, it is easy to go too far and backfire, which will bring harm to oneself. The book "the I Ching" seems to be warning people: "Cash is the king, deposits are noble, and loans are regrettable.".

Upon comprehending this, we cannot help but marvel that all things are interconnected and the Tao is the only one truth. The eight diagrams in the book "the I Ching", from the first to the last, are ever-changing and recurring. The artificial currency, from version 1.0 to version 6.0, also fits in with the laws and aesthetics of nature.

VI. Currency Types and Their Conversion under the Modern Financial System

The cash issued by central banks in various countries are mainly the 4.0 version of "Contract Currency". People deposit the "Contract Currency" they earn into commercial banks in exchange for version 5.0 of "Deposit Currency" (A deposit certificate that is not based on a loan but rather on cash deposits, with a passbook or an internet system serving as the medium for

---

[2] Jin Jingfang, Lv Shaogang. Complete Interpretation of the I Ching[M]. Jilin: Jilin University Press, 2015.

recording deposit information). Commercial banks own the right to issue loans to social entities, and the commercial bank deposit certificate held by borrowers based on their loan contract with commercial banks is the 6.0 version of "Loan Currency". After borrowers receive the deposit certificate, they can either hold it in cash or deposit it in commercial banks (represented by the commercial bank deposit certificate recorded in a passbook or Internet system). In either case, this part of money is newly created by debt. When borrowers choose to withdraw cash, the "Loan Currency" changes into "Contract Currency", and when borrowers choose to transfer money to others, the "Loan Currency" changes into the other person's "Deposit Currency", but before the change, the "Loan Currency" has already been created and brought into the market by the borrower.

In other words, under the modern financial system, there are three types of currencies used in the market: version 4.0 Contract Currency, version 5.0 Deposit Currency, and version 6.0 Loan Currency. Among them, version 4.0 Contract Currency can be understood as existing in two forms in the market: one is direct existence, which refers to the cash on hand of various units outside the banking system and the cash held by residents, and the other is indirect existence, which refers to the deposits people make in commercial banks in exchange for bank deposit certificates issued by commercial banks, including demand deposits and fixed deposits, which are version 5.0 Deposit Currency. Version 5.0 Deposit Currency is a substitute for version 4.0 Contract Currency. Since the issuers of Deposit Currency and Loan Currency are commercial banks, and the forms of expression are all commercial bank deposit certificates, the total amount of currency that can be used for trading in the market is the sum of the cash held by non-commercial bank market entities and the total amount of deposits shown on commercial bank deposit certificates. It should be noted that the carriers of Deposit Currency and Loan Currency are both deposit certificates, which appear in various forms in the market. Our bank passbooks, account interfaces on online banking or mobile banking, banker's checks, bills of exchange, and checks are essentially deposit certificates. When we use these deposit certificates for transactions, we only need to transfer or change the information on the deposit certificates, without having to use cash from commercial bank inventory.

Since Contract Currency in version 4.0, Deposit Currency in version 5.0, and Loan Currency in version 6.0 are all issued based on the borrower's liabilities, unlike previous versions of currencies based on physical value, these three currencies do not have any physical backing. We collectively refer to these three currencies as "Credit Currencies", and we will further explore the credit connotation of credit currencies in the next chapter, "The Essence and Logic of Credit Currencies".

It should be noted that there are certain mutual conversion relationships between these three credit currencies. Loan Currency only exists when the commercial bank transfers the loan amount to the borrower's account opened at the bank when issuing the loan. At this time, the borrower obtains a deposit certificate from the commercial bank. When the borrower withdraws cash with this deposit certificate, Loan Currency disappears, and the nature of the currency in the borrower's hand has been converted into a Contract Currency. When the borrower transfers this deposit certificate amount to another person's account, this part of Loan Currency also disappears, and its nature has become a Deposit Currency. Although Loan Currency has changed its nature, its function has been completed. It is through the creation and conversion of Loan Currency that the borrower leaves the debt on the account book of Currency Issuer and brings the money supply to the market. Contract Currency and Deposit Currency also undergo mutual conversion during the holder's deposit and withdrawal process.

VII. Classification Method of Current Money Supply and Improvement Direction

We refer to the total amount of currency that can be used for circulation and payment by the whole society at a certain point in time as the money supply. Currencies are used for transactions, based on the state in which currency is stored, it is possible to roughly estimate the time when the currency was used for exchange, and thus deduce the total amount of currency actually used for transactions in the market during a certain period of time. For example, if a family has a total of 1 million yuan in cash in their safe, but they only plan to use 100,000 yuan per year, then the actual amount of money supplied to the market by this family each year is only 100,000 yuan, not 1 million yuan. Therefore, people classify the total money supply of the entire society during a certain period of time in an attempt to judge the impact of money on the economy. Countries usually divide the money supply into three levels:

First, M0, refers to the sum of cash held by various units outside the banking system and the cash held by residents, that is, the part of the 4.0 version contract currency in the market that has not been saved by commercial banks.

Second, the narrow money supply M1, refers to M0 plus the current deposits of enterprises, institutions, organizations, troops, schools, and other units in banks. That is, each unit deposits part of the Contract Currency into commercial banks and receives a current deposit certificate issued by the commercial bank, which is part of Deposit Currency in version 5.0 and Loan Currency in version6.0.

The third is the broad money supply(M2) which refers to the cash outside the banking system plus corporate deposits, household savings deposits, and other deposits, including: M1 (narrow money supply, including cash in circulation and corporate demand deposits), corporate fixed deposits, urban and rural residents' demand and fixed deposits, foreign currency deposits, and trust deposits. The total amount of money that can be used for transactions, which we define as the sum of the 4.0 version of Contract Currency, the 5.0 version of Deposit Currency, and the 6.0 version of Loan Currency, is the sum of cash and deposits, which coincides with our classification of money supply based on the nature of money.

This traditional division of the money supply is based on several assumptions: First, individuals usually use cash for short-term money usage, so as long as they deposit money in the bank, whether it is demand or fixed, it represents that they will not use it in the short term. Second, units usually use cash or bank transfers for short-term money usage, and the money they intend to use in the short term will be placed on demand deposits. Third, units that do not intend to use money in the short term will place it on fixed deposits. Therefore, it is generally believed that M0 represents purchasing power closely related to consumption, while M1 reflects the actual purchasing power in the economy; M2 not only reflects the actual purchasing power, but also reflects the potential purchasing power. The rapid growth of M0 represents that residents have become richer, and consumption may also be active, which may reflect active market transactions and strong liquidity. f the growth rate of M1 is relatively fast, the consumption and terminal market will be active, which is prone to inflation. If M2 growth is rapid, investment and the intermediate market will be active.

Obviously, this classification of money supply does not distinguish based on the essential differences between currencies, or people simply do not recognize the essential differences between currencies. In fact, there is no other person in the world who has made an essential distinction between cash and commercial bank deposits and commercial bank loans based on the logic of this book, and then classified currencies based on their essence. This current classification method only superficially believes that there is no essential difference between bank deposit certificates, bank deposits, and cash, all of which are the same "legal currency", so it can only speculate on the intention and plan of the currency holder based on the different forms of storage. This classification based on the appearance of currency storage will inevitably lead to biased judgments. No wonder people frequently ask: why is the growth rate of M0 so rapid, but society is in a consumption downgrade? Why is M1 soaring, but the economy is experiencing a contraction? Why is the central bank "releasing water", and M2 soaring, but investment has been sluggish? The traditional classification method of money supply seems to be frequently in a state of failure and offline.

In fact, with the development of technology and the highly developed electronic payment, units and individuals have rarely used cash, and M0 can no longer represent the purchasing power of consumption. With the richness of financial products provided by various commercial banks and various payment software, many currencies intended for short-term use are also deposited in banks in the form of fixed deposits. The conversion between M1 and M2 is becoming more and more flexible, the ability to judge payment intent through this classification method is becoming increasingly weak. In addition, the current classification method does not distinguish Loan Currency from bank deposit certificates, nor does it distinguish between currencies held by financial units and currencies held by the real economy. These factors are the internal reasons for the increasingly insensitive judgment of the economic impact of traditional M0, M1, and M2 classifications.

In order to more accurately judge the impact of various currencies on the economy, a more scientific and reasonable classification method for money supply should be based on the different nature of currencies: first, Contract Currency, which are cash outside the banking system, similar to the current M0. Second, Loan Currency, which are deposit certificates issued by commercial banks to borrowers through external loans. Third, Deposit Currency, which are deposit certificates issued by commercial banks through absorbing deposits rather than issuing external loans.

The borrower of Loan Currency has a clear and strong intention to use the currency, and Loan Currency can be further classified based on the borrower's identity, loan term, and credit enhancement method to further assess the expected use of Loan Currency. For Contract Currency and Deposit Currency, they can also be classified based on whether the holders are banks, non-bank financial institutions, or entity enterprises, and then subdivided based on demand and fixed deposits. It should be noted that it should not be simply assumed that deposits held by urban and rural residents in commercial banks are not intended to be used in the short term, nor should it be simply assumed that cash is intended to be used in the short term. Through electronic payment platforms, residents can deposit money in commercial banks for use at any time, while cash deposited in their own hands is often not intended for short-term use, but for other reasons or purposes. Many large-value cash are stored in the hands of residents and units for a long time and are not intended for short-term use. In particular, it should be noted that M2 includes deposits from commercial banks themselves, according to the analysis and classification in this book, commercial banks are the main Currency Issuers, and their own deposits should be considered as currency within Currency Issuer system and are not brought into the market by borrowers. This part of currency can only be considered as semi-finished currency and cannot truly enter the market circulation, which has little significance for analyzing market expectations. After we have made a distinction between currencies in essence, we can more scientifically refine and classify currencies to provide support for economic forecasting and economic decision-making. We look forward to economists and policymakers continuing to explore in this direction.

Chapter 4: The Essence and Logic of Credit Currency

All currencies currently used by countries can be collectively referred to as credit currencies. Credit currencies are traditionally viewed as central bank credit or national credit. The original meaning of credit is to fulfill obligations as promised. Does the central bank or government have obligations to the currency holder? If so, what are the legal obligations of the central bank and the government on credit currencies? If not, what rights do we own in the credit currencies we hold? Who are the corresponding obligors? Credit currencies are just a symbol, why are they considered as the main form of wealth? Where is the source of its value? It is crucial to explore the credit essence and underlying logic of credit currencies.

I. Total Savings Always Equal to Total Liabilities

After the occurrence of story 3, the coiners successfully promoted economic growth on Island Z by increasing loan disbursements, while also allowing some people to save money and others to have unpayable debts. At the end of the year, the farmer received 2000 worth, paid 1800 worth, and saved an additional 200 worth. Adding the cash retention of 500 worth from story 2, after paying off the coiners' loan, his drawer had a savings of 700 worth. This year, the blacksmith received 1800 worth, paid 1700 worth, and after paying off the coiners' loan, he also had a cash savings of 100 worth for the first time. This year, the masseuse received 1700 worth, borrowed 2000 at the beginning of the year, and settled the repayment at the end of the year, her debt at the coiner increased by 300 worth to 800 worth. The 800 worth that the masseuse could not pay off at the coiner was exactly the savings of 700 worth and 100 worth in the drawer of the farmer and blacksmith.

In Story 4, the farmer invested his savings in transactions, which also promoted the economic growth of Island Z. In that year, the farmer's income was 2000 worth and his payment was 2300 worth. At the end of the year, the farmer paid an additional 300 worth. In fact, the farmer had a loan of 300 worth that could not be repaid that year. Fortunately, there was still 700 worth of cash left in his drawer, which he used to pay for the 300 worth. Therefore, his drawer's cash balance changed from 700 worth to 400 worth. The blacksmith's income was 2300 worth, expenditure was 2200 worth, and there was a deposit of 100 worth. Adding the 100 worth from Story 3, the blacksmith now had a deposit of 200 worth. The masseuse's expenditure was 2000 worth and income was 2200 worth, with an additional 200 worth, her debt of 800 worth that could not be settled at the coiner in previous years was reduced to 600 worth. The 600 worth that the masseuse could not settle at the coiner was also the cash balance of 400 worth and 200 worth in the drawer of the farmer and the blacksmith.

Through the above two examples, we found that no matter how the three people spend and earn, the amount of "Z coin" left in the drawer on the

Island and the unpayable figure on the white wallboard of the coiner are always equal after the year-end settlement. Deposits and liabilities are always a zero-sum game. Of course, in this type of analysis, we did not include the factor of interest charged by Currency Issuer, but regardless of whether interest is charged or not, the corresponding rule of deposits and liabilities will never change. In the case of interest charged, we will provide a detailed introduction in the chapter on the operation and impact of interest.

After the case analysis, we can make a logical deduction and come to the same conclusion. Any currency that appears in the market is generated through the lending of the Currency Issuer (central bank or commercial bank) to the borrower. If the liability on the Currency Issuer's account book is to be eliminated, the corresponding currency in the market must be retrieved. According to the principle that the original proposition and its inverse negation proposition are equivalent, if the original proposition is true, the inverse negation proposition is also true. Therefore, it can be inferred that if the currency is not retrieved, that is, it remains in the hands of market participants, then the debt at the Currency Issuer's place is not eliminated. Every penny of money in people's hands is a liability of another person to the Currency Issuer. Of course, if the money in people's hands comes from their own loans, then they themselves are the debtors. In short, "savings and liabilities always correspond", every penny of deposit in our hands corresponds to a penny of liability. In the trading market outside the Currency Issuer system, the total savings of all market participants always equals the total liability of all market participants to the Currency Issuer, that is, "total savings always equals total liabilities", which we can call the second law of monetary economics.

It should be noted that when Currency Issuer issues loans to the borrower and collects them back, it needs to charge interest to the borrower. On the surface, this part of interest will cause the total debt outside Currency Issuer to be higher than the total savings. When the currency savers lend their money back to Currency Issuer, that is, store their money with Currency Issuer, Currency Issuer will pay interest to them. On the surface, this part of interest will cause the total debt outside Currency Issuer to be lower than the total savings. In both cases, it seems that the second law of money has been broken. However, after in-depth analysis, we found that the interest charged by Currency Issuer is the profit of Currency Issuer, and this part of money can be directly used for market transactions, which is essentially different from the semi-finished currency within Currency Issuer system. This part of money is actually the service income of Currency Issuer (which will be discussed in Section 5, "The Essence and Role of Issuance interest and Renting Interest," of Chapter 8, " Currency Issuer and Issuance of Credit Currency," in the following text). When Currency Issuer collects this part of money, it is in the capacity of a general market entity providing services outside Currency Issuer system. Therefore, this part of money should not belong to Currency Issuer system, but should belong to the trading market system outside Currency Issuer system. Similarly, when market entities store their money with Currency Issuer and Currency Issuer pays interest for them, this behavior is that Currency Issuer appears as a general borrower outside Currency Issuer system, and the currency used for payment is not the semi-finished currency within Currency Issuer system, but the currency available for direct use owned by the issuer. Therefore, this part of money should also belong to the trading market system outside Currency Issuer system. We strictly limit the identity, behavior, and boundaries of Currency Issuer to "relying on the borrower credit, having the borrower creditor's rights, lending and recovering an equivalent amount of currency to the borrower." Any identity, behavior, or currency outside this definition should belong to the general trading market system outside Currency Issuer system. The second law of money has not been broken.

Money is a commodity produced by the issue. The process of Currency Issuance is the process of exchange between the borrower and Currency Issuer. The borrower hands over their debt to Currency Issuer, and the issuer hands over the currency to the borrower. Therefore, every deposit in the market corresponds to a liability, and every liability corresponds to an expectation of future goods. Once this expectation is not met, the currency becomes redundant.

II. The Evolution of Currency Forms is Essentially the Evolution of Rights Categories

In the previous article, we classified currencies into six forms based on their historical evolution. Now, let's take a look at the differences between these six currencies in essence. Why can we say that they are six different currencies in essence? Because the monetary system is a contract system, a system of rights and obligations, and the analysis of the essence of currency should be defined from the perspective of rights and obligations.

According to the role of civil rights, civil rights can be divided into the right of domination, the right of claim, the right of formation, and the right of defense. The right of domination, also known as the right of control, refers to the exclusive right of the holder to directly control the properties, and property rights are typical examples of the right of domination. Other rights such as quasi-property rights, personal rights, and intellectual property rights are also typical examples of the right of domination. The right of claim refers to the right of the obligee to require others to perform certain acts or refrain from performing certain acts. The obligee cannot directly control the subject matter of rights and can only request the obligor. The right of claim arises from basic rights and can be divided into claims on creditor's rights, claims on property rights, claims on personal rights, and claims on intellectual property rights, depending on the basic rights. Creditor's rights are typical examples of the right of claim. The right of formation refers to the right of the holders to change the legal relationships between themselves and others by their own actions. The main function of the right of formation is that the right holder can, by unilateral declaration of intent, cause the effectiveness of an already established legal relationship to arise, change, or extinguish. The right of revocation, the right of ratification, the right of dissolution, and the right of choice are all examples of the right of formation. The right of defense refers to the right to counter the claim of the opposite party or other rights. The broad definition of the right of formation also includes the right of defense. The defensive nature of the right of defense makes it different from the right of claim and becomes a separate category of rights, including the right of defense of simultaneous performance, the right of defense of prior performance, and the right of defense of unease.

Material Currency in version 1.0 belongs to the property right in the right of domination, which is a universal absolute right. Receipt Currency in version 2.0 is a right of claim for the return of physical goods to the banknote shopkeeper, which is a relative right against the shopkeeper. People generally accept banknotes (Receipt Currency) based on their trust in the banknote shopkeeper. Promise Currency in version 3.0 still has the claim right to Currency Issuer to give physical goods, and has a relative right against Currency Issuer. The credit of modern central banks has made Promise Currency more widely trusted and used. The US dollar under the Bretton Woods system is the most typical representative of Promise Currency. Contract Currency in version 4.0, which is the central bank note after the collapse of the Bretton Woods system, although completely identical to Promise Currency in version 3.0 in terms of Currency Issuer and appearance, has completely lost any claim right against Currency Issuer, that is, the central bank.

Due to the legal requirement that no unit or individual may refuse to use or accept cash for non-legal reasons, people believe that Contract Currency has lost the right to claim debts from its issuer but gained the right to claim debts universally. People believe that holding a piece of paper currency in a free market can request the exchange of goods from anyone. However, this is a misconception, as the law only stipulates that people can only receive specified currencies if they want to sell goods, but it does not compel anyone to sell their goods to anyone who requests a transaction, nor does it compel anyone to sell their goods at a specific price. Even in today's extremely commercialized and marketized world, it is not possible to trade anything at any time, under any circumstances, and at any price. For example, when you want to buy a luxury house, if you have enough money, you can probably buy a certain type of villa, but the law does not guarantee that you can buy a specific villa, because the owner of that villa may not sell it at all or may simply refuse to sell it to you. In extreme inflation situations, people are simply unwilling to accept legal currency and refuse to sell any goods to currency holders, and there is no law that can hold these individuals accountable for any responsibilities. Therefore, the civil rights of Contract Currency are not a claim to anyone's creditor's rights.

What exactly are the civil rights of Contract Currency? When people hold Contract Currency, they only have the right to control Contract Currency itself. Yes, you are right, they only have the right to control a piece of paper. This is a kind of property right. People can claim exclusive rights such as possession, income, and non-infringement of this piece of paper based on the property right. It can be said that the emergence of Contract Currency has completed the return of the essence of monetary property rights. The only difference is that this property has changed from a piece of gold to a piece of paper marked with numbers. This piece of paper may contain extraordinary value, or it may be worthless. Contract Currency is a right of dominion.

Of course, if you hand over this piece of paper to a commercial bank and obtain a deposit certificate from the commercial bank, your ownership of this piece of paper will disappear, and the currency in your hand will become Deposit Currency. According to the deposit contract between you and the commercial bank, you have the right to request payment of this piece of paper from the commercial bank.

Deposit Currency in version 5.0 and Loan Currency in version 6.0 are commercial bank deposit certificates issued by commercial banks based on the central bank notes in version 4.0. Due to their external issuance using real-name registration, they can be transferred or changed by people for use. Holding a commercial bank deposit certificate only gives the holder the right to claim the central bank cash in version 4.0 from the commercial bank. Therefore, Deposit Currency in version 5.0 and Loan Currency in version 6.0 are claims against the commercial bank. Further, the holder of a commercial bank deposit certificate cannot claim possession or income from the deposit certificate itself. If you find a bank deposit certificate on the street, you cannot actually possess the full value of this paper. Legally, this paper still belongs to the owner registered with the commercial bank, and the person who registered on the deposit certificate can also go to the commercial bank to report the loss and apply for a new deposit certificate. Deposit Currency and Loan Currency are both the right of claim.

The transfer behavior of people through online banking, mobile banking, ATM machines or bank counters is not the transfer of property rights, but the right to request cash from commercial banks, that is, the right to demand cash from banks. We can regard the transfer behavior between commercial bank accounts as the transfer behavior of the creditor's rights of the holder of commercial bank deposit certificates. If the transfer-out account and the transfer-in account are opened in the same commercial bank, when the commercial bank receives the notice of payment, it only changes the name and amount of the creditor on its account book. If the transfer-out account and the transfer-in account are opened in two different commercial banks, it is equivalent to the holder of commercial bank deposit certificates, that is, the creditor, notifying the deposit commercial bank, that is, the debtor, to transfer its own creditor's rights to the receiving commercial bank. Then the receiving commercial bank transfers the creditor's rights to the final recipient, and finally completes the transfer of creditor's rights from the transferor to the recipient.

The value of Deposit Currency in version 5.0 and Loan Currency in version 6.0 is not only due to the claim of creditor's rights, but also because the items that the holder can request are the central bank notes in version 4.0, which have the value of property rights.

III. The Essence of Credit Currency and Three Layers of Credit

Contract Currency in version 4.0, Deposit Currency in version 5.0, and Loan Currency in version 6.0 are all credit currencies that are just a piece of paper or bank deposit certificate. With the advancement of technology, bank deposit certificates even eliminate the need for paper, and the promotion of central bank digital currency by central banks is also eliminating the need for the piece of paper of Contract Currency. People only need to log in to the corresponding APP account or official website account to view and operate. It seems that we can assert that the value of cash is definitely not the value of that dispensable piece of paper, but the value of the rights it is endowed with. However, we have analyzed that all your rights over cash is only the ownership of this piece of paper, so the value of this piece of paper is the full value of cash.

We cannot use the cost of producing cash by Currency Issuers as a standard for evaluating their value, which is too narrow and unreasonable. Just like our valuation of a famous painting, we cannot say that the cost of the paper used to produce the painting is 100 yuan and the ink is 50 yuan, so we can only value it at 150 yuan. We cannot simply add the labor cost of the painter to assess the value of the painting. Leonardo da Vinci's work "The Savior" was sold for $400 million on the evening of November 15, 2017. People believe that the value of this painting lies in its culture and the arts. Similarly, the cost of a bottle of Guizhou 53-degree Feitian Maotai Liquor in China is around 100 yuan, but the market price is around 3,000 yuan. People believe that the value of this bottle of wine lies in its brand and craftsmanship. The reason why cash have value is not in the paper, but in its rich purchasing power. Similarly, the value of the piece of paper in a commercial bank deposit certificate also lies in its rich purchasing power.

Where does the purchasing power of Credit Currency come from? Just as the ownership of a house includes the rights of possession, use, income, and disposal, we believe that purchasing power is a specific right of Credit Currency. Rights and obligations promote and complement each other, and correspond to each other. Specific rights correspond to specific obligations, and specific obligees correspond to specific obligors. " Rights come from obligations", what is the obligation corresponding to purchasing power? Only by finding this specific obligation can we expect the fulfillment of the obligation. We follow the path of the creation, use, and circulation of Credit Currency to find the specific content of the obligor and obligation of purchasing power. In this process, the state has enacted currency legislation, Currency Issuer has issued loans, the borrower has signed a loan contract, the seller of goods has accepted payment from the borrower, and it can be concluded that the obligor must be among these participants.

Since the promise to exchange physical goods was abolished, Currency Issuer has no obligation to pay any goods to the holders of Credit Currency, nor does the government. However, we cannot assume that Currency Issuer and the government have no other obligations to the holders of currency, because the law gives Currency Issuer the right to issue currency and also gives the government the right to formulate monetary policies and supervise. There must be obligations for those who have rights. We have found the borrower, Currency Issuer, and the government as obligors, but their respective obligations have different importance and different priorities.

In the economic field, especially in the monetary field, we are used to using credit to replace obligation. So what is credit? We call the expectation of the obligor to fulfill its obligations as credit, and the reality of this expectation is regarded as the obligor's compliance with credit. Therefore, the purchasing power of Credit Currency originates from credit, and from the specific obligor's compliance with their own credit.

The essence of Credit Currency is "a social commodity produced by Currency Issuer using the borrower credit". The raw material of Credit Currency is not gold or paper, but the borrower credit. The manufacturer of Credit Currency is a legal Currency Issuer, as its manufacturing behavior is an exclusive monopoly, Credit Currency incorporates the issuer's credit into its formulation during the manufacturing process. The manufacturing license of Credit Currency is issued by the state, which puts on the coat of national credit for Credit Currency through legislation.

1. The Borrower's Commitment is the Core Credit of Credit Currency

As mentioned earlier, any cash originates from the central bank and is issued by the central bank through lending. Therefore, Contract Currency originates from a corresponding liability to the central bank from the root. Deposit Currency is a substitute for Contract Currency, Deposit Currency is stored in commercial banks in exchange for commercial bank deposit certificates. Deposit Currency also originates from a liability to the central bank from the root. Loan Currency is independently issued by commercial banks through lending to the outside, it originates from a liability to the commercial bank from the borrower.

The issuer of Contract Currency is the central bank, while the issuer of the Deposit Currency and Loan Currency is the commercial bank. Regardless of who the issuer is, there is no legal or contractual requirement that the issuer of these three types of credit currencies and the government directly exchange any physical goods or provide any services to the currency holder. That is to say, the owner of Credit Currency cannot command any goods with Credit Currency from the issuer and the government. So, the credit of the Currency Issuer and the state in Credit Currency is abstract, vague, and illusory. In countries where currencies have significantly depreciated, the issuers and governments are not held to clear legal accountability.

This raises a question worth pondering: why do people willingly accept Credit Currency? The promise of converting currency into gold had long been broken, and people accept Credit Currency certainly no longer because it is linked to gold. Is it because of the "legal currency"? Obviously not. In many Latin American countries and developing countries with their own legal currencies, it is a common phenomenon to sign contracts using US dollars as the currency of payment, and it is also common for private transactions to be paid in US dollars. Even in countries where the US dollar is explicitly resisted and declared illegal by the government, it is widely accepted by people. However, the "legal currency" under severe inflation is also widely despised by people. Traditional textbooks may still have such an explanation: people accept their own currency because they believe that others will accept it. This is even a superficial and perfunctory answer. Even when a girl who is in love loses her rational thinking and asks her lover the question: "Why do you love me?", she will not be satisfied with such an answer: "Because I think others will love you too". Modern monetary theory confidently claims to have found the secret answer of "tax-driven currency", which believes that because the government only accepts designated credit currencies when collecting taxes, such credit currencies are widely accepted by people. Such an answer is not as acceptable as the answer given by the lover just now, which is equivalent to saying: "Because the most powerful boy I know loves you very much". We can completely continue to ask: "Why does the government accept it?" If Credit Currency cannot ultimately purchase the required goods or service, including the government, no one will accept it, and Credit Currency must be widely accepted because of its inherent value.

Any economy, including government, enterprises and individuals, will examine the environment and make decisions based on their own needs. What can ultimately meet people's needs is inevitably goods or service, that is, commodities. The fundamental reason why people accept Credit Currency is that Credit Currency has purchasing power, that is, there are commodities needed by the holders of the currency behind the Credit Currency. So who will provide the commodities needed by the holders of Credit Currency? We believe that it should be provided by the borrower of Currency Issuer. Is there any legal basis for this? Yes, there is.

When a borrower borrows money from a Currency Issuer, Credit Currency is created. At this point, a loan contract is established between the borrower and Currency Issuer, the borrower having a "source of repayment" is a necessary condition for successfully applying for a loan. The loan contract stipulates that Currency Issuer provides currency for the borrower to use, and the borrower is required to repay the principal and interest within a specified period of time. So, when the currency is consumed by the borrower, what does the borrower rely on to repay the principal and interest? Only by creating wealth through his own labor, that is, providing goods or service to the market, can he earn income and exchange it for currency to repay the principal and interest. The loan contract directly stipulates that "the borrower has the obligation to repay the principal and interest to Currency Issuer", which is equivalent to indirectly stipulating that "the borrower promises that he will provide goods or service with a value not less than the sum of the principal and interest to the market". Of course, if the borrower only borrows money for investment and uses the investment income to repay the debt of Currency Issuer, it is also possible. At this time, the borrower is simply putting the currency he has obtained from others into his own pocket. The borrower may also sell his own property on the market to obtain income for repayment. In any case, as long as the borrower adheres to the credit agreement and repays both the principal and interest, there will always be someone providing tradable goods or service to the market. We imagine that if all borrowers only consume, do not produce, and do not sell after obtaining currency, then there will soon be no tradable commodities in the market and the currency will lose its value. At this point, we have found the core obligor of Credit Currency purchasing power, "the borrower", the core obligation of "repaying the principal and interest", and the core credit of "borrower credit".

The issuer of Credit Currency requires the borrower to repay in the currency issued by the issuer. In order to fulfill the repayment obligation, the borrower must provide commodities to the market. When a seller of commodities in the market faces a buyer holding Credit Currency, the currency holder has only two legal sources of money: one is the income from transactions, which has already provided commodities to the market; the other is the income from loans, in which the borrower promised to provide commodities to the market in the future. In either case, when Credit Currency is initially brought to the market by the borrower from the issuer, it is accompanied by the borrower's promise to provide sufficient commodities to the market. Unlike the promise made by the issuer of old-age currency that holders can exchange gold for it, the promise of Credit Currency is made directly by the currency borrower, promising that "those who accept the currency will be able to exchange other people's commodities for it in the market." This broad promise is constructed by the direct commitment of numerous individual borrowers to the issuer. The credit of Material Currency is its own physical value, while the credit of Receipt Currency and Promise Currency is provided by a single issuer. The credit of Credit Currency is provided by all borrowers collectively. People believe that most borrowers are honest and able to fulfill their promises, and can earn income through their own products to repay the principal and interest. The market has or will have corresponding commodities for all money, and the "gold content" of Credit Currency is its "credit content," with the main credit content being the credit of the borrower. This is the fundamental reason why people generally accept Credit Currency. If we must say that legal regulations, government taxes, and so on are also reasons, these are only external factors, while the internal factor is the credit of the borrower behind Credit Currency.

The prevalent view is that the reason why the currency issued by the central bank is widely accepted is because of the central credit of the central bank. This is a major misunderstanding. Since Promise Currency was declared to be unable to exchange any wealth from the central bank, the center of gravity of the currency credit has shifted from the promise of the central bank to the promise of the borrower. Receipt Currency and Promise Currency have a central credit, which is the credit of Currency Issuer, while Credit Currency is issued based on the promise of the majority of borrowers, which is decentralized and decentralized credit and public credit.

All currencies are borrowed by borrowers from Currency Issuers based on their own credit. If the borrower does not have credit, Currency Issuer should not issue currency. If the borrower does not have the willingness to borrow, Currency Issuer cannot complete the Currency Issuance. If the borrower does not fulfill its commitment, the creation of currency will bring consumption and enjoyment to the borrower itself, while consuming wealth and creating excess currency for society.

The Currency Issuer is a water tank that cannot turn on the faucet by itself, while the borrower is the one who introduces water into the market and is obliged to return the water to the tank. The borrower and Currency Issuer jointly create the currency, and in this process, Currency Issuer is passive and selective, while the borrower is active and creative. At the same time, both are responsible for the currency in the market, the borrower should strive to create wealth for society through their own efforts, while Currency Issuer should be virtuous and ensure that the currency circulates throughout the market and maintains stable purchasing power. The issuer is the mother of credit money, while the borrower is the father of credit money.

Credit Currency implies debt. Debt implies contracts. The essence of Credit Currency is a multilateral commitment, representing the multilateral contractual relationship between Currency Issuers, borrowers, and sellers of commodities. The circulation of currency among the three groups is an exchange process under multilateral commitment. The borrower owes a debt to Currency Issuer, handing over his own credit to Currency Issuer, directly promising to repay the principal and interest to Currency Issuer, which is equivalent to directly promising to Currency Issuer that it will provide sufficient commodities to the market in the future. Currency Issuer hands over the currency to the borrower, directly providing the purchasing power to the borrower, indirectly promising to the existing seller of commodities that "the borrower will provide sufficient commodities to the market in the future" for their exchange in the currency. The seller of commodities believes in the indirect commitment of Currency Issuer and indirectly promises to Currency Issuer that "they are willing to accept the currency in the hands of the borrower". Therefore, the borrower hands over the currency to the seller of commodities, and the seller of commodities hands over the commodities to the borrower. The borrower gets the current commodities, and the seller of goods gets the expectation of future commodities. The market economy circulates under multilateral commitment.

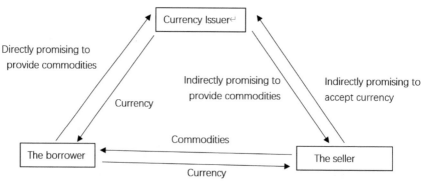

Human beings need the assistance of their compatriots almost anytime and anywhere, and it is definitely not feasible to rely solely on the kindness of others. If he can stimulate their self-interest and make it beneficial to them, and tell them that it is beneficial to them to work for him, it will be much easier for him to achieve his goal. No matter who it is, if he wants to do business with others, he should first propose this: Please give me what I want, and at the same time, you can get what you want. This is the general meaning of trading. Most of the mutual help we need is obtained in this way[3]

Adam Smith believed that self-interest is human nature, and people's pursuit of personal interests would promote social development. People would act altruistically in order to obtain more benefits. The borrowing and

---

[3] Adam Smith. An Inquiry into the Nature and Causes of the Wealth of Nations[M]. Beijing: The Commercial Press,2015.

repayment of money is the concrete practice of this egoistic and altruistic code of conduct. This code widely observed by social subjects forms the principle of honesty and credit in society. Based on this, wealth is constantly created and benefits mankind through exchange, and Credit Currency is created in exchange.

2. Currency Issuer Provides Intermediary Credit for Credit Currency Based on Their Judgment of the Borrower

When Currency Issuer no longer bears any debt on its own, Currency Issuer has no obligation to pay the currency holder. The payment of Credit Currency depends on the credit of the borrower. Currency Issuer has changed from the wealth custodian of the currency holder to the credit intermediary of the currency holder.

In a free market, when people face a currency holder, they can infer that this currency is either borrowed from Currency Issuer by the person or earned by the person through previous labor. However, even from earned income, someone must have borrowed the currency from Currency Issuer at the source. People cannot know who borrowed the money from Currency Issuer in the market at the source, and they cannot judge whether the borrower has the willingness and ability to fulfill his promises. So how can people judge whether the borrower will provide commodities to the market as agreed? At this time, the role of the Currency Issuer is reflected. The Currency Issuer relies on its own loyalty, diligence, and professional skills to identify those who have the ability to create wealth in the future and have the true willingness to fulfill their obligations to repay principal and interest among the people who apply for loans, that is, those with good credit.

It is believed that borrowers selected by Currency Issuer are expected to provide sufficient goods or service to the market, and the currency created through the borrower can be expected to purchase sufficient commodities from the market in the future. When each borrower can provide commodities equivalent to their loan amount to the market as promised, the market commodities are also supplemented when the borrower purchases other people's goods and brings their currency in the market, then the amount of money in the market will not be excessive relative to the amount of commodities, and the purchasing power of the currency can be guaranteed.

We often say that the central bank issues currency out of thin air to complete the water release to the market, this merely indicates that the Currency Issuer did not incur any costs for the currency, rather than suggesting that there is no basis for issuing the currency. The Currency Issuer must rely on the credit of the borrower when issuing currency to the outside world. When the central bank and commercial banks issue currency to the outside world, they must have sufficient understanding and evaluation of the borrower. People believe in the credit of the Currency Issuer based on the intermediary credit of the issuer, and then jointly establish the credit of the currency. In short, people believe in the believing of the Currency Issuer in the borrower, and accept the currency of the issuer brought by the borrower.

Today, the general public and even the central bank itself believe that Credit Currency is issued by the central bank, and the credit of Credit Currency comes from the credit of the central bank. Therefore, in order to maintain the authority and credibility of the central bank, the central bank refuses to directly issue currency to the public or even the government, but gives monetary support and policy guidance to commercial banks, and indirectly completes Currency Issuance through various policy tools. In order to enhance the public's confidence in themselves, central banks around the world also reserve a large amount of gold as a show of their strength. Such practices are actually self-love and worrying about troubles that don't exist by the central bank, because the core of credit in currency has long been shifted from the central bank to borrowers, and such practices are superfluous and unnecessary. Central banks can widely and directly lend to the public commercial banks are doing so, there is no sufficient reason to believe that issuing loans to the public through commercial banks is more accurate, scientific, and safe than issuing loans directly by the central bank. As the lender of last resort, the central bank actually indirectly issues currency to the market through commercial banks. The indirect issuance of currency is an act of self-destruction, self-restraint, and even circumvention of responsibility by the central bank. The central bank gives up the power to directly issue loans to various economic entities in society, resulting in many monetary policies that are beneficial to the country and the people but not beneficial to bank commercial profits not being effectively implemented. As for the strategy of reserving a large amount of gold and foreign exchange to enhance their own credit, it is an ancient practice of the Rialto Bankers in the late Middle Ages in Italy to establish their own credit. They showed their strength through grand opening performances, and the climax of the performance was the bankers showing bags of gold and silver coins. It should be noted that that was the era of Material Currency, and the backing behind banknotes was gold and silver promised by bankers. Now we have entered the era of Credit Currency, and the backing behind Credit Currency is the credit of borrowers. Even if the central bank has sufficient inventory of gold, it has no obligation to exchange it for holders of Credit Currency, and it cannot also guarantee the market purchasing power of Credit Currency.

3. The Government-led Countries Provide the Catch-all Credit for Credit Currency

The concept of a country is a broad one, and it is a political and geographical term. In a broad sense, a country refers to a social group that shares a common language, culture, ethnicity, territory, government, or history. In a narrow sense, a country is a form of community formed by a certain range of people. A country does not specifically refer to a particular social entity, especially not to the government. The stronger the comprehensive strength of a country, the more stable Credit Currency circulating in that country.

Money comes into the market through a specific borrower, allowing it to trade commodities with everyone in the market. To achieve this state, in addition to the borrower's compliance with providing sufficient commodities for the market as described earlier, there are also a prerequisite and a remedial condition.

The prerequisite condition is that all people in the market need to form a consensus that "others also recognize this unified payment method", which requires a clear legislation within the country. Credit Currency must establish its own position within the country in the form of legislation, and the law must stipulate the rights and obligations of various subjects within the country when facing currency. Because of this, modern Credit Currency is also known as "legal tender". Article 16 of "People's Bank of China Law of the People's Republic of China" stipulates that "The legal tender of the People's Republic of China is the Renminbi. All public and private debts within the territory of the People's Republic of China shall be paid in Renminbi, and no unit or individual shall refuse to accept it."

The condition for remediation is that even if the borrower fails to comply with credit, there needs to be a sufficient supply of commodities in the market. This means that even if the borrower fails to provide the commodities that he should provide to the market, it can ensure that the purchasing power of the currency will not decline and will not seriously affect the transactions of currency holders. To achieve this, one of three conditions needs to be met. First, the market is large enough that the currency can be used throughout the country, and world currencies like the US dollar are even circulated throughout the entire planet. Local and partial borrower defaults will be diluted by the market, and the impact on the purchasing power of the currency will not be particularly significant. Second, not all market participants have borrowed from Currency Issuer, and a considerable number of entities only invest their own goods or service in the market without bringing in currency. Third, as time goes on, new producers and service providers will provide commodities for the market. The greater the inclusiveness of the currency circulation market, the stronger the resilience of the purchasing power of the currency. The production and service capabilities of all market entities within the entire currency circulation range endorse and guarantee the purchasing power of the currency.

There is also a popular saying in the market that money is the credit of the central government, because under the current monetary system, the central government is usually the main target of the central bank's money supply. The central bank completes loans to the central government by directly or indirectly purchasing central government bonds. During the debt period, the central government prepares funds through its own service fees, taxes, or other operating income to ensure repayment of principal and interest when due. The central government is the main borrower of the central bank, and its fulfillment of repayment commitments has a significant impact on the purchasing power of money. Therefore, there is a concept in the market that money is the credit of the central government. Even so, this statement is incomplete and not comprehensive. The central bank also lends money to commercial banks, which in turn lend money to a wide range of economic entities in the market. The credit of all borrowers ensures the strong purchasing power of money.

In the three-tier credit system of Credit Currency, the borrower credit is the core and foundation, the issuer's credit is the assessment and verification of the borrower credit, and the state's credit is the backup and supplement to the borrower credit.

Credit Currency is a chocolate-covered candy made by the issuer and borrower of the currency. The raw material is credit, the center candy is the borrower credit, the chocolate coating is the issuer's credit, and the outer packaging is the national credit.

IV. Labor and Exchange are Two Hands of a Human Being for Creating Wealth

Most of the help we need from each other comes through contracts, exchanges and purchases. Therefore, it is also the tendency of humans to exchange with each other that has led to the division of labor. For example, in hunting or nomadic peoples, there is a person who is good at making bows and arrows. He often exchanges his own bows and arrows with others for livestock or meat. As a result, he finds that it is better to exchange with hunters than to hunt in the wild, because the exchange is more profitable. For his own benefit, he has to make bows and arrows as his main business, and thus becomes a weapon maker. Another person, who is good at building the framework and roof of small huts or mobile houses, is often hired to build houses and gets paid with livestock and meat. He finally realizes that it is beneficial for him to devote himself entirely to this work, and thus becomes a house builder. Similarly, a third person becomes a blacksmith or copper smith, and a fourth person becomes a tanner or leather maker. In this way, everyone can exchange the surplus of their own labor products that they cannot consume for the surplus of others' labor products that they need. This encourages everyone to devote themselves to a specific business, allowing them to hone and develop their respective talents or abilities in their respective businesses. Various other animals must now and in the past be separated and defended by themselves. Nature has given them various talents, but they cannot benefit from them. The situation of humans is completely different. They can use each other's talents even if they are very different.

They rely on the general tendency of exchanging goods and service, bartering, and trading to combine the different products produced by their various talents into a common resource that everyone can use to freely purchase the goods produced by others that they need[4]

Adam Smith believed that the unique tendency of humans to "exchange goods, barter, and trade with each other" has contributed to the division of labor among humans. This division of labor has led to specialized skills, streamlined production processes, and sophisticated production tools, resulting in increased labor productivity and human wealth. Labor creates goods or service, but without division of labor, goods or service are necessarily single and inferior, making it impossible to achieve accumulation. When division of labor occurs, goods or service become diverse and sophisticated, and at the same time, their numbers are also growing rapidly, human wealth is accumulated. The division of labor among humans enables different people to provide different goods or service, providing transactional objects for exchange.

Money is precisely the "common resource" formed by human beings through their own wisdom. When money appears, extensive and diverse transactions are carried out, and goods and service are exchanged and distributed between people. Human beings connect different goods or service through the "common resource" of money, so that each can do their best and get what they need, and the division of labor is supported and continued. Without exchange, products cannot achieve extensive and diverse exchanges, and the division of labor cannot continue. Human exchange is achieved through money.

Labor creates wealth, and division of labor optimizes labor; exchange guarantees division of labor, and money optimizes exchange. Labor and exchange support and collaborate with each other, promoting the continuous accumulation of human wealth, ensuring that humans can satisfy each other's needs.

Labor and exchange are two hands of a human being for creating wealth, division of labor and money are respectively the magic gloves on these two hands. The implementation of the rule of law removes the handcuff from these hands and gives them full freedom in market economy.

V. Currency Helps Human Beings to Achieve Overdraft and Reserve of Wealth

The fundamental difference between humans and other animals lies not only in the division of labor, but also in the ability of humans to remember the past and plan for the future. Time is the fourth dimension above three-

---

[4] Adam Smith. An Inquiry into the Nature and Causes of the Wealth of Nations[M]. Beijing: The Commercial Press,2015.

dimensional space. People not only live in the present, but also live in the future. For the future, people have two preparations. One is to consume now and provide goods for society in the future, and the other is to work now and purchase other people's goods in the future. Based on the first plan, people will borrow money from the Currency Issuer. Based on the second plan, people will store the earned currency in a digital accounting way in commercial banks, or in cash in safes.

Debts are for current transactions, and savings are for future transactions. It can be inferred that if people believe they cannot provide what society needs in the future, they will not incur debt now; if people believe society cannot provide what they need in the future, they will not save now. Whether it is debt or saving, the existence of currency has enabled commodity transactions to not only achieve spatial and subjective leaps, but also temporal leaps.

When people borrow money from the issuer and use it for transactions, money is issued and they overdraw the future labor achievements. When people store the money they have earned from transactions, savings are generated and they store the achievements of their current labor. Credit Currency, a virtual concept created by humans, is stored by people like gold, grain, nuclear bombs and other physical goods for future transactions. Through savings, people expect to purchase future goods from unspecified entities in the market in the future. Currency has enabled the optimization of resources not only spatially and among different entities but also over time.

VI. The Essence of Several Typical New Currencies

With the development of economy and technology, in recent years, many new forms of currency have emerged. Cryptocurrencies represented by Bitcoin have become popular, and the issuing authorities of legal tender have also launched central bank digital currencies in response to the trend. Various third-party payment platforms offer a rich array of financial products and loan products. It is necessary for us to explore their essence in order to better understand and grasp these new things.

1. Cryptocurrencies Represented by Bitcoin

A cryptocurrency has become a product with stronger privacy and higher security due to its anonymity and decentralization. At the same time, it is generated and exists on the Internet, and the transfer of ownership is very convenient. These characteristics of cryptocurrency make it have strong transaction attributes, thus playing a role in currency transactions within a certain range. Just as our definition of currency as " the most universally used commodity in society", cryptocurrencies were invented solely to meet the needs of human transactions, and the realization of this function is based on people's consensus.

Material Currency in version 1.0 establishes people's consensus on themselves through its natural practical value, thus having the function of transaction. A cryptocurrency itself has no practical value, and this consensus comes from extensive publicity. The highly developed information network, the promotion of media reports, and the rise of self-media communication make the formation of this consensus possible. Cryptocurrencies were generated through computer algorithms and computing power, which are computer programs and technological products, and are specific labor achievements. Therefore, the essence of a cryptocurrency is a new type of "Material Currency". It should be emphasized that this "Material Currency" is different from traditional gold, shells, and cloth. Cryptocurrencies have no practical value, and the consensus that people can "use them for transactions" is only based on public opinion propaganda, which has natural vulnerabilities.

Based on the understanding of the evolution and legal nature of money, we have given a precise definition of Credit Currency: " a social commodity produced by Currency Issuer using the borrower credit ". A cryptocurrency is not a product of credit, nor is it issued by lending. It is not a Credit Currency. According to the historical trajectory of the evolution of money, Material Currency is followed by Receipt Currency. We can infer that after cryptocurrencies, someone should provide storage services for various types of cryptocurrencies and issue cryptocurrencies deposit certificates for people to trade. Then, without realizing storage, someone should issue deposit certificates for borrowers and promise the market that their deposit certificates can be exchanged for cryptocurrencies. In this way, we can develop Receipt Currency and Promise Currency based on cryptocurrencies. Let's wait and see.

The global financial crisis broke out in 2008. On November 1 of the same year, a person who claimed to be Satoshi Nakamoto published the Bitcoin white paper "Bitcoin: A Peer-to-Peer Electronic Cash System on the P2P foundation website", stating his new vision of electronic currency - Bitcoin was introduced.

Bitcoin is a cryptocurrency, consisting of a complex series of codes generated by computers through preset programs. Compared to fiat currencies, Bitcoin does not have a centralized issuer, but is generated by the calculations of network nodes. Anyone can participate in the production of Bitcoin, and it can circulate worldwide. It can be traded on any computer connected to the internet, regardless of location. Anyone can mine, purchase, sell, or receive Bitcoin, and the user's identity information cannot be recognized by outsiders during the transaction process.

The Bitcoin network generates new bitcoins through "mining". Essentially, "mining" involves solving a complex mathematical problem with computers to ensure the consistency of the Bitcoin network's distributed ledger system. The Bitcoin network automatically adjusts the difficulty of the mathematical problem, ensuring that the entire network receives a qualified answer approximately every 10 minutes. Subsequently, the Bitcoin network generates a certain amount of new bitcoins as a reward for those who provide the answer.

The initial price of Bitcoin was $0.0025 per coin, and on July 5, 2013, the price was $65.63 per coin. As of May 27, 2024, the quoted price of one Bitcoin is $69,263.6.

2. The Central Bank Digital Currency Represented by the Digital RMB

The paper currency issued by the central bank is only a carrier for information display. Compared to its purchasing power, no one cares about the value of the paper itself. Since it is only used to carry information, there is no need to use paper, and electronic pages can also display information. Just like we used to read paper books, now we start reading e-books, there is no essential difference between the two.

The information displayed electronically needs to be registered and accounted for in a specific location, and there are two ways to do this. One is centralized accounting. Just like the assets we own, such as real estate, cars, stocks, etc., are all registered with a government-designated authority, a specific center has a centralized account book to record relevant information. When the asset owner needs to make a power transfer or change information, they must go to this specific center. We store Contract Currency issued by the central bank in commercial banks and operate accounts through the commercial banking network system. This is the digitization of currency, and the digitization of currency adopts this centralized accounting method. The other is distributed accounting, which is a database technology shared, copied, and synchronized among network members. It synchronizes the transactions between network participants, such as the exchange of assets or data. Unlike centralized accounting, which has only one universally recognized account book, all participants in distributed accounting have an account book, which means all transfers and changes are recorded on the account books of all participating members simultaneously. Each node in the system can participate in processing transaction records and updating the shared database in real time to ensure data consistency and security. This shared account book reduces the time and expense costs incurred by mediating different account books, thereby improving the efficiency of data exchange. At the same time, it provides a transparent, traceable, highly centralized blockchain, where all records are encrypted, digitally signed, and verified for their integrity. Therefore, it has the characteristics of decentralization, high reliability, high security, and high transparency.

The central bank digital currency adopts the same distributed accounting method as cryptocurrencies in technology to achieve decentralization and enable offline storage and transactions. However, the same accounting method does not mean that the central bank digital currency and cryptocurrencies have any similarities in nature. The essential difference between currencies lies not in the accounting method, but in the acquisition method. cryptocurrencies are generated through algorithms and computing power, while the central bank's legal currency and central bank digital currency are generated through borrowing. The digitization of currency is the embodiment of centralized accounting for paper currency, while the central bank digital currency is the embodiment of distributed accounting for paper currency. The difference between currency digitization and central bank digital currency lies in the different accounting methods, and there is no essential difference between them. The central bank digital currency and cryptocurrencies only share similarities in their accounting methods, but they are fundamentally different in nature. The former is Contract Currency, while the latter is Material Currency.

As the first country to study the digital currency of the central bank, China started research on digital currency as early as 2014. With the establishment of the Central Bank Digital Currency Research Institute in 2016, China became the first country in the world to establish an official research and development institution for the legal central bank digital currency. At the end of 2017, the People's Bank of China organized some commercial banks and relevant institutions to jointly carry out research and development of the Digital RMB system (DC/EP).

At the end of 2019, the Digital RMB was launched in Shenzhen, Suzhou, Xiong'an New Area, Chengdu and the future Winter Olympic Games. Since then, the pilot areas, application scenarios and application methods have been continuously expanded, enriched and upgraded.

At present, the Digital RMB adopts a two-tier operation system. That is, the People's Bank of China does not directly issue and exchange central bank digital currency to the public, but first exchanges Digital RMB to designated operating institutions, such as commercial banks or other commercial institutions, and then these institutions exchange it to the public. The operating institutions need to pay 100% reserve to the People's Bank of China for 1:1 exchange.

The Digital RMB uses blockchain technology combined with other high-end technologies. The distributed ledger accounting method means that transaction data is recorded in multiple locations and is not easily tampered with. Each transaction of the Digital RMB can be tracked and verified on the blockchain, greatly enhancing the transparency and traceability of transactions. The encryption features of blockchain technology provide a strong guarantee for the security of the Digital RMB. Each transaction needs to be verified through complex algorithms, and once the transaction is completed, it is encrypted and stored, and cannot be modified. This mechanism significantly improves the ability to resist external attacks and internal errors.

The Digital RMB combines multiple advantages of blockchain technology, providing a safer, more efficient, and transparent payment and transaction tool for modern financial systems. It not only helps to improve the quality of financial services, but also is expected to change the landing mode of monetary policy through subsequent development and upgrading, and promote the development of financial innovation and inclusive finance.

Under the current circumstances, the Digital RMB promoted by the People's Bank of China can only be exchanged for cash notes or deposits of cash notes. The People's Bank of China does not lend the Digital RMB directly to the outside world. The Digital RMB used by commercial banks to issue Digital RMB loans to the outside world is also exchanged from the People's Bank of China with their own 100% reserve funds. Therefore, the current release of Digital RMB will not result in an increase in money supply, but only the replacement of the original Contract Currency and Deposit Currency. It is a Contract Currency displayed in electronic information rather than paper.

As Digital RMB is obtained through the exchange of existing currencies rather than borrowing, and holding Digital RMB can claim to exchange cash or withdraw cash to bank cards at any time, Digital RMB can be seen as a voucher for Contract Currency. However, it should not be considered as a Receipt Currency, because according to our definition, Receipt Currency is a voucher for Material Currency, while Deposit Currency is a voucher for Contract Currency. Therefore, the central bank digital currency essentially belongs to Deposit Currency in version 5.0. When the central bank starts to issue central bank digital currency through direct lending to the outside world one day, its nature will become a new type of Contract Currency with the same status as cash. After that, if commercial banks allow the issuance of "central bank digital currency deposit receipts" to complete external loans, such deposit receipts of commercial banks will become a new type of Loan Currency.

The holders of existing Contract Currency or deposit currencies can only open accounts in commercial banks and cannot open accounts in the central bank. The holders of Digital RMB directly open accounts in the central bank and record their holding information on the distributed ledger provided by the central bank. These distributed ledgers can be installed on user terminals in offline state, supporting users to conduct offline operations on Digital RMB.

At present, commercial banks are unable to store central bank digital currency for customers and issue central bank digital currency deposit certificates for people to trade. Some people mistakenly believe that central bank digital currency can be deposited into bank cards, in fact, it can only be exchanged into Contract Currency at any time. People's central bank digital currency is not stored in commercial banks, and commercial banks handle relevant procedures, but only serve as a channel for the central bank to manage central bank digital currency. That is to say, commercial banks are not yet able to issue Deposit Currency based on central bank digital currency.

3. Deposits in Third-party Payment Platforms Represented by Alipay

Deposits and loans on third-party payment platforms have brought new topics to our discussion on the nature of money. When we transfer bank deposits to third-party payment platforms such as WeChat and Alipay, we essentially transfer Deposit Currency to the companies that own these platforms, namely Tencent or Alibaba. These platforms, like commercial banks, present their own deposit certificate information to prove that we have the right to request money on the platforms. Therefore, deposits on third-party platform companies are essentially a new form of Deposit Currency in version 5.0, which does not constitute an increase in the money supply. When third-party platforms issue loans based on customer credit, because they are not given the authority to lend based on partial deposit reserve, every cent of money they lend out is their own funds or funds borrowed through their own debts. When it is their own funds, the essence of external loans is private lending, which does not increase the overall market money supply; when it is funds come from lending, it is equivalent to helping commercial banks complete the evaluation and lending of borrowers. At this point, it can be considered that third-party platforms help banks achieve new money supply to the market while promoting inclusive finance.

Chapter 5: Current Misconceptions of Money

With the continuous progress of human practices, money has completed the purification of transaction functions and undergone a transformation in essence. Humanity has already entered the era of Credit Currency, but human monetary theory and monetary concepts have lagged far behind the pace of the times. This widespread and profound mistake has caused most current economic theories to remain at the level of assumptions or exploration, often unable to accurately predict economic crises and accurately solve practical problems.

I. The Concept behind the Balance Sheet of the Central Bank is Outdated

As mentioned earlier, the currency used for transactions in practice has evolved from Material Currency in version 1.0, Receipt Currency in version 2.0, and Promise Currency in version 3.0 to Credit Currency in version 4.0, 5.0, and 6.0. However, our understanding of Contract Currency still remains in the era in version 3.0. The most typical mistake is that the issuance of currency is always recorded as a liability on the balance sheet of most countries in the world, including the Federal Reserve System, the European Central Bank, or the People's Bank of China, which is a clearly outdated practice.

In the era of Promise Currency represented by the Bretton Woods system, the US dollar was pegged to gold and other currencies were pegged to the US dollar. People could indeed exchange their currency for gold by presenting it to the Federal Reserve System. At that time, the issuance of currency was recorded as the liability of Currency Issuer, based on the actual liability of Currency Issuer, which was in line with facts and legal provisions.

It was based on this real debt that President Charles de Gaulle asked

France to convert all its foreign exchange reserves into gold in 1968. As European countries follow suit with France's approach, the crisis of gold payment in the United States led to the collapse of the Bretton Woods system in 1971. Since then, other currencies can be exchanged for US dollars, but the US dollar can no longer be exchanged for gold at the Federal Reserve System. The debt of Currency Issuer has long lost its verbal commitment and has no legal basis. However, as of today, the central bank's balance sheet still records the currency issued by the central bank as a liability. How to understand this worldwide practice?

Balance Sheet of the Federal Reserve System

asset	liabilities
security	cash in circulation
Loans issued to financial institutions	reserve

Federal Reserve System Banknotes (USD) are IOUs issued by the Federal Reserve System to their holders and are considered liabilities. However, unlike most liabilities, the Federal Reserve System only promises to repay the holder with Federal Reserve System Banknotes (USD), which means that these IOU can only be repaid with other IOU. If you hold $100 in banknotes and request the Federal Reserve System to repay, you may receive 2 $50 banknotes, 5 $20 banknotes, 10 $10 banknotes, or 100 $1 banknotes, or a total of $100 in different denominations of banknotes[5]

The above paragraph is the most authoritative and world-wide accepted explanation of the US dollar as a liability of the Federal Reserve System. You hold a IOU to claim repayment from me, and I will take back your IOU and issue several new ones to you. As long as the total amount of these new notes equals the original one, the debt is considered settled. Seeing this, as someone holding US dollars or other types of cash, do you feel absurd? Do you feel deceived? Do you feel angry? Do you want to question: "What kind of logic is this? This is gangster logic! It's rogue logic!"

So, please wait a minute, calm down and think carefully. Is it true that "the currency issued is the liability of Currency Issuer"? If it is indeed the liability of Currency Issuer, and the obligation that Currency Issuer can fulfill when paying off the debt is only to replace the old loan note with a new one, and the replacement of the loan note is at most a continuation of the debt, it cannot be considered as a repayment of the debt in any way. A debt that will continue forever and cannot be repaid cannot be considered as a true liability! Simply put, "if it is indeed a liability, it is not a true liability". At this point, we

[5] Frederic S. Mishkin. The Economics of Money, Banking, and Finance Market[M]. Beijing: China Renmin University Press, 2018.

CURRENCY 6.0: The Essence, Principles and Reconstruction of Money

can assert that it is a clear misunderstanding to regard the currency issued by the central bank as the liability of the central bank to the currency holder, which is a misunderstanding of the nature of the central bank's issuance of currency, as well as a misunderstanding of the nature of cash in circulation. Those who still claim that the central bank has a liability to the currency holder and will make a "rigid payment" are only deceiving themselves and others.

As we have discussed before, the currency issued by the central bank is what we call Contract Currency. When Contract Currency is issued, Currency Issuer does not have any commitment to the currency holder. The job of Currency Issuer is only to complete the investigation of the borrower and accept the commitment of the borrower. The obligor of Contract Currency is the borrower, not Currency Issuer. The borrower directly promises to repay the principal and interest to Currency Issuer on schedule, and indirectly promises to all holders of currency in society that they will provide sufficient goods or service to the market within the time limit. The essence of Contract Currency has evolved from debt vouchers to credit symbols. If we insist on viewing it as debt, then it can only be said that the contract currency originates from the borrower's debt to the Currency Issuer, but itself is not a debt.

We have previously analyzed the types of rights associated with Contract Currency in our discussion. Contract Currency, like Material Currency, represent the right of dominion and the property right, not the right of claim and the creditor's right. This fundamentally determines that Contract Currency is not anyone's debt. Just as in the era of metal currency, when people acquired a gold coin through exchange, the gold coin itself was wealth. There was no reason for the holder to hold this gold coin to demand any debt repayment from the mint that made this gold coin.

Now we can be calm. It turns out that the money in our hands is not the debt of Currency Issuer from beginning to end. Currency Issuer claims that the money that is not their debt is their debt, and then they show through practical actions that it is not their debt.

We believe that the fundamental reason for such confusion is not deliberately dishonesty of Currency Issuer or the intentional deception of Currency Issuer, but the lack of understanding of the evolution of currency and the misunderstanding of the essence of Contract Currency among the general public, including economists, bankers, and government officials.

This common mistake on the balance sheets of central banks around the world is enough to show that human understanding of money has lagged far behind the development of money itself. Human bodies have entered the era of Contract Currency, but their thoughts are still stuck in the era of Promise Currency.

It should be noted that although commercial banks also indirectly have the right to issue currency, however, the currency it issues possesses a claim on central bank notes. Deposit Currency in version 5.0 is essentially a certificate for the holder to reserve cash, while Loan Currency in version 6.0 is essentially a promise for the holder to withdraw cash. Those who hold Deposit Currency or Loan Currency, that is, those who hold commercial bank deposit certificates, have the right to request commercial banks to withdraw cash, that is, Contract Currency. Therefore, when commercial banks lend money externally, they record creditor's rights on the asset side and liabilities on the liability side, without any errors.

II. The Accounts in the Balance Sheet of the Central Bank Should be Corrected

Since Contract Currency is determined not to be the liability of the central bank, how should the balance sheet of the central bank be set? Is it the owner's equity? If there are only liabilities and owner's equity on the liability side of the central bank's balance sheet, then without a doubt, Contract Currency is the issuer's owner's equity on the liability side. Currency is a commodity and asset for the social subject outside Currency Issuer, but for Currency Issuer, currency is created out of thin air based on laws and the credit of borrowers. However, as mentioned earlier, the law should not allow Currency Issuer to directly use currency to trade with other social subjects. Currency should not have any practical value for Currency Issuer itself, and it is not logical to regard it as owner's equity.

Given that Currency Issuance is a unique and special power in a country, only Currency Issuer has the right to issue Contract Currency, and Currency Issuer should be distinguished from other legal entities in this project. Therefore, in addition to liabilities and owner's equity on the liability side of the central bank's balance sheet, a special account for " The Exercise of Currency Issuance right" should be set up specifically for the central bank. It is this " The Exercise of Currency Issuance right" that gives currency users recognition of the currency, and this "Currency Issuance right" originate from the legal confirmation of the identity of Currency Issuer.

The special subject " The Exercise of Currency Issuance right " in the balance sheet distinguishes the central bank from all other socio-economic entities, highlighting the unique position of the central bank in a country's political and economic system. This is a symbol of the central bank as a bank for the whole people. As a unique power, "Currency Issuance right" also corresponds to unique obligations. The state should regulate this through detailed legal provisions to ensure that "Currency Issuance right" serves the whole people and is subject to supervision by the whole people. We will discuss in detail the setting and exercise of Monetary Power as the fourth political power in the last chapter "Principles and Construction of an Equal Rights Monetary System ".

The issuance of currency by a Currency Issuer based on the "Currency

Issuance right" granted by the entire people is essentially an exercise of political power rather than an economic liability. If the issuance of currency is recognized as a liability of Currency Issuer, not only will Currency Issuer be unable to actually repay the debt, but it will also give Currency Issuer a false excuse, which can be used to claim that "the debt can be repaid in the future", and then use the issued currency to purchase goods or service for themselves. This will lead to the destruction of the neutrality and public welfare of the Currency Issuance right. Currency Issuer should not use the Currency Issuance right to seek profits for themselves, which should become a basic monetary principle. Regarding " the principle of non-self-interest for Currency Issuers", we will also discuss it in detail in the chapter " Principles and Construction of an Equal Rights Monetary System ".

III. The Obligations of Currency Issuer Are Not in Exchange but in Independent, Impartial and Serious Lending

When the currency is decoupled from the physical goods, the currency is no longer a liability for its issuer. Currency Issuer has no obligation to exchange it when issuing a currency. This is an objective fact and logical. Because the transaction is the need of the whole society, the function of Currency Issuer is to provide a currency that meets this need. It is not obliged or able to use its own wealth to provide sufficient tradable goods for these currencies. Just like the car manufacturer has fulfilled its mission by producing high-quality cars according to market demand, it is not obliged to create roads for cars to drive on according to the needs of car buyers.

Money can only be exported through lending. Money issued by the issuer cannot be used for the issuer's own purchases of goods or service, but only for obtaining the borrower's commitment to provide goods or service as agreed.

Rights and obligations are a natural pair of partners, existing in equal measure. Currency Issuer has no obligation to exchange, and therefore no right to purchase from the outside world. The law never allows Currency Issuer to directly use the currency to conduct transactions with other social entities. Currency Issuer has no right to trade in currency, only the right to issue currency. Currency Issuer's right to issue currency only includes the right to lend and recover currency from the outside world.

The obligation of Currency Issuer is not to exchange physical goods, but to independently and impartially issue currency. As discussed earlier, the essence of modern currency is the credit of the borrower rather than the credit of Currency Issuer. Therefore, the responsibility of Currency Issuer is to conduct a professional and rigorous assessment of its borrowers. Should a Currency Issuer issue money to a particular loan applicant? there is only one standard: "There are sufficient reasons to believe that the borrower can provide commodities to society in the future in exchange for other people's currency, and repay Currency Issuer in full." Serious lending is the obligation corresponding to the right of issuance, and it is also the core mission and responsibility of Currency Issuance.

IV. The Unit of Currency is Mistakenly Used as the Unit of Wealth

The basic topics of economics are what wealth is, how much its value is, and how its price is formed. We will discuss these topics in the chapters "The Nature of Wealth and the Measurement of Wealth Value" and "The Price of Commodities" later. Now our focus is on how to express the value of wealth.

If someone asks you, "Are price and value the same thing?" you will most likely answer with certainty that they are not. It is obvious that they are not the same thing, and this is already common knowledge among people. No matter how people measure value and comment on it, they are always expressing value in terms of price, even though they have clearly known that price and value are two different concepts and have clearly stated the relationship between them.

In the Tang Dynasty of China, a horse was probably worth about 35 pieces of silk, estimated to be 70 taels of silver; in the Song Dynasty of China, a horse with a shoulder height of 133 centimeters was worth 40 taels of silver, and then the estimated value increased by 10 taels of silver for every inch increase in shoulder height, with the highest price reaching 70 taels. In the Ming Dynasty, a horse was equivalent to only 20 taels of silver. Currently, the price of one tael of silver is 500 yuan RMB, so a horse in the Ming Dynasty is equivalent to 10,000 yuan RMB today. Nowadays, the price of an ordinary horse is around 15,000 to 20,000 yuan RMB, and the price of a foal is around 8,000 yuan RMB. Similar expressions include the following examples, the United States' gross domestic product reached 27.4 trillion US dollars in 2023; on February 6, 2023, two 7.8-magnitude earthquakes occurred in southeastern Turkey, affecting neighboring countries such as Syria and Lebanon, causing direct economic losses exceeding 429 billion US dollars. These are common and obvious mistakes in expressing commodity value in ancient and modern times, people have clearly known that the value and price of wealth are not the same thing, but they still use price to express value.

William Petty, the originator of classical economics, proposed that "land is the mother of wealth and labor is the father of wealth",[6] and also proposed the use of land and labor to measure the value of cattle and grain. However, he did not and could not use land and labor to measure the value of all commodities, because the value of land and labor themselves is also uncertain. Adam Smith created the "labor theory of value", and Karl Marx further

---

[6] William Petty. A Treatise of Taxes and Contributions[M]. Beijing: China Social Sciences Press, 2010.

proposed that the value of commodities is not determined by the labor time consumed by individual producers, but by the socially necessary labor time. However, they also never used labor time as a unified standard to measure the value of commodities.

If we have the opportunity to point to a specific piece of land and ask them, "What is the value of this piece of land in your town now?" William Petty would probably answer, "This piece of land is worth about 500 pounds," and Karl Marx would probably answer, "This piece of land is worth about 50 thalers." The pound and thaler are respectively the currency units of Britain and Germany at that time, we can see that economists have at most discussed the factors that determine the value of a thing, but have not discussed the measurement standards of value. When they need to measure value, they naturally use monetary analogies like the public, but they do not talk about how much the value exactly is.

when you meet a female old friend at a business event, and you vaguely know that she got married a few years ago and raised a child, you ask her, "I heard that you have a child. How tall is your child?". She answers you very seriously, "The answer is very accurate. I just measured it last night. He is exactly one-third as tall as his father now". Do you know how tall her child is? Does this answer sound vague? You don't know whether the father of the child is tall or short, and you don't know how tall his father is exactly. What you want to know is the specific height of this child. In fact, this answer is not particularly outrageous. At least there is a standard for the general height of a man, and you can probably guess the height range of his child. If she answers "His height is exactly one-third of the tree in our yard", do you know what kind of tree is in her yard? How old is it? What is its growth rate? How tall is it now? When we use major currencies such as US dollars, euros, and Chinese yuan to express the value of a product or the amount of wealth a person has, we can probably establish a basic understanding of the described object. However, When someone uses minor currencies such as the Brazilian real, Argentine peso, Austrian schilling, or even Uzbekistan som to make similar statements, we will completely lose our waymarks on the road of evaluating value.

We cherish wealth very much, but in the development of human society, we still use the ancient analogy method to measure the value of wealth. When we answer "this dress is worth $10", what we really mean is "the value of this dress is equivalent to the value of $10". When we ask "how much is this dress worth", we are also using the analogy method to ask about the value of the dress. Obviously, humans lack a common, stable, and accurate unit for measuring wealth value.

We have become accustomed to using money value to compare the value of everything, as if we only care about the proportional relationship between things and money, but not the true value of things. In people's eyes, money is wealth, and other forms of wealth can only show their value compared to money. This is the ancient "mercantilist" view of wealth. In the era of mercantilist economics, gold and silver were seen as the only form of social wealth, and the amount of gold or silver was used as the only standard to measure a country's wealth. Such a view reflects the fervor for pursuing gold that was popular in Western Europe at that time, and is a typical view of wealth in the era of "Material Currency". Such outdated concepts have long been abandoned by people.

The measurement units used by humans for metrology and statistics possess inherent fixity and definability. The length of 1 meter is initially defined as one ten-millionth of the distance from the equator to the North Pole on the meridian passing through Paris, while 1 kilogram is the mass of 1 cubic decimeter of water. However, the monetary units of one dollar and one cent have no fixed definition. Looking back at our monetary units such as "pound", "dollar", and "yuan", they are all extensions of the number of silver dollars, gold coins and silver coins. However, it is unknown that the names of Material Currencies still exist, and their essence is irrelevant. There is no doubt that human beings have entered the era of Credit Currency, but their thoughts about how to measure currency, still remain in the era of Material Currency.

V. The Measurement Unit of Contract Currency does not Competently Perform the Function of Wealth Measurement

In the era of Material Currency, the value of Material Currencies such as gold and silver changes with the increase or decrease in production and people's demand, but such changes are moderate and subtle, and overall, their value is quite stable. However, the value of current credit currencies fluctuates greatly, and a policy, an event, or a public opinion can easily trigger a huge change in the purchasing power of the currency. Even in calm and peaceful times, the value of the same 1 pound, 1 dollar, and 1 yuan at different times and under different circumstances is constantly changing, and the unit of measurement of the currency itself has lost its accurate definition, which brings a serious problem: "The unit of measurement itself cannot be measured." Even in countries with normal economies, the 100 dollars in commercial bank account 20 years ago cannot be said to be equivalent to the current 100 dollars in terms of wealth. When we measure GDP, we usually use the US dollar as the unit of measurement. Over the past few decades, we have only seen the growth of numbers, but rarely considered the increase or decrease in the value of the US dollar itself. The current unit of currency measurement cannot accurately reflect the value of the currency itself, let alone the true value of other things. In this situation, we still use the unit of currency measurement to measure the value of wealth, which is a huge disregard for our own interests.

People mistakenly regard money, the most widely accepted form of wealth, as a synonym for all types of wealth, which is a serious generalization from one example. No matter how special money is, it is only one type of wealth, and it is the most single-functioned type of wealth. Humans are biased and mistakenly regard the monetary unit as the wealth unit, which seriously distorts the amount of wealth. Wealth has not been measured in a fixed, lasting, and accurate way. When all wealth is clothed in the garb of money, they lose their true looks. The value of 1 kilogram of gold or 1 kilogram of rice, when measured in a specific currency unit such as US dollars, will vary significantly across different markets, times, and buyers and sellers. Because we do not have an effective method for measuring wealth value, we can only use the price of goods as a measure of the wealth value of goods.

Money makes transactions extremely convenient, but it also makes the value of wealth extremely ambiguous and unmeasurable. This is the most common unscientific phenomenon in human society, and it also brings hidden and unavoidable injustice to human society. Human technology and civilization have been highly developed, but we have not established the basic units of the International System of Units for the wealth that we value most and that is most directly related to our interests.

Chapter 6: The Nature of Wealth and the Measurement of Wealth Value

We all care about wealth, pursue wealth, and manage wealth. Wealth is our vital interest. From ancient times to the present, people's understanding and understanding of wealth are quite different and even completely opposite. If we do not have a full and thorough understanding of what wealth is, how can we strive for wealth, protect wealth, and enjoy wealth? Is money wealth? Maybe money is just a tool to exchange wealth? If money cannot serve as a yardstick to measure wealth, how can we grasp the amount of wealth? Human beings should be aware that money is only one kind of wealth. All wealth has its own intrinsic value. Correctly understanding the essence and quantity of wealth value is not an optional philosophical issue but a realistic issue of gains and losses. When gold and silver are no longer our means of measuring wealth and the current currency is extremely unreliable, it is urgent to find a fixed unit of measurement for our wealth.

I. The Nature and Variety of Wealth

Mercantilist economics emerged and flourished in Western Europe from the 15th century to the mid-17th century, with Thomas Mun as its leading figure. During the rise of mercantilism, the form of money was gold and silver. Mercantilist economics advocated that money is wealth, and believed that the essence of wealth is money. They emphasized that gold and silver are the only forms of wealth, and that the purpose of all economic activities is to acquire gold and silver.

Classical economics was formed in the United Kingdom from the second half of the 18th century to the early 19th century. The main representatives were Adam Smith and David Ricardo, who are also known as liberal economists. In the perspective of classical economics, wealth is usually understood as material products, which are directly or indirectly derived from the gifts of nature. These material products have the utility of satisfying human needs and desires. Classical economics further points out that the essence of wealth lies in its productivity and scarcity. Productivity means that these material products can be produced through labor and capital investment, while scarcity emphasizes that these products are not infinite, their quantity is limited, and they need to be rationally distributed through market mechanisms and price systems.

Neoclassical economics emerged in the late 19th and early 20th centuries, represented by Alfred Marshall, Léon Walras. Neoclassical economics has developed and deepened its understanding of wealth and its essence. Under the framework of neoclassical economics, wealth is no longer limited to material products, but extends to a broader range of fields, including knowledge, skills, services, and other resources that can meet people's needs and desires. Neoclassical economics believes that the essence of wealth lies in its ability to meet people's needs and desires, and that this satisfaction can come from various types of resources and services. Compared with classical economics, neoclassical economics emphasizes the importance of intangible things such as knowledge and technology in wealth creation.

Keynesian economics was proposed by John Maynard Keynes in the 1930s, Keynesian economics believes that wealth includes not only material products and financial assets, but also people's confidence and expectations in future economic prospects. This confidence and expectations have a significant impact on economic activity and investment decisions. When people are optimistic about the future economic prospects, they will increase investment and consumption, thus promoting economic growth and wealth accumulation. Conversely, when people are pessimistic about the future economic prospects, they will reduce investment and consumption, leading to economic recession and wealth reduction. Therefore, in Keynesian economics, the essence of wealth lies not only in its current ability to meet needs and desires, but also in its expectations and confidence in future economic activities. Therefore, the government should stimulate aggregate demand by adopting expansionary economic policies, increase investment and consumption, improve people's confidence and expectations in future economic prospects, and thus promote economic growth and wealth accumulation.

neoliberal economics emerged after the 1970s, with representatives such as Friedrich August von Hayek and Milton Friedman. From the perspective of neoliberal economics, wealth is mainly seen as material and non-material resources obtained by individuals through free choice and market competition. These resources include but are not limited to currency, assets, skills, knowledge, etc., which can be used for production, consumption, and exchange. Neoliberal economics believes that the essence of wealth lies in its ability to provide people with more choices and freedom. This freedom and choice are not only reflected in the material level, but also in the spiritual, cultural, and social levels. Neoliberalism emphasizes that through free competition in the market and individual free choice, people can better realize their self-worth, meet their own needs and desires, and maximize their wealth.

In Marxist economics, wealth is understood as a good or service with use value. This use value can be natural, such as sunlight and beaches, or man-made, such as tents and chairs. These goods or service can satisfy people's needs and desires. The essence of wealth lies in its use value, which originates from the use of goods or service by people to meet their own needs. Money, as a general equivalent, enables the exchange of goods and service. Therefore, in Marxist economics, wealth includes not only material wealth but also monetary wealth. In general, Marxist economics believes that the essence of wealth is use value, which originates from people's labor and the use of natural resources.

By reviewing and sorting out the history of human thinking about wealth, it is not difficult to find that different economic schools have significant differences in their definitions and views of money and wealth. However, with the progress of the times, there is a trend of continuous improvement and more in line with the truth. Human understanding of wealth is becoming more comprehensive and profound, and the scope of wealth is gradually expanding, from the initial theory of only gold and silver to later material products, to knowledge, skills, services, and finally to confidence and expectations for the future. People's perception of wealth has gradually shifted from the pursuit of material objects to respect for their own needs. It can be said that human's perception of wealth is accompanied by the awakening of their own needs. With the progress of society, human's perception and affirmation of their own needs have undergone a process from single to multiple, from one-sided to comprehensive, from concrete to abstract, and from the present to the future. Human's perception of wealth has also undergone a process of gradually expanding its scope from money to agriculture, then to commerce, industry, and service industries.

Today, our understanding of wealth has far exceeded the idea that "gold and silver are the only wealth", and we have also recognized that many famous quotes from economists have obvious limitations in their time. For example, William Petty once said that "Land is the mother of wealth, and labor is the father of wealth", and Pierre Le Pesant Boisguillebert proposed that "Agriculture and commerce are the two nipples of wealth". In the era of these sages, t was inconceivable that the world we live in today would allow

92

humans to bring minerals back from the moon, extract combustible ice from the seabed, with industry becoming a major sector of the economy, and the poles and outer space being viewed as treasures due to humanity's expectations for the future.

Starting from human needs, it is not difficult to judge that wealth refers to all things that can meet human needs, including all tangible things, intangible things and human labor that are effective for people. Nature is the mother of wealth, and labor is the father of wealth. This is a humanistic perspective on economics. We believe that wealth can truly benefit the vast majority of people only when it is understood based on satisfying human needs. Wealth and demand are a dialectical and unified contradiction, and wealth and demand are one-to-one correspondence. People's needs are diverse and complex, so the types of wealth are also diverse and complex. People need housing, and real estate is wealth. People need spiritual comfort, and art works are wealth. People are crazy about tulips, and tulips are a symbol of wealth.

In a highly market-oriented society, where there is demand, there will be things or services that are stimulated to be sold as commodities in the market to meet customer needs. Transactions allow humans to exchange goods and service, and goods or service that can meet the different needs of different people through transactions are collectively referred to as commodities. Unneeded goods or service will not become the object of transactions, so they are not commodities. In general, commodities are wealth. Currency is the product of human intelligence and labor, widely needed by humans in market transactions, and also widely stored by people due to its availability for trading. Of course, it is also a form of wealth.

II. Money is a Unique Form of Wealth

The classical economic school believes that money itself does not have intrinsic value, but is only a medium of exchange. Its value comes from the goods and service it represents. Adam Smith elaborated on the function of money as a medium of exchange in his book "An Inquiry into the Nature and Causes of the Wealth of Nations", and pointed out that the main role of money is to facilitate the exchange of goods and service. David Ricardo also held a similar view, believing that money is only a representation of value and does not create wealth itself. On the one hand, classical economists fully affirmed the efficacy of money, but on the other hand, they saw its difference from other forms of wealth and thus denied that money belongs to wealth. The transactional needs of human beings, which are significantly different from other human needs, have entered the eyes of classical economists, but they have not been fully respected. Transactional needs are instrumentalized in their eyes, which is their discrimination against human transactional needs.

As we discussed in Chapter 4, "The Essence and Logic of Credit Money," Section 4, " Labor and Exchange are Two Hands of a Human Being for

Creating Wealth ", the importance of human transactions is evident, compared to other human needs, the need for transactions is the most common, profound, and important need of human beings. If this need is not met, all other needs will be seriously affected, or even impossible to achieve. The form of money in human society has undergone many changes. Shells, grains, animal bones, gold nuggets, coins, paper money, network data, or cigarettes in concentration camps and prisons. There are always things that perform the function of money under different productivity or social situations. The form of money has evolved from Material Currency in version 1.0 to the modern version 4.0 Contract Currency, namely central bank paper money, and the commercial bank "Deposit Currency" and "Loan Currency" in versions 5.0 and 6.0. Excluding their practical attributes, their commonality is that they can all meet the human transaction needs. There is no doubt that money is the most special and important wealth of human beings.

From the perspective of the efficacy of wealth, the efficacy of money is the most different. The fundamental efficacy of money is to meet the needs of human exchange, but the exchange object is all other wealth including money itself. Money is the intermediary for all wealth to exchange, and money becomes the most significant wealth because it can meet the most common transaction needs. Therefore, we can divide wealth into two categories: one is practical wealth, which can meet various material and spiritual needs of human beings. To distinguish it from money, we call such resources, goods or service as commodities. The other is transactional wealth, which is used for the exchange of various practical wealth. We call it money. Essentially, commodities are not money, but money is a commodity. However, for the convenience of expression, the commodities referred to in this book are narrowly defined as other resources, goods or service excluding money.

If we use the concepts of "virtual" and "real" to define commodities and money, commodities are real wealth, while money is virtual wealth. Money is used to exchange commodities, and without commodities, money cannot survive and lose all its value. Just like King Midas in Greek mythology, who gained a magical power to turn anything he touched into gold. As a result, he starved to death because all the food he touched turned into gold. Similarly, commodities must be exchanged to reach the people in need, and without money, commodities lose their legs and the market becomes a stagnant pool, and the utility of commodities cannot be fully utilized. Whether it is the economic crisis in the UK from 1837 to 1843, the Great Depression in 1929, or the "money shortage" that once occurred in the Chinese market, these historical facts all warn people that insufficient supply of money will bring heavy drags and even devastating blows to the economy. Human happiness is based on the satisfaction of human needs, and the excellent partnership between commodities and money makes human needs fully satisfied.

III. The Measurement Standard of Wealth Value

Different schools of economics have different views and methods on how to measure the value of wealth. Classical Economics emphasizes the importance of the real economy and believes that the value of wealth should be based on physical production and services. They tend to use labor time or production costs to measure the value of wealth. William Petty, the founder of classical economics, was the first to propose the "Labor Theory of Value," which posits the principle that labor time is determinant of commodity value. He left behind the famous dictum, "Labor is the father of wealth.". Pierre Le Pesant Boisguillebert, the founder of French classical economics, believed that agricultural products are the true wealth, and agriculture is the source of wealth. Adam Smith criticized the views of mercantilism and physiocracy, arguing that all material production sectors create wealth, and that the value of wealth should be measured based on labor time and labor intensity, and determined through market mechanisms and supply and demand relationships. In the early 19th century, the French economist Jean-Baptiste Say proposed the famous theory of the three factors of production, which states that labor, capital, and land jointly create the utility of goods, and the utility determines the value of commodities. This theory emphasizes that in addition to labor, capital and land also participate in the creation of value. The neoclassical school of economics emphasizes the theory of marginal utility, arguing that the value of wealth depends on its marginal utility. They also advocate measuring the value of wealth through market supply and demand relationships and price mechanisms. Marxist economics believes that the value of wealth is created by labor, especially abstract labor. On the basis of the "labor theory of value", Karl Marx proposed the view that the value of commodities is determined by socially necessary labor time. Keynesian economics believes that the value of wealth depends not only on physical production and services, but also on monetary and financial factors. They advocate regulating the economy through macroeconomic and fiscal policies to affect the value of wealth.

These views only discuss the role of various factors in the determination of wealth value, but they do not address what the value of wealth is and how to measure it specifically. Taking the most academic source of "labor theory of value" as an example, it claimed that the value of a commodity is determined by the socially necessary labor time spent in producing it, and that commodity exchange is based on the value of the commodity and is carried out on the principle of equal exchange. We inevitably have doubts about whether the value of a product produced through a specific amount of labor time will remain unchanged if it is no longer needed by people due to changes in market conditions. For example, during the COVID-19 pandemic, Pfizer spent a lot of manpower to develop and produce the oral medicine Paxlovid, which is a combination of the antiviral drug Natafuratib and the antiretroviral drug Ritonavir. When people had achieved herd immunity and the COVID-19 pandemic was over, they no longer needed any treatment, so was there still value in this specific drug? Another opposite example is that a local farmer in Hotan city, Xinjiang, China, accidentally picked up a piece of Hotan Jade with excellent color, appearance, and volume from the river while playing. He did not pay any labor for it, so is this piece of jade worthless?

Obviously, these seemingly measurable methods of measuring the value of commodities do not fundamentally explain and solve problems. Most of them are merely discussing issues through analogy, which is equivalent to using specific production factors as a yardstick when comparing the value of two pieces of wealth. However, wealth is diverse, and the origins of various types of wealth are also different, which fundamentally determines that it is impossible to measure it uniformly through specific production factors. The reason why there had been such views as "land and labor determinism", " labor theory of value ", and "three-factor theory" in the history of economics is mainly because the types of wealth at that time were single and the production factors were convergent. However, with the progress of human civilization and the improvement of productivity, agriculture, industry, and service industries have all developed comprehensively, and the types of human wealth are too numerous to measure value from the production factors of wealth itself.

Let's revisit the essence of wealth: "items that satisfy human needs". We can see that the common characteristic of all wealth is that it can satisfy human needs. Therefore, the only reasonable and feasible way to measure the value of wealth is to judge it based on its satisfaction of human needs.

Jeremy Bentham, a British legal reformer, utilitarian philosopher, and economist, argued that the value of wealth should not be based on the wealth itself, but on the degree of satisfaction and happiness that the wealth can bring, namely utility. The marginal utility school, represented by Austrian economist Carl Menger and British economist William Stanley Jevons, also holds a similar view. They believe that when consumers purchase goods or service, they will decide the quantity based on the marginal utility of the goods or service. Therefore, the value of wealth should be measured based on its marginal utility (i.e., the additional satisfaction brought by the last unit of goods or service) to people.

IV. Proposal for Establishing the Eighth Fundamental Unit of the International System of Units

When we find the measurement standard of wealth value: "the degree of meeting people's needs", we have a clear direction for exploring the basic unit of wealth value. It is necessary for us to analyze and learn from the origin and characteristics of the existing seven basic units of the International System of

Units (SI), and to conceive the establishment of the eighth basic unit of the International System of Units - the basic unit of wealth value.

Today, there are seven basic units in the International System of Units (SI): meter, kilogram, second, ampere, kelvin, mole, and candela. In order to establish a basic unit of value, establish the basic unit of value, let us understand and analyze the existing basic units. The basic unit of length, the meter (m), was originally defined as one ten-millionth of the distance from the equator to the North Pole on the meridian passing through Paris; The unit of mass kilogram (kg) was originally defined as the mass of one cubic decimeter of pure water at 4°C, this sample is loaded in the "International Kilogram Prototype" made of platinum-iridium alloy, serving as the international standard unit of mass, and is stored in a heavily guarded vault in the suburbs of Paris, France. The basic unit of time is the second (s) When cesium-133 atoms are at sea level, in an undisturbed ground state, transitioning between two hyperfine energy levels, they emit electromagnetic waves with a fixed period. This period, multiplied by 9,192,631,770, is defined as one second. In short, seconds are defined by the frequency of cesium. The basic unit of current, ampere (A), was originally defined as a constant current that can electrolyze 1.11800.02 milligrams of silver from a silver nitrate solution within a time interval of 1 second. The basic unit of thermodynamic temperature, kelvin (K), is defined as a thermodynamic temperature corresponding to the Boltzmann constant of $1.380649 \times 10^{-23} J \cdot K^{-1}$. The basic unit of amount of substance, mole (mol), contains Avogadro's constant (about 6.02×10^{23}) particles in any substance (microscopic substances such as molecules and atoms). The basic unit of light intensity, candela (cd), 1 Candela refers to the luminous flux emitted by a light source within a unit solid angle in a specified direction. Of course, the definition of the fundamental units of the International System of Units (SI) is not static, but has undergone multiple revisions. The most recent revision was the adoption of the resolution "Revision of the International System of Units" by the 26th International Conference on Weights and Measures on November 16, 2018, which officially updated four basic unit definitions including the international standard mass unit "kilogram". The reason for multiple revisions is that the original definition "is still not precise enough".

Most of these definitions involve esoteric physics concepts, which are quite obscure and difficult to understand. However, here we don't need to concern ourselves with the deep connotations of these professional concepts. We are only analyzing the methods and logic of defining these basic units. Through the analysis of existing basic unit definitions, we found that there are four processes when measuring a certain quality of a thing. First, extract the common essential characteristics of such things. For example, the essential characteristic of length is space, the essential characteristic of mass is inertia, the essential characteristic of time is position change and its process of change, and the essential characteristic of temperature is energy. Second, use a specific sample to accurately fix the quantity of this characteristic. Each basic unit is a sample under strict constraints that fixes the quantity of the essential characteristic. Third, compare the quantity of the characteristic of the thing to be measured with the quantity of the same characteristic in the sample. When the sample is fixed, the quantity of related characteristics of all other items can be expressed in terms of the ratio to the sample. Fourth, human beings strive for perfection in their requirements for accuracy. Various basic units have been modified many times to be more precise, and the definition of the meter has been changed to the wavelength of orange-yellow light emitted by a krypton 86 isotope lamp in a vacuum under specified conditions, while the definition of the kilogram has been changed to be based on the Planck constant in quantum mechanics. The specific improvement methods are of little significance for our attempts to establish a basic unit for wealth value, but inevitably lead us to lament once again that people are so extreme and demanding in their requirements for the accuracy of other things, yet careless about the measurement of wealth value. We find that humans, by simply substituting price for value, are in fact comparing the items that need to be valued with a specific currency. This approach is equivalent to only performing the third step of the complete measurement process, which is a fragmented and careless method of measurement.

We try to define the basic unit of wealth value with the same logic and steps, in order to scientifically measure the value of wealth. Based on the fundamental characteristic of value, which is "the degree of satisfaction of needs", we need to accurately understand and measure human needs to extract this characteristic. With the development of human technology to such a high level today, we find that most of the human's eyes for exploring truth are looking at the outside of the human body, and human's understanding of their own body is still at a preliminary level. However, understanding and grasping human needs is related to many disciplines that study human beings, such as anthropology, biology, physiology, psychology, etc., which are precisely the weakest links in human technology. No wonder our measurement of wealth value still remains in a primitive state. It is also because of the backwardness of human technology in related fields that our efforts to establish the basic unit of the International System of Units for wealth value are inevitably difficult. However, no matter how far and difficult the road is, as long as we fully understand the importance and necessity of accurately measuring wealth value, we have enough courage to explore. As long as we find the direction and steps to go to our destination, we will eventually make progress and success.

V. Attempt to Build the Basic Unit of the International Unit System of Wealth Value

One kilogram of rice can make people no longer hungry, one liter of water can make people no longer thirsty, one bicycle can make people walk faster and farther, one piece of music can make people daydream and feel happy, and one dollar can make people trade with each other. Without moral evaluation, and without causing harm to oneself and others, any kind of human needs should be respected and deserve to be satisfied. Any goods or service that can meet human needs are wealth. The value of wealth lies in being able to meet human needs. Starting from needs, evaluating and measuring the value of wealth is our clear direction. The premise of measuring wealth is to measure human needs. If we can measure needs, we can measure wealth. But needs seem to be the most abstract, complex, changeable, and non-standard category of human beings.

Perhaps we can map the ultimate needs of people to energy and material, and establish the basic unit of wealth value through the solidification of samples of energy and material. However, it is clear that energy and material can only measure human material needs, and intangible assets and services that can meet human spiritual needs cannot be defined and measured by physical means. A song, a painting, a movie, and an antique can bring satisfaction to people, and they are inevitably valuable. So how to measure them? Perhaps we need to classify and evaluate the wealth that meets human material and spiritual needs? Perhaps with the advancement of technology, we find that human material and spiritual needs have fundamental connections and roots, and the degree of satisfaction of both can be measured by the same indicators. In that case, the bottleneck problem of constructing the basic unit of wealth value will be solved. These ideas and efforts are left for the future!

Here, we initially set human needs as the essential characteristic of calculating wealth value. As for how to measure and calculate human needs and how to measure and calculate the degree of wealth satisfaction, we also leave it to the future. Currently, the popular "dopamine secretion ranking list" on the Internet ranks the happiness levels of various human behaviors and sorts them according to dopamine secretion: falling in love (760 units), getting married (231 units), smoking (220 units), exercising (142 units), getting a massage (93 units), watching sports games (61 units), etc. We know that this is just a loose online joke, but it may provide a way for us to explore, discover, and measure human needs.

The measurement of human needs and the measurement of wealth value appear in pairs and have the same origin. Now Let us establish a preliminary sample for human needs and wealth value respectively. We have found that the degree of satisfaction of the same quantity of commodities varies depending on the person, time, and place. The measurement of needs and wealth must establish a specific situation and use it as a standard. We set the basic unit of human needs and the basic unit of wealth value as "Need", because they are essentially the same. We first set up a sample for the basic unit of wealth value: a healthy man with a height of 1.80 meters, a weight of 75.00 kilograms, and an age of 22 years old, who has just graduated from the Master of Finance program at the Shanghai Advanced Institute of Finance of Shanghai Jiao Tong University. In defining his basic needs, we assume that after being fully fed and hydrated, he does not eat or drink for 24 hours. During this period, he simply sits and has 8 hours of normal sleep. At the same time, it is assumed that this man has no other needs besides food, including any other material needs and spiritual needs, we define the basic unit of human needs "1 Need" as "the basic needs of this man in this situation". After defining the basic unit of wealth value, we can define the basic unit of wealth value 1 Need in the same way: "the effect of food that satisfies his basic needs by restoring his physiological balance and eliminating his hunger". If 1 kilogram of sweet potatoes can satisfy this level, we can measure the wealth value of 1 kilogram of sweet potatoes as 1 Need, and then the wealth value of 5 kilograms of sweet potatoes is 5 needs.

1 kilogram of sweet potatoes can basically satisfy the basic needs of the man in the sample, which is only the hunger that humans can feel. If beef is used instead of sweet potatoes, it can not only satisfy hunger and thirst, but also provide a more delicious taste and a high-quality protein that cannot be tasted. These can keep people healthy and free from illness, which is a more long-term and deep-seated need. We assume that humans have mastered the scientific method of "measuring human needs and the degree to which goods satisfy these needs". Through measurement, it is found that the degree to which 1 kilogram of beef can satisfy needs is 5 times that of our defined basic unit, so the wealth value of 1 kilogram of beef is 5 needs. When a farmer produces 1 ton of sweet potatoes and 1 ton of beef in a year, we can accurately express that the total wealth value produced by this farmer in a year is 6000 needs. The total number of value measurements is stable and constant because the sample we set is fixed. We no longer use currency to express the wealth value created by this farmer in a year, because even if he produces 1 ton of sweet potatoes and 1 ton of beef every year, last year, we would say he created 104000 yuan of wealth, and this year, we would say he created 123000 yuan of wealth, because last year beef was 100 yuan per kilogram and sweet potatoes were 4 yuan per kilogram, while this year beef is 120 yuan per kilogram and sweet potatoes are 3 yuan per kilogram.

Of course, some people may raise such a question: 1 kilogram of sweet potatoes can meet the needs of this young man, so we believe that the wealth value of 1 kilogram of sweet potatoes is 1 need. According to this standard, the wealth value of 1 ton of sweet potatoes is 1000 needs. However, the marginal effect of human enjoyment of wealth is diminishing. The needs of this man satisfied by 1000 times of sweet potatoes are not 1000 times of the original needs, but less than 1000 times. Such a question essentially does not understand our purpose and method of establishing a basic unit for wealth value. Our purpose is to establish an objective standard for measuring the wealth value of goods, rather than discussing how goods meet the needs of a person in any way. We define the basic unit of wealth value as 1 need by satisfying the needs of the sample man. We calculate the wealth value of 1 ton of sweet potatoes as 1000 needs by comparing it with our established basic unit. The definition of this basic unit is strictly constrained by circumstances, and the marginal effect decreases only when goods continue to meet the needs of people. If we have to compare the wealth value with the degree of satisfaction of human needs in the same proportion, we can consider that 1 ton of sweet potatoes satisfies the needs corresponding to the basic unit, which is equivalent to satisfying the man in the sample 1000 times. In this way, the wealth value of 1000 times also satisfies the needs of 1000 times, rather than being calculated as less than 1000 times under the condition of diminishing marginal effect.

VI. The Wealth Value of the Currency Itself Should also be Measured by the Basic Unit of Wealth Value

Contract Currency has become an independent object, a special type of commodity. So how should we measure the wealth of the currency itself? What is the wealth of one yuan? Like all other goods, the wealth value of the currency should be measured by its ability to meet a person's needs. In modern society, all of a person's needs are rarely met through self-reliance and direct production and self-service. Most of them need to be acquired through transactions. The more prosperous the demand for transactions, the higher the wealth value of the currency. Regarding the measurement of human transaction needs, we also need to establish a specific sample. The 22-year-old young man mentioned earlier，When we define the demand for money in transactions, we assume that his relatives and friends will not provide any financial assistance. He has no savings and comes to Shanghai alone with only daily necessities. He earns money through his own work. The desire of this young man for all goods is limited to rent, food, and books, and he has no interest or need for anything else. Through advanced technology and means of calculation, we find that the total demand of this sample is 100,000 times the basic unit of wealth value, so, the total transaction demand of this young person is 100,000 needs. That is to say, we define the basic unit of the wealth value of money "1 Need" as "one hundred thousandth of the transaction demand of this young man in the sample". Transaction needs are fulfilled through currency, and in his living environment, the amount of RMB that can meet his transaction needs is 150,000 yuan. At this point, we consider the wealth value of this 150,000 yuan to be 100,000 needs. The wealth value of one yuan is 0.667 Need. After determining the basic unit of wealth value of currency, we can assess the wealth value of any currency. For example, if his supervisor's annual income is 300,000 yuan, we can say that his supervisor earns a wealth value of 200,000 needs in a year.

When the basic unit of wealth value of money is defined, we can measure the true wealth value of money not by its monetary amount but by its satisfaction of transaction needs. In this way, we can get rid of the influence of changes in purchasing power of money on our calculation of the true wealth value of money.

Understanding transaction needs is quite laborious. We may simply understand it as "comprehensive money desire", which does not refer to the need for a specific thing, but refers to the need for money generated by a person's entire material and spiritual needs. For example, in the second year of the market, this young man needs 200,000 yuan to complete the same purchase as the previous year. This means that inflation occurred this year, and the purchasing power of the RMB has declined. We can say that the real wealth value of 200,000 yuan currency at this time is still 100,000 needs. The wealth value of 1 yuan has become 0.5 needs. And this 100,000 needs is the transaction needs of this young man for one year.

VII. Using the Price Index as a Reference to Define the Basic Unit of Wealth Value

Under the current technological conditions, human intelligence and technical means are not sufficient to measure human needs and the extent to which commodities meet human needs, and We hardly have the possibility to measure the value of commodities in reality. However, people have generally recognized the impact of changes in the purchasing power of money itself on human beings' measurement of the real wealth value of commodities. When inflation occurs, the same amount of money can only purchase a smaller number of commodities which means that we earn the same amount of money, but the true wealth value we obtain is reduced. In order to reflect the true wealth value of money and commodities, countries have adopted price indexes to measure and adjust the wealth value of goods measured in monetary units in people's production and life. We can fully learn from the scientific method of price index to define the basic unit of wealth value.

Human economic statistics have been quite developed, and the statistics and application technology of price index have been quite advanced. Price index is an economic indicator that reflects the direction, trend, and degree of change in the price level of a group of commodities in different periods. It is a type of economic index, usually expressed as a relative number comparing the reporting period with the base period. Common price indexes include Consumer Price Index (CPI) and Producer Price Index (PPI). In order to ensure the continuity and comparability of price indexes, a "basket" of goods and service is usually fixed for a certain period of time, commonly known as a "fixed basket". We can consider that during this period, the wealth value of this "fixed basket" is fixed, moreover, at a specific point in time during this period, the total price of this "fixed basket" can be statistically determined, and thus the wealth value corresponding to 1 unit of currency at that time point can also be statistically fixed. We can define 1 unit of currency at that time point as equivalent to 1 unit of wealth value.

In order to measure the wealth value of all commodities more comprehensively and accurately, the "fixed basket" we choose when defining the wealth value unit should be more comprehensive than the "fixed basket" of CPI and PPI, and the weight of various commodities in the basket also needs to be different. However, the basic ideas and methods used in current statistics of CPI and PPI can be adopted.

Drawing on the statistical methods of price index, after defining the basic unit of wealth value as one unit of currency at a specific point in time, the basic unit of wealth value has a name that is independent of the currency unit. When we express the wealth value of commodities and currencies in different situations at different times, we can use the basic unit of wealth value to express them separately, independent of the currency quantity.

Now let's take the US dollar as an example. Since 1913, the purchasing power of the US dollar, that is, the wealth value of its currency, has been steadily declining. At that time, one US dollar was defined as 1/20 of one ounce of gold. Up to now, one US dollar can only buy about 1/2100 ounces of gold, and the total amount of goods and service purchased with one US dollar is also getting smaller and smaller. The following chart demonstrates the rise and fall of the purchasing power of the US dollar since 1913.

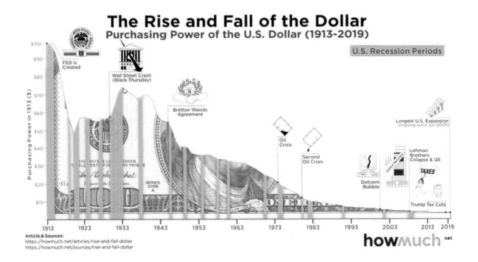

The Rise and Fall of the Dollar
Purchasing Power of the U.S. Dollar (1913-2019)

year	1913	1923	1933	1943	1953	1963
quantity $	100	57.89	76.15	57.23	37.08	32.35
year	1973	1983	1993	2003	2013	2019
quantity $	22.30	9.94	6.85	5.38	4.25	3.87
year	1913	1923	1933	1943	1953	1963
quantity $	100	57.89	76.15	57.23	37.08	32.35
year	1973	1983	1993	2003	2013	2019
quantity $	22.30	9.94	6.85	5.38	4.25	3.87

In terms of actual purchasing power, $100 in 2019 is equivalent to $3.87 in 1913. Now, we define the basic unit of wealth value as "1 need": "1 dollar in 1913". After defining the basic unit of wealth value, we can measure the wealth value of $1 in 2019 as 0.0387 needs. Therefore, on September 10, 2019, the iPhone 11 with a storage of 64GB released by Apple was priced at $699, which can be expressed as its wealth value of 27.05 needs (0.0387*669=27.05). When the US Department of Commerce announced that "the nominal GDP (GDP) completed by the United States in 2019 was $21431.6 billion, taking 2012 as the base year, and the actual GDP of the United States in 2019 was $19060.5 billion", another announcement can be added: "calculated in the basic unit of the International System of Units for wealth value, the actual GDP of the United States in 2019 was wealth value of 8294.03 billion needs" (214316*3.87/100=8294.03).

Different from the actual GDP statistics currently used in various countries, the definition of the basic unit of wealth value aims to establish a more unified, accurate, fixed, and long-lasting standard measurement unit worldwide, in order to avoid the confusion caused by various economic terms to the general public, and also to achieve a unified measurement of the true wealth value of various commodities and currencies worldwide. It can help the general public to see the actual value of various commodities directly, and also reflect the dynamic changes in the intrinsic value of various currencies.

As a book that focuses on money, we strive to remind people that the price and value of wealth are completely different, and the value of wealth should be clearly defined and accurately measured. At the same time, we provide feasible ideas and methods for determining the basic unit of wealth value. As for how to measure people's needs and the procedures for satisfying them in defining the basic unit, as well as how to determine the base period rotation and other scientific and reasonable institutional measures, or whether there are other more scientific definition methods, it is beyond our research capabilities. We leave these questions to those smart scientists, economists, statisticians, and government officials. We look forward to the future when someone can use advanced technology to scientifically and accurately define the basic unit of wealth value for money and commodities.

Chapter 7: Prices of Commodities

Price refers to the amount of money that can be exchanged for a commodity, essentially the proportional relationship between the wealth value of money and the wealth value of the commodity. Price is an economic concept directly used in people's daily life and production, but people's understanding of price is based on traditional wealth concepts and value measurement standards, which cannot correctly understand and manage prices. After establishing a new wealth concept and basic unit of wealth value, we can understand prices more scientifically.

I. The Quantity of Wealth Value is Fixed, While the Perception of Value is Variable

We have established a sample of wealth value for commodities and currencies by extracting "human needs" and defined it as the basic unit for measuring the wealth value of commodities and currencies. At the same time, we have also established a basic unit for the wealth value of commodities and currencies by drawing on the statistical methods of price indexes. We are well aware that such a definition is not scientific and precise enough, and we are only providing a method and idea to achieve the goal of unifying the basic unit of wealth value. Only when this basic unit is established can we achieve a stable evaluation of the wealth value of currencies and commodities.

The definition of the basic unit enables humans to accurately evaluate and express the wealth value of money and commodities. Using the basic unit of wealth value as a yardstick, the wealth value of a specific commodity or a specific currency can be accurately measured and specifically expressed. We call the wealth value of a unit quantity of commodities and currency "Objective Wealth Value" (OWV), including "Objective Wealth Value of Commodities" (OWVC) and "Objective Wealth Value of Money" (OWVM). For example, the "Objective Wealth Value" of 1 kilogram of sweet potato mentioned earlier is 1 need, while the "Objective Wealth Value" of 1 yuan of RMB is 0.667 needs.

The price of a commodity we refer to in our daily lives is essentially the value ratio between the commodity and a specific currency. For example, when we say that a piece of clothing costs $10, we are essentially saying that "the value of this piece of clothing is 10 times the value of $1". Now that we have introduced the measurement of wealth value, we can conclude that the ratio of a unit quantity of commodity to a unit quantity of currency, measured by objective wealth value, is the price of this unit quantity of commodities in this currency. We refer to this ratio as the objective price (OP)of the commodity when priced in this currency.

OP= OWVC/ OWVM

For example, through scientific and accurate measurement and calculation, we conclude that the objective wealth value of a hat is 50 needs, while the objective wealth value of 1 dollar is 10 needs. The ratio between the two is 5, and 5 dollars is the objective price of this hat.

The objective price of a commodity is determined by the objective wealth value of the commodity and the currency used for pricing. At the same time, we must also recognize the fact that different people and situations have different perceptions of the same wealth value of commodities and currencies. This is equivalent to the same 10kg iron block, which has a constant mass and weight, but is heavy for a 6-year-old child and light for a 30-year-old man. In the eyes of men in northeastern China, a girl who is 170 centimeters tall is not considered tall, while in the eyes of men in southern China, this girl is called a tall beauty.

In order to reflect the different perceptions of the objective value of commodities and money among different individuals, we have set up a new economic concept, "Value Perception" (VP). Due to different needs, environments, internal ideas, and wealth they possess, people have different value judgments on the same commodities. A painting that is considered a treasure by collectors may be worthless in the eyes of farmers. People also have different value judgments on the same amount of currency. Some people choose to give up treatment due to the medical expenses of 1 million yuan for a serious illness, while some person has just purchased a unique Louis Vuitton handbag for 7 million RMB, and then "collected" a Boucheron jewelry "artwork" for 28 million RMB. The same commodity, the same currency, with the same objective value, after the basic unit of wealth value is determined, there is also an objective wealth value with the same quantity. However, in the eyes of different people, their subjective wealth values are not the same. We refer to people's different cognition and feelings about wealth as "value perception", including "Value Perception of Commodities" (VPC) and "Value Perception of Money" (VPM).

For specific individuals, the more commodities or money they have, the weaker their "value perception" becomes; the greater their own demand for commodities or money, the stronger their "value perception" becomes. If we define rich and poor based on the amount of money they hold, we have a basic life experience that selling our labor and products to rich people is easier to obtain satisfactory prices, while using money to purchase the labor and products of poor people is easier to obtain satisfactory quantities of commodities. For example, for the same amount of 10,000 yuan of currency, once the basic unit of wealth value is defined, its total objective wealth value is fixed. However, for a billionaire, his "value perception" of this 10,000 yuan of currency is extremely weak, while for a beggar, his "value perception" of this 10,000 yuan of currency is extremely strong. Similarly, for 10 kilograms of sweet potatoes, when the basic unit of wealth value is defined, the total objective wealth value is fixed. However, for a person who is well-fed and has a full granary, his "value perception" is extremely weak, while for a person who is hungry and in need of food, his "value perception" is extremely strong.

The "value perception" is also affected by economic expectations, social environment, scene atmosphere and other factors. We will discuss in detail in the third section of this chapter" Calculation Formula and Influencing Factors of Subjective Price of Commodities" which factors and how they affect people's "value perception" of commodities and currencies.

Quantifying the impact of this "perceived value" leads to the same amount and objective wealth value of money and commodities perceiving different subjective wealth values in different individuals' hearts. Just like the sweet potato mentioned above, for the same person, in a non-hungry state, the total wealth measurement may only be 0.1 or 0.5 needs, rather than 1 need. If the 22-year-old graduate is replaced by an 88-year-old single elderly person who already has all the items they need, does not want to buy a house or car, and even has a weak appetite, and has no children, and the doctor has diagnosed her with pancreatic cancer and she has three months to live, she does not consider anything after death, and there is basically no need for transactions. And her bank account still has 100 million yuan in cash, then 150,000 yuan may only be 100 needs for her wealth measurement, rather than 100,000 needs which is its OWV.

We define the different wealth values of a specific commodity or currency unit due to differences in "Value Perception" between individuals as "Subjective Wealth Value" (SWV), including the Subjective Wealth Value of Commodities (SWVC) and the Subjective Wealth Value of Money (SWVM)。 Let us set A as the coefficient of SWVC, and B as the coefficient of SWVM.

Then we can derive the relationship between SWV and OWV of commodities and money

SWVC= OWVC*VPC*A

SWVM= OWVM*VPM*B

From this, we can further calculate the ratio of the subjective wealth value of a unit quantity of commodities to the subjective wealth value of a unit quantity of money. We call this ratio the subjective price (SP) of the commodity when priced in this currency.

SP= SWVC/SWVM

=(A/B)*(OWVC/OWVM)* (VPC/VPM)

Using the hat with an objective price of $5 mentioned earlier as an example, in the eyes of a bald rich man, its subjective wealth value is 100 needs, while the objective wealth value of the hat is just 50 needs. On the other hand, for a $1 bill, the subjective wealth value is only 1 Need, while the objective wealth value of this 1 dollar is 10 needs. Then the ratio of the subjective wealth value of the hat to the dollar is 100, and $100 is the subjective price of this hat for the rich man. Yes, it is not an exaggeration to say that the subjective price of this hat for this rich man is 20 times its objective price. There is a popular saying on the Internet: "Poverty limits my imagination." In the world of the rich, the transaction prices of commodities are always amazing.

II. Economists' Views on Prices

There are many views on the formation of commodity prices in the economic community. The labor value theory believes that the price of a commodity is mainly determined by the labor time required to produce it. The longer the labor time, the higher the value of the commodity and the higher the price. The marginal utility theory believes that the price of a commodity depends on its marginal utility, which is the degree of satisfaction consumers obtain from the last unit of the commodity. If the marginal utility of a commodity is high, then the price consumers are willing to pay is also higher. The supply and demand theory is the foundation of modern microeconomics. It believes that the price of a commodity is determined by its supply and demand in the market. When supply equals demand, the commodity reaches an equilibrium price. If supply exceeds demand, the price will decrease; if demand exceeds supply, the price will increase. The market competition theory believes that the price of a commodity is determined by the degree of competition in the market. In a perfectly competitive market, every seller is a price taker, and the price is determined by the competitive supply and demand relationship in the market. In an imperfectly competitive market, sellers have certain pricing power, and the price may be higher or lower than that in a perfectly competitive market.

Adam Smith pointed out that when the supply of commodities in the market equals the demand, the price will reach a balance point. If the supply exceeds the demand, the price will fall because sellers will compete to reduce prices to attract buyers; on the contrary, if the demand exceeds the supply, the price will rise because buyers will compete to raise prices to compete for limited commodities. Adam Smith also believed that the price of commodities can be decomposed into these three parts, representing the wages of laborers in the production process, the profits of capitalists, and the land rent of landlords. This view reflects the understanding of price formation in classical economics, that is, prices are determined by various costs in the production process. Karl Marx believed that the value of commodities is determined by socially necessary labor time, while prices are the monetary expression of the value of commodities. In market competition, prices will fluctuate around the value due to the influence of supply and demand, but in the long run, prices and values tend to converge.

Through analysis, we found that there is a common and obvious deviation in these past views on the formation of commodity prices, which only discusses the commodity itself without discussing the currency. However, price refers to the amount of currency that can exchange for a commodity, that is, the proportional relationship between currency and commodity. When analyzing prices, it is completely inappropriate to only consider the commodity and ignore the currency. This is like discussing a couple's relationship by focusing solely on the wife without mentioning the husband. It's also like, when reporting on the UEFA Euro 2024 final between Spain and England, only the match process of the English team is described in detail, while the performance of the Spanish team on the field is not mentioned at all. In the end, it directly informs the audience that the Spanish team won the championship with a score of 2:1. The reason for the deviation and neglect of economists lies in their habit of using currency as a yardstick for measuring wealth, mistakenly regarding the basic unit of currency as the basic unit of commodity value. Obviously, they fail to see that currency itself is also a commodity, nor do they attach importance to the phenomenon that the same commodity has huge price differences among different people or under different circumstances. In fact, prices are jointly determined by buyers and sellers during the transaction process. People who engage in buying and selling simultaneously consider their dual needs for currency and commodities, linking commodities and currency together, thus determining the price of commodities. Only by treating currency as other commodities, assessing the wealth value of commodities and currency separately, and taking into account the different "value perceptions" of currency and commodities among different people and under different circumstances, can we fully understand the formation mechanism of prices. We will discuss the true formation process of commodity prices in detail below.

III. Calculation Formula and Influencing Factors of Subjective Price of Commodities

In the real world, not all borrowers pay off their loans at the same time, and the claims of Currency Issuers will not be cleared. Due to the existence of bankruptcy laws, a significant number of debtors have their debts discharged. Additionally, there are some debtors who, even without filing for bankruptcy, are practically incapable of repaying their obligations to the issuers of currency. At the same time, new borrowers are constantly bringing money into the market from Currency Issuers. In these cases, money is left in the market as savings, Contract Currency issued by the central bank, Deposit Currency issued by commercial banks, and Loan Currency circulate together in the market. At the same time, the goods produced by people are not completely consumed, and a large amount of production capacity is constantly producing new products. The employees in the service industry are always waiting for customers' purchases. These stocks of commodities and stocks of money, as well as the continuous consumption or increase of commodities and money, are important factors affecting the price of commodities. The free exchange of commodities and money in the market, people's general feelings and choices about them determine the proportional relationship between them, driving the rise and fall of commodity prices. The supply of commodities, the supply of money, the demand for commodities, the demand for money, and other factors simultaneously determine the trend of commodity prices. Now let us conduct a more detailed analysis.

The price of a commodity in the individual's mind, that is, the subjective price (SP) of the commodity, has been discussed in the previous article.

$$SP = SWVC/SWVM$$
$$= (A/B)* (OWVC/OWVM)* (VPC/VPM)$$

After the basic unit of wealth value is defined, the objective wealth value of commodities (OWVC) and the objective wealth value of money (OWVM) under the International System of Units are fixed, and the only variables that affect the subjective price (SP) of commodities are the value perception of commodities (VPC) and the value perception of money (VPM). The higher the VPC, the higher the SWVC, and the higher the SP, and vice versa. The higher the VPM, the higher the SWVM, and the lower the SP and vice versa.

When a buyer faces the market price of a product, the higher his subjective price (SP) for the product, the more cost-effective he feels it is, and the more inclined he is to purchase. The lower his subjective price (SP) for the product, the less cost-effective he feels it is, and the more inclined he is not to purchase.

Let's further analyze what factors affect people's perception of the value of commodities and currencies. Demand determines perception, whether it is commodity or currency, he greater the demand, the higher the perception of value, and the lower the demand, the lower the perception of value. People are four-dimensional creatures, and they not only consider the present, but also consider the future. Therefore, the demand for commodities and currencies should not only consider the current demand, but also consider the future demand. Rareness is valued, whether it is commodities or currencies. The more there are, the cheaper they are, and the less there are, the more expensive they are. Similarly, this "more" and "less" not only depends on the current stock, but also on future expectations.

People's value perception of commodities (VPC), is directly proportional to the person's "Current Personal Demand for Commodities" (CPDC) and "Expected Personal Demand for Commodities" (EPDC), and inversely proportional to the "Current Market Supply of Commodities" (CMSC) and "Expected Market Supply of Commodities" (EMSC).

People's value perception of money (VPM), is directly proportional to the "Current Personal Demand for Money" (CPDM) and the "Expected Personal Demand for Money" (EPDM), and inversely proportional to the "Current Personal Saving"(CPS) and the " Expected Personal income " (EPI).

When analyzing the "value perception", in addition to existing and future demand and supply, we also need to pay attention to another important factor, which is Interest Rate (IR). When we store goods, no one gives us any reward, but when we choose to store money in commercial banks or central banks, we receive interest returns. The law is set up in this way, giving monetary policy makers the power and means to adjust people's value perception of money (VPM), which is directly proportional to interest rate (IR). At the same time, Interest Rate (IR) is not strongly correlated with the existing supply, expected supply, existing demand, and expected demand of specific individual commodities, so it has little impact on the value perception of commodities (VPC).

The positive and negative relationships between these variables that affect individual subjective prices may not be linear proportional relationships. Regarding existing and future demand and supply, they also need to be calculated based on the total time that goods and money satisfy individuals. There may be other factors beyond these variables that affect the relationship. We will not further analyze these factors in this book.

Among the factors affecting the value perception, the "Current Personal Demand for Money" (CPDM) and the "Expected Personal Demand for Money" (EPDM) are relatively difficult to understand. We will discuss this further. A person living in a specific market environment is influenced by various internal and external factors, forming a sum of material and spiritual needs in their current life. This sum of needs, excluding the part that can be produced and provided by themselves, can only be met through market transactions, which forms the overall demand for money, which is the "Current Personal Demand for Money" (CPDM). For example, a farmer, aged

40, expects to work for another 30 years and retire at the age of 70, with a life expectancy of 80 years. Now he needs 60 kilograms of grain, 30 eggs, 1 piece of clothing, and 60 tablets of antihypertensive drugs per month. However, he can only produce 10 kilograms of grain and 10 eggs per month through farming and raising hens, and the rest needs to be purchased from the market. At this time, the market prices are 10 yuan per kilogram of grain, 2 yuan per egg, 100 yuan per piece of clothing, and 1 yuan per tablet of antihypertensive drugs. Therefore, the farmer's monthly needs are 700 yuan (50*10+20*2+100+60*1), which is the "Current Personal Demand for Money" (CPDM) of the farmer.

This farmer has raised a son who is now 18 years old and very intelligent. He just passed the entrance exam for a prestigious university. He plans to cultivate him well until he obtains a doctoral degree. The budget for tuition and miscellaneous expenses is 500,000 yuan. He also wants to rebuild a house with a budget of 500,000 yuan. The budget for future medical expenses is 200,000 yuan, and he plans to save 300,000 yuan for his pension when he can no longer work. The total amount of money needed to be earned by the farmer during the remaining 30 years of working life is 1.5 million yuan. Therefore, his "Expected Personal Demand for Money" (EPDM) can be calculated as 50,000 yuan per year (1500,000/30). If the farmer has a dream since childhood that he must take a round-the-world trip during his lifetime and budgets 300,000 yuan, then the amount of money he needs to earn during the next 30 years of working life is 1.8 million yuan. In this case, his "Expected Personal Demand for Money" (EPDM) can be calculated as 60,000 yuan per year (1800,000/30).

In addition, each factor affecting the value perception has its own sub-level influencing factors, which we will not further analyze in this chapter. We will further analyze the relevant deepening factors in Chapter 10, Section 4 " Composition of the Amount of Money and Commodities in the Market and the Market Transaction Equation".

IV. The Price Formation Mechanism in a Non-fully Competitive Market

Having grasped the essence of wealth, we no longer consider currency as a standard for measuring wealth, making it easier to understand the essence of trading. Let's explore the process of confirming the objective wealth value of commodities and currencies in the hearts of the two parties involved in the transaction and forming a consensus between them. We illustrate with an example of a grain transaction between a farmer who has plenty of grain but not enough money and a merchant who is wealthy but desperately hungry. We assume that, based on the defined basic unit of wealth value, the objective wealth value (OWVC) of 1 kilogram of rice is 8 need, while the objective wealth value (OWVM) of 1 yuan is 2 need. Then the objective price (OP) of

this 1 kilogram of rice is 4 yuan (OP= OWVC/OWVM).

Compared to businessmen, the farmer has a lower "Current Personal Demand for Commodity" (CPDC) for rice, a lower "Expected Personal Demand for Commodity ", a higher "Current Market Supply of Commodity" (CMSC), and a higher "Expected Market Supply of Commodity"(EMSC), this results in the farmer having a lower "Value Perception of Commodity" (VPC) for rice.

At the same time, compared to businessmen, the farmer has a higher "Current Personal Demand for Money" (CPDM), a higher "Expected Personal Demand for Money" (EPDM), a lower "Current Personal Saving" (CPS), and a lower "Expected Personal Income" (EPI), this results in the farmer having a higher "Value Perception of Money " (VPM) for money.

According to the formulas for the subjective wealth value of goods, the subjective wealth value of money, and the subjective price discussed in the previous text:

SWVC= OWVC*VPC*A
SWVM= OWVM*VPM*B
SP= SWVC/SWVM

The farmer's SWVC is relatively low. We assume that the subjective wealth value of 1 kilogram of rice in the farmer's mind is 5 needs. The farmer's SWVM is relatively high. We assume that the subjective wealth value of 1 yuan in the farmer's mind is 2.5 needs. Therefore, the subjective price (SP) of rice formed by the farmer is 2 yuan per kilogram, which means that if someone offers to exchange 1 kilogram of rice for 2 yuan or more, the farmer is willing and satisfied.

At this time, the merchant's OWVC is higher, while the OWVM is lower. In the heart of the merchant at this time, the subjective wealth value of 1 kilogram of rice is 10 needs, while the subjective wealth value of 1 yuan is 1 need. The subjective price (SP) of rice formed by the merchant is 10 yuan per kilogram, which means that if someone offers him 1 kilogram of rice in exchange for money equal to or less than 10 yuan, the merchant is willing and satisfied.

We can see that for this 1kg of rice, the farmer and the merchant have formed their own subjective prices, and any price between 2 and 10 yuan is likely to be the transaction price for both parties.

At this time, the businessman thinks that he has rich experience in trading and has a good grasp of the psychology of the counterparty. He thinks to himself, "I can't reveal my psychological price, I have to keep his price down." The businessman speaks first and offers the farmer 5 yuan for 1 kilogram of rice. Unexpectedly, this is significantly higher than the farmer's psychological price of 2 yuan. The farmer agrees and is quite satisfied. So, 5 yuan forms the market price of this kilogram of rice in this situation, but there is only two people in this market.

If the farmer previously learned about the merchant's monetary savings or inner thoughts and replied, "A minimum of 10 yuan," the merchant would agree. Then 10 yuan would be the price of 1 kilogram of rice in this specific situation. What would happen if the farmer started by offering 3 yuan? the merchant would agree, 3 yuan would be the price. What if the merchant insisted on offering 1.5 yuan, or the farmer insisted on offering 12 yuan? Then, without any change in the subjective wealth value of the rice or currency of the other party, the transaction would not be able to proceed and the price would not be formed.

Generally speaking, the demand for rice and currency from merchants and the farmer is stable under specific circumstances, but it is not excluded that their on-site performance will temporarily change each other's "value perception". For example, the performance of the merchant may affect the farmer' own demand judgment for rice and currency. For example, the merchant says, "You may not understand the market? Nowadays, it is difficult to make money in the market. Recently, recently, all items have been reduced in price, and local other farmers have achieved high-yield varieties this year, resulting in a bumper harvest of rice，rice is sold everywhere. ". The farmer, solely because of the merchant's remark, might reassess the subjective value of wealth for 1 yuan to 3 need, and adjust the subjective value of wealth for 1 kilogram of rice to 4 need. Consequently, the merchant could make the farmer satisfied with the transaction price by using only 1.33 yuan. At this time, if the merchant quotes 1.5 yuan to buy 1 kilogram of rice, the farmer will agree. In this small market of two people, the price of 1.5 yuan can be formed.

The above is just a short story we wrote to illustrate the principle of price formation. In fact, the price formation mechanism in this non-fully competitive market operates everywhere in our daily lives, even in the stock market where we think there should be full bidding. On April 9, 2024, China's Tianrui Cement (01252) in Hong Kong stocks plummeted 99.04% in the last 15 minutes before the market closed, falling from the previous day's closing price of HK$5.00 per share to HK$0.048. The total market value evaporated from over HK$14 billion to only HK$140 million in an instant. However, its latest financial report shows that the net asset value per share is HK$5.264. The parent company responded on the same day that they were not aware of the reason for the sharp decline in share price and that the company's production and operation were normal. According to public information, Tianrui Cement was one of the national key cement enterprise groups, ranking ninth in the country. The parent company Tianrui Group ranked 380th among China's top 500 enterprises and 195th among China's top 500 manufacturing enterprises. Tianrui Cement's business mainly covered Henan province, Liaoning province, Anhui province, Tianjin city, and the eastern coastal areas, and currently had more than 30 production enterprises across the country. In addition, the company was also a major supplier for key projects such as the South-to-North Water Diversion Project, the Harbin-Dalian High-speed Railway, the Beijing-Hong Kong High-speed Railway, the Beijing-Hong Kong-Macao Expressway, the Lian-huo Expressway, the Yellow River Bridge, and Dalian Port. Such a huge fluctuation in share price has shocked the world. No matter what kind of unexpected events have occurred in the company's own management, we cannot believe that the stock price fluctuation truly reflects the changes in the company's own value.

The reason is that the subjective price (SP) of the stock has changed for both the seller and the buyer. For the seller, they may have obtained significant negative information about the company's dramatic changes in operations, so the seller's "value perception of the commodity" (VPC) for the stock at the time of sale is extremely low, and their willingness to sell is extremely high. It may also be that the stock has been pledged, and the pledgor has not paid the required margin, and the brokerage firm has liquidated the position according to regulations. In this situation, as a seller, the brokerage firm has a high "value perception of money" (VPM) due to legal liability considerations, and is willing to recover funds at all costs. Regardless of the situations, it will lead to a very low subjective price SP for the stock for the seller. For the buyer, due to the lack of liquidity in the Hong Kong stock market in recent years, some stocks have extremely low daily trading volumes, and the buyer's currency holdings are extremely limited, resulting in a high "value perception of money" (VPM), which also leads to a very low subjective price (SP) for the stock. The subjective price (SP) for both the buyer and seller of the stock decreases significantly at the same time, resulting in an epic crash in the stock.

Why is the stock price formation in this example considered to be under a non-fully competitive market? Although the Hong Kong stock market is open and transparent, with a large number of investors, due to the lack of liquidity and poor trading in the Hong Kong stock market in recent years, some stocks have not received much attention from market participants. Regardless of the number of shareholders in the company or the number of stock investors in the market, only a very small number of stock holders and fund holders in the market were concerned about this stock. It was this very small number of people that made up the market for this stock during that specific 15-minute period. Therefore, we believe that during that emergency period, this stock was under an insufficient market. This stock announced the suspension of trading on the second day after the sharp decline. We can predict that due to the shocking decline of this stock, it had attracted the attention of the entire market. When trading resumes, it will be in a fully competitive market, and its price formation will be a different scene. This stock cannot stay at such an outrageous price for a moment and will surely return to its reasonable market price.

V. The Price Formation Mechanism in a Fully Competitive Market

People's perception of the value of their currency and commodities is not only affected by their own physiological and economic characteristics, but also by external factors such as the legal environment, public opinion, and economic situation. However, overall, people's perception of the value of currency and commodities is stable. For a specific commodity at a specific time, people's perception of the value of the commodity is stable. People will use the information they can get to form their own comprehensive judgment of the commodity, and form a relatively stable subjective wealth value for a certain commodity in their hearts. At the same time, in general, people have formed a relatively stable judgment of the amount of money in their pockets and future income based on their living environment, and have a stable subjective wealth value judgment for a certain amount of money. When it comes to trading, people will use the ratio of the two subjective wealth values of commodities and currency that have been formed in their hearts as a standard to judge the price of the commodities on sale and decide whether to buy.

As mentioned earlier, we refer to the ratio of two subjective wealth values formed by people for commodities and currencies as the "subjective price" (SP) of commodities. For example, under normal market conditions, an ordinary citizen forms a subjective wealth value of 15 needs for 1 kilogram of pork and a subjective wealth value of 1 need for 1 yuan of RMB. This citizen's " Buyer's Subjective Price" (BSP) is 15 yuan per kilogram. If the butcher's price is 10 yuan per kilogram of pork, it indicates that the butcher's "Seller's Subjective Price " (SSP) is 10 yuan per kilogram of pork. At this time, the BSP of the citizens is higher than the SSP of the butcher shop. The citizen will think that the pork in this butcher shop is worth more than it costs, and her willingness to buy is strong. On the contrary, she will think that the pork is "not worth the money", and her willingness to buy is low. We can see that the ratio of BSP to SSP directly determines whether the product can be successfully sold. We call this ratio the "Transaction Ratio"(TR)。

We usually think that the Cost Performance (CP) of a commodity determines whether it will sell well. We define Cost Performance as the ratio of the performance value of a commodity to its price. We can see that Cost Performance is actually the ratio of the objective wealth value of a commodity to the seller's external quotation. The seller's external quotation will not be lower than its subjective price for the commodity. Therefore, the maximum value of Cost Performance is OWVC divided by SSP.

$CP_{(Max)}=OWVC/SSP$.

If it is true that the Cost Performance of a commodity determines its popularity, then the same product with the same quotation should sell equally

116

well. However, in reality, the same product with the same price does not have the same acceptance among different people and under different circumstances. Cost Performance cannot fully reflect the possibility of transaction for a commodity.

Through analysis, we found that when buyers decide whether to purchase a commodity, they are not only influenced by the "objective wealth value" or " Cost Performance " of the commodity, but also by their own perception of the value of the commodity and their perception of the value of money. The "transaction ratio" is the ultimate and comprehensive decision-making basis. The larger the "Transaction Ratio", the more likely they are to purchase, and the smaller the "Transaction Ratio", the more likely they are to refuse.

The subjective wealth value of the purchaser for the commodity is recorded as SWVC, and the subjective wealth value of the purchaser for the money is recorded as SWVM. The "Subjective Price" of the purchaser is recorded as BSP, then

BSP=SWVC/SWVM

The subjective wealth value of the seller for the commodity is recorded as SWVC', and the subjective wealth value of the seller for the currency is recorded as SWVM'. The seller's "Subjective Price" is recorded as SSP, then

SSP=SWVC'/SWVM'

Then we can calculate the Transaction Ratio (TR) of the commodity when facing specific potential customer。

TR =BSP/SSP= (SWVC/ SWVC') * (SWVM'/SWVM)

When the Transaction Ratio (TR） of a commodity is greater than or equal to 1, it indicates that the selling price is lower than the buyer's price expectation, and the transaction will proceed smoothly. The higher the TR of a commodity, the higher the buyer's willingness to purchase and the lower the seller's willingness to sell; the lower the TR of a commodity, the lower the buyer's willingness to purchase and the higher the seller's willingness to sell.

When people purchase an unconventional item, such as a villa in a strange city for investment purposes, they will consult online historical transaction prices, average transaction cycle, and listing prices for properties in the same region, neighborhood, and type. They will listen to the evaluation of the property by real estate professionals, and will ask friends from the government planning department about future construction plans, industrial plans, population plans, and other information for the location. They may even consult economists on their views on the relationship between supply and demand of real estate, economic policies, population trends, and housing price trends, thus forming their own subjective wealth value for this particular villa. If the person is relocating for work and family reasons and purchasing this villa purely for personal use, then their evaluation system for their own property needs will change. They will focus on factors such as vegetable

117

markets, school districts, and landscapes, thus forming their own subjective wealth value for this particular villa. Regardless of an individual's intrinsic factors, in a fully competitive market environment, information is abundant and transactions are free. The general consensus of the public's subjective wealth value for money and for a specific commodity will form a collective subjective price for this specific commodity. This collective subjective price is usually the market price of the commodity.

Whether we are in an imperfectly competitive market or a perfectly competitive market, and whether we are buyers or sellers, when conducting transactions, we should fully consider the subjective wealth value of both parties to commodities and currency, so as to form a comprehensive and profound understanding and management of the transaction ratio of commodities. For example, if the seller's subjective price remains unchanged, they can adjust the variables in the buyer's subjective price calculation formula upwards to achieve the goal of increasing the transaction ratio and enhancing the purchasing intention. The seller can increase the buyer's value perception of the commodity by exaggerating the shortage of the commodity, thereby increasing buyer's SWVC; or by exaggerating the expectation of inflation, reducing the buyer's value perception of the currency, thereby reducing buyer's SWVM. In fact, top business negotiators rarely facilitate transactions by offering discounts or seeking to buy at high prices. Instead, they create various influences and design different rhetoric strategies to adjust the opponent's subjective price of the commodities according to their own interest demands. Their adjustment affects the transaction ratio calculation results, thereby enhancing the opponent's willingness to transact at a satisfactory quote for themselves.

A partner in a law firm with a strong business acumen has established the firm in a top-tier office building in the city and has secured various prestigious titles for himself. He consistently ranks at the top of various legal rankings, projecting an image of professionalism and busyness in his career. He clearly outlines the service time required for representing cases. Through these measures, he enhances clients' Value Perception and Subjective Wealth Value associated with the legal services provided. Simultaneously, during negotiations on attorney fees, he emphasizes the significant amount of the case, illustrates with examples that the charging standards for representing other cases are higher, jokingly states that high-quality representation may secure substantial benefits for clients, and even compares court litigation costs with legal service fees to reduce clients' value perception and subjective wealth value of money. By adjusting clients' SWVC and SWVM in the formula, he comprehensively enhances the subjective price of his own legal services in the minds of clients, ultimately increases the Transaction Ratio (TR) and facilitates case commissions.

Chapter 8: Currency Issuer and Issuance of Credit Currency

After discussing the commodities and the ratio of money to commodities, we return to the discussion of Credit Currency itself. Material Currency in version 1.0 is the existing gold and silver wealth, Receipt Currency in version 2.0 is the storage voucher of the existing gold and silver wealth, and Promise Currency in version 3.0 is the extraction commitment of the existing gold and silver wealth. All three currencies rely on "existing gold and silver wealth", where "existing" means the wealth formed in the past and was currently owned, and "gold and silver" means the single variety of wealth. The emergence of credit currencies in versions 4.0, 5.0, and 6.0 has freed humanity from the constraints of existing gold and silver wealth when creating trading mediums for commodities.

The emergence of Credit Currency expands the wealth corresponding to Currency Issuance to a comprehensive range of wealth types. People no longer believe that currency is issued based on gold and silver. The Currency Issuer issues money to borrowers who can provide various commodities to the market in the future. Currency is no longer based on a single gold and silver commodity, but on a comprehensive range of commodities. At the same time, the emergence of Credit Currency expands the promise implied by Currency Issuance from exchanging existing wealth to exchanging future wealth. Before the emergence of Credit Currency, to obtain currency, one must first have existing wealth. Credit Currency allows people who promise to own wealth in the future to obtain currency by borrowing on credit, gaining the power to trade their future wealth with others' existing wealth.

Next, in order to enhance our understanding of credit currencies, we will introduce the establishment of Currency Issuers and the mechanism of Currency Issuance under the current monetary system in a unique way. It should be emphasized that the existing monetary system is a product of practice rather than scientific design, maintained and controlled by dominant entities and vested interests. The global monetary system has been gradually established by relatively underdeveloped countries and emerging nations emulating advanced economies. The current monetary system should not be regarded as authoritative or truthful. We should think independently, innovate boldly, to explore and establish more rational, fair and scientific monetary theories and monetary systems based on facts and logic. Our thinking and ideals about money should not be constrained by the existing monetary system.

I. Relationship Between the Central Bank and Commercial Banks

The law directly grants the central bank the right to issue currency within a country through clear provisions, and also stipulates that commercial banks can absorb deposits and issue loans under the deposit reserve system, thereby indirectly granting commercial banks the right to issue currency.

Under the current monetary system, commercial banks worldwide have three identities at the same time:

First, commercial banks are the monetary storage institutions of social entities. Commercial banks initially existed as ordinary market entities, which in our Z Island model are equivalent to the shared drawers of the farmer, the blacksmith, and the masseuse, only playing the role of storing cash "Z coin". Of course, if commercial banks also have "Z coin", they can be seen as storing "Z coin" for themselves. When commercial banks issue deposit certificates equivalent to the amount of "Z coin" they store externally, they still only have the identity of a "warehouse".

Second, Commercial banks are the assistants of the central bank in completing Currency Issuance. We can regard the central bank and commercial banks as a Currency Issuance community. When the central bank lends money to commercial banks, the currency is not issued and still exists within Currency Issuer, unable to be controlled and used by social entities in the real economy. When we discuss the fact that the massive increase in M2 has not played a role in stimulating the economy, we misunderstand the main body and process of Currency Issuance. When the central bank lends money to commercial banks, the currency is only a semi-finished product. Only when the non-Currency Issuer entity acts as the borrower does this semi-finished product get infused with the borrower credit through the hands of the borrower, thus being shaped into complete currency and entering market circulation. At this point, when commercial banks issue the currency borrowed from the central bank to other social entities, the currency is issued finally and the commercial banks act as assistants for the central bank to issue currency externally.

Third, Commercial banks are independent Currency Issuers. When commercial banks issue loans based on borrower credit, borrowers acquire commercial bank deposit certificates in return for their liabilities to the commercial bank. In the transaction, borrowers only transfer the deposit certificates, and the commercial bank deposit certificates become new money in the market. Commercial banks issue new money as independent Currency Issuers, and they have the status of the second central bank. In reality, commercial banks issue loans with extremely low or even zero reserve requirements, and commercial bank loans have become the main way of money supply worldwide. Therefore, under the current monetary system, Commercial banks bear the direct and primary function of Currency Issuance, while the central bank takes a backstage role, focusing more on formulating and controlling monetary policy.

How do banks issue currency? Modern banks do not have the authority to issue paper money and coins, which is still the prerogative of the monetary authority. Banks can issue a new bank loan and add a number in the unit of public currency (pound, dollar, euro) to the bank account. These money are magical because no one knows where they come from. Banks claim that everyone can get a loan and the money can be transferred normally, which everyone takes for granted. Loans enable borrowers to obtain funds immediately and of course they also have the obligation to repay the loan with interest before the agreed date. If the entire process of borrowing, consumption and repayment is completed through bank accounts, then there is no need to involve cash currency issued by the state, such as paper money and coins. If borrowers really need cash, banks can use their own cash reserves or withdraw cash by deducting from their accounts at the Bank of England (the central bank). In today's Britain, most currency exists in the form of bank accounts, which are just a record. Only 3% of currency is cash (paper money and coins). As people use less and less cash, bank accounts have become the main way of currency circulation[7]

It is precisely because of the special position of commercial banks in Currency Issuance and operation that the banking industry is known as the "mother of all industries". As a mother, its nature should be selfless. However, it is regrettable that the "mother of all industries" commercial banks are essentially commercial institutions that aim to make profits. As a company, its nature is to "make profits". Commercial banks compete with all industries in the market for profits, and these profits are generally recognized by laws in various countries. It has to be said that this is a defect and fault of the monetary system. We will further discuss the contradiction between the profitability of commercial banks and the public welfare of Currency Issuers in other chapters.

As commercial banks actually exercise the function of independent Currency Issuers, and they are commercial institutions, the state must bring their behavior into the scope of management of the central bank, making them subordinate to the central bank in management. The specific manifestation is the deposit reserve system stipulated by law. Deposit reserve refers to the deposits of commercial banks in the central bank. The proportion of deposit reserve required by the central bank to the total deposits of commercial banks is the deposit reserve ratio. The initial significance of this system is to ensure the payment and settlement of commercial banks, and later it gradually evolved into a policy tool for the central bank to regulate the money supply. When the central bank increases the deposit reserve ratio, commercial banks need more funds as reserves, which will reduce the available funds of banks and thus reduce the money supply in the market. On the contrary, when the central bank reduces the deposit reserve ratio, the reserves required by commercial banks decrease, and

---

[7] Mary Mellor. Money: Myths, Truths and Alternatives[M]. Beijing: China Social Sciences Press,2022.

the available funds of banks increase, and the money supply in the market will also increase accordingly. In fact, this regulation of the central bank on the money supply is not only indirect but also theoretical, because the available funds of commercial banks are only the funds that they may lend to others. Whether commercial banks can complete loan disbursement depends not only on their willingness and ability, but also on the willingness and ability of borrowers.

The central bank is also the lender of last resort for commercial banks. Since the Loan Currency issued by commercial banks do not have a corresponding reserve of central bank cash, in order to prevent banking panics and financial crises and ensure the balanced and orderly operation of commercial banks, the central bank provides loans to commercial banks through various means. The specific methods will be discussed in Section 3 of this chapter " Main Ways of Currency Issuance and Regulation in the World ".

It is worth mentioning that in order to implement the government's economic policies, countries around the world have established professional financial institutions that do not aim to make profits and carry out financial business in specific fields, namely policy banks. Due to their status and role in Currency Issuance, which are similar to those of commercial banks, we will include them in the discussion of Currency Issuance as part of the commercial banks and will no longer list them separately.

II. Establishment of Central Banks in Countries Around the World

The main functions of the central bank include formulating and implementing monetary policies, maintaining financial stability, and providing financial services. Among them, formulating and implementing monetary policies is the core function of the central bank, aiming to influence economic operations through adjusting monetary policy instruments to achieve predetermined macroeconomic goals. Maintaining financial stability is also an important responsibility of the central bank, responsible for supervising financial markets and financial institutions to ensure the stability and security of the financial system. Providing financial services is an important means for the central bank to support the operation of the financial market and promote the smooth operation of the financial system.

Today, issuing currency is one of the important functions of the central bank, but it is not its main function. It is more of a means to implement monetary policy and maintain financial stability. The central bank regulates the supply of currency in circulation by issuing currency to meet the demand for currency in circulation and ensure the normal circulation of currency. Meanwhile, issuing currency is also one of the important means for the central bank to act as the government's bank, treasury agent, and centralized manager of government revenue and expenditure.

The establishment of central banks in various countries around the world varies depending on factors such as national systems, historical traditions, and economic development conditions. Currently, there are three common organizational forms of central banks: (1) the single central bank system, which refers to a system in which a country establishes a central bank institution independently to fully and purely exercise the functions of a central bank and supervise all financial enterprises. Currently, most central banks in the world, especially developed countries such as the United States, Britain, France, and Japan, implement the single central bank system. (2) the composite central bank system, which refers to a central bank system in which the state does not establish a separate institution exclusively for central banking functions. Instead, a national mega-bank that combines both central and commercial banking roles undertakes the responsibilities of a central bank. This system usually appears in the initial stage of the development of central banks or in countries with a planned economic system. For example, the former Soviet Union and former Eastern European countries, as well as China's banking system before 1983, had all implemented this system. (3) the quasi-central bank system, which refers to a system in which some countries or regions do not have a central bank in the usual sense, but only establish financial management institutions similar to central banks to partially exercise the functions of a central bank, such as the Monetary Authority of Singapore and Hong Kong.

The establishment of central banks in various countries around the world has shown characteristics of diversity and flexibility to meet the needs of economic development and financial stability in their respective countries. At the same time, with the continuous development of global economic integration and financial markets, the role and status of central banks have become increasingly important.

Through the investigation of the structure and independence of the central banks of major countries, we can find that there has been a significant trend towards greater independence in recent years. In the past, except for Germany and Switzerland, the Federal Reserve System was more independent than almost all central banks in the world. Now, the newly established European Central Bank is more independent than the Federal Reserve System, and the Bank of England and Bank of Japan have also been given greater independence, almost on par with the Federal Reserve System. At the same time, many central banks in countries such as New Zealand, Sweden and the eurozone countries also have greater independence. Both theory and practice show that the more independent the central bank is, the better monetary policy it can formulate, which in turn promotes the trend of independence[8]

[8] Frederic S. Mishkin. The Economics of Money, Banking, and Finance Market[M]. Beijing: China Renmin University Press, 2018.

III. Main Ways of Currency Issuance and Regulation in the World

As we have discussed before, the current issuers in various countries are central banks and commercial banks. The ways commercial banks issue currencies to the outside world have been explained through the generation of deposit currencies in version 5.0 and Loan Currency in version 6.0. The deposit currencies in version 5.0 are essentially a substitute for the currencies issued by the central bank, without generating new additions to the money supply. The issuance of Loan Currency in version 6.0, broadly speaking, is: "Issuing bank deposit receipts to borrowers for market transactions based on the borrower's commitment and credit.", commercial banks' external loans directly cause new additions to the market's money supply, which is complete money creation. The main ways for commercial banks to issue loans to the outside world are credit loans, mortgage loans, pledge loans, guaranteed loans, and commercial bill discount loans. The difference between these methods lies in the different ways of enhancing the creditworthiness of borrowers, but the essence of the loans is the same, which is to lend out money to the outside world, obtain creditor's rights from the borrowers, and achieve Currency Issuance.

Under the current monetary system, central banks typically do not issue currency to non-banking entities. Currency Issuance is usually carried out through commercial banks making loans to the public. For example, Article 29 of the People's Bank of China Law stipulates that, " The People's Bank of China shall not make overdrafts for the government's fiscal expenditure, nor shall it directly subscribe to or underwrite treasury bonds and other government securities. " Article 30 stipulates that " the People's Bank of China shall not provide loans to local governments, government departments at all levels, non-bank financial institutions, or other units or individuals, except for specific non-bank financial institutions that the State Council has decided that the People's Bank of China may provide loans to. ".

We have discussed the way in which central banks issue currency externally in the previous article, mainly focusing on the emergence of the 4.0 version of the currency contract. At the same time, we also mentioned that some central banks would issue their own currencies based on reserves of gold or currencies issued by other countries. Now it is necessary for us to fully understand the ways in which central banks issue currency and the essence of these Currency Issuance methods.

When the central bank provides loans to commercial banks based on the credit of the commercial banks themselves, by holding claims on commercial banks, even if the commercial banks use these funds to complete loans to other market entities, we believe that the central bank is not indirectly providing loans to market entities including the government, because at this time the central bank does not hold claims on market entities. However, when the central bank pays transfer fees to commercial banks or other bondholders by purchasing bonds from other market entities, we believe that it is essentially indirectly completing the loan to the corresponding market entities through the channel of commercial banks or other bondholders, because at this time the central bank actually holds the claims of the bond issuers and pays money for them, while the original bondholder does not hold the bonds or pay money after completing the bond transfer.

1.Central Banks Provide Loans Directly to Commercial Banks

First and foremost, it should be reiterated that the issuance of currency refers to the entry of currency created by the issuer into the market for trading. Therefore, if the loan issued by the central bank to the commercial bank does not enter the market through the channel of the commercial bank, it is not considered as the issuance of currency, but only as the internal circulation of currency within the issuer.

Article 23 of the "People's Bank of China Law" in the "Business" chapter stipulates that "the People's Bank of China may use the following monetary policy instruments to implement monetary policy: (3) handling rediscount for banking financial institutions that have opened accounts at the People's Bank of China; (4) providing loans to commercial banks". Article 28 stipulates that "the People's Bank of China may decide the amount, term, interest rate and method of loans to commercial banks according to the needs of implementing monetary policy, but the term of the loan shall not exceed one year ".Central banks in other countries around the world also directly provide loans to commercial banks to directly deliver currency to commercial banks, which is used to solve the shortage of funds of commercial banks or support their expansion of credit scale. The direct loan methods of central banks to commercial banks mainly include the following:

(1) Re-lending, which is the main way for central banks to provide loans to commercial banks. Most of the re-lending is credit loans, but there are also mortgage loans and pledge loans. The reason why it is called "re-lending" is that such loans usually require commercial banks to provide "claims obtained from providing loans to other social entities" or government bonds and corporate bonds as collateral. Re-lending can be called loans to the lender, which essentially belongs to the central bank's "credit loans" or "pledge loans" to commercial banks, which are usually divided into short-term re-lending and medium-term re-lending.

(2) Pledged Supplementary Lending (PSL), is a supplement to re-lending provided by the central bank to policy banks with a longer term (3-5 years) and low-cost funds. It is mainly used to support specific national economic projects or construction. Pledged Supplementary Lending is issued through pledge, and the collateral includes high-grade bond assets and high-quality credit assets. Essentially, it is a "pledged loan" from the central bank to

commercial banks.

(3) Standing Lending Facility (SLF), mainly serves to meet the large-scale liquidity needs of commercial banks with longer terms, ranging from 1 to 3 months, and is issued in the form of pledge. Qualified collateral includes high-credit-rating bond assets and high-quality credit assets. Therefore, it is essentially a "pledged loan" provided by the central bank to commercial banks.

(4) Medium-term Lending Facility (MLF), typically offers loans with terms of 3 months, 6 months, or 1 year. These loans are issued through pledge, and commercial banks are required to provide treasury bonds, central bank notes, policy-related financial bonds, high level credit bonds and other High-quality bonds as qualified collateral, so they are essentially still "pledged loans" provided by the central bank to commercial banks.

2.Indirect loans from central banks to governments

Although central banks do not usually lend directly to governments, they usually achieve the release and withdrawal of money by buying and selling valuable securities on the open market. Such valuable securities are usually identified as central government bonds and government agency bonds, especially treasury bonds, because the treasury bond market has the most liquidity and the largest trading volume, and is capable of absorbing the huge trading volume of central banks.

The government borrows money by selling government bonds to the society. Government bonds are essentially certificates of creditor's rights held by the holder to the government. When the central bank purchases government bonds, it pays money to the government bond holder and actually owns the creditor's rights to the government. The essence of this behavior is that the central bank's creditor's rights are transferred, which is equivalent to the central bank indirectly issuing loans to the government through the hands of the government bond holder.

When the central bank wishes to purchase government bonds and inject money in a short-term manner (1 to 15 days), the central bank will reach an agreement with the seller when purchasing the bonds, requiring the seller to buy back the bonds after the maturity date. The central bank will withdraw the money upon maturity. This complete operation of buying and selling is called "reverse repo". When the central bank implements "reverse repo", it buys bonds and injects money. When the "reverse repo" matures, it sells the bonds and withdraws the money.

The central bank can also sell the government bonds it has bought on the open market to achieve the purpose of withdrawing money from the market. When the central bank wishes to sell government bonds and earn money in the short term (1 to 15 days), the central bank will reach an agreement with the buyer when selling the bonds. The central bank promises to buy back the bonds after they expire and put the money back into the market. This complete operation of selling and buying back by the central bank is called "central bank repurchase". When the central bank implements "central bank repurchase", it sells bonds and earns money. When the "central bank repurchase" expires, it buys bonds and puts money into the market.

The central bank's "reverse repo" has the same purpose as purchasing government bonds, through which the central bank releases money into the market; the central bank's " repurchase " has the same purpose as selling government bonds, through which the central bank withdraws money from the market too.

These names and connotations are quite confusing to non-financial professionals, as the subject and perspective constantly change. Since the central bank does not directly purchase bonds from the government or issue loans to non-bank entities, initially, the bonds can only be held by traders in the open market. Therefore, when the bonds return to traders in the market, equivalent to the dealer "buying again", they are naturally called "repurchase", which is viewed from the perspective traders in of the market. However, what we call open market operations are usually described from the perspective of the central bank, therefore, there are awkward names such as " central bank repurchase " and " reverse repo ", which left the public feeling very puzzled. We view these names from the perspective of the original bondholder, and the subject and predicate are unified, making it easier to understand. " central bank repurchase "refers to the original bondholders in the market buying back, while the central bank sells. "Maturity of a repurchase agreement" means the original bondholders in the market sell, and the central bank buys. "Reverse repo" is when the original bondholders in the market sell, and the central bank buys. "Maturity of a reverse repo" is when the original bondholders in the market buy, and the central bank sells.

The financial industry is not inherently complex. It is just a relationship of rights and obligations. However, it is often made mysterious and difficult to understand by some difficult-to-understand terms and abbreviations. It seems that if it's not this way, it won't appear upscale enough. In fact, the financial industry is not upscale and mysterious. Finance, when detached from the real economy, cannot meet any of people's needs at all.

Similar to " central bank repurchase " and " reverse repo ", there is also the Short-term Liquidity Operations (SLO), this is also a tool provided by the central bank to provide short-term liquidity support, but with a shorter term, usually 7 days.

3. The Central Bank Indirectly Provides Loans to Non-bank Financial Institutions and Other Private Sectors

The central bank usually releases and withdraws money by buying and selling valuable securities in the open market, mainly government bonds, but also other securities, especially under the monetary quantitative easing policy implemented by various countries, where the securities are expanded to include some high-quality corporate bonds. After the central bank completed the bond purchase, it actually owned the creditor's rights of the bond issuing company, and released money to the market. However, the original bond holders received the money back, and lost their creditor's rights to the bond issuer. This is equivalent to the central bank indirectly granting loans to the issuers of securities through the transfer of securities from their original holders.

The way in which the central bank indirectly provides loans to non-bank financial institutions and other units and individuals is through "rediscount". When commercial banks need funds, they can apply to the central bank for rediscount using commercial bills which they discounted but not yet matured, and then obtain funds. The reason why it is called "rediscount" is because the commercial bills transferred by commercial banks to the central bank are obtained through their own external "commercial bill discount" business. The payer of commercial bills is indebted to the bank, and the bank actually has an indirect loan relationship with the payer. In the "rediscount" business, commercial bills that commercial banks provide are transferred to the central bank, rather than mortgaged. Once the bills are rediscounted by the central bank, the commercial banks lose ownership of these bills, and the central bank becomes the legal holder of these bills. When the bills expire, the central bank will collect funds from the original debtors who issued these bills. Therefore, "rediscount" is essentially a loan that the central bank indirectly extends to the payer of commercial bills through the hands of commercial banks.

With the development of society, the types of similar behaviors implemented by central banks are constantly innovating. Because central banks are usually designed as the makers and implementers of monetary policy, their behaviors are often considered to be the regulation of money supply rather than the direct issuance and recovery of loans to the market. Therefore, these behaviors are known in the economic community as open market operations, rediscount, or "unconventional monetary policy and quantitative easing" of "conventional monetary policy tools".

4. Central Banks Exchange Currencies with Other Assets as Anchors

The central bank can export currencies by purchasing special types of assets from market entities. These types of assets mainly include gold and other countries' currencies. In this case, the central bank releases its own currency through exchange rather than lending.

As we have analyzed before, "the issuer is the mother of credit money, and the borrower is the father of credit money". The creation of currency is jointly completed by the issuer and the borrower. In this case, the Currency Issuer actually has a dual identity, it creates a non-issuer market trading entity and participates in currency creation as a borrower. It can be seen that the Currency Issuer lends its own currency, and at this time, the Currency Issuer

128

has a hermaphroditic function. The Currency Issuer uses its own dual identity to complete currency creation, and uses the created currency to purchase other countries' currencies, gold or other commodities in the market.

Among them, the issuance of domestic currency based on the storage of other countries' currencies does not produce new currency additions worldwide, but only completes currency substitution. However, we do not consider this part of currency to be essentially Deposit Currency in version 5.0, because the issuer of Deposit Currency has a rigid obligation to honor its payment to the holder, that is, when the holder requests payment, the issuer must return the original currency to the holder, the central bank is clearly not obliged to pay foreign exchange to the holder of its own currency when they request it. Therefore, this part of currency is still essentially Contract Currency in version 4.0, but the borrower participating in currency creation is the Currency Issuer itself.

Under normal circumstances, countries that issue their national currencies in this manner stipulate that the use of foreign currencies for payment settlements in domestic market transactions is prohibited. Therefore, the foreign currencies held by market entities do not inherently possess liquidity. The national currency that the central bank injects the into the domestic market, by acquiring foreign currencies, constitutes an increase in the money supply within the domestic market.

The central bank of a country that issues its own currency based on the reserves of foreign currencies is, to some extent, a vassal of the foreign central banks, just as commercial banks are vassals of the central bank when they issue Deposit Currency. However, the issuance of Loan Currency by commercial banks is an independent Currency Issuance behavior that produces new currency additions. Central banks that anchor their currencies to foreign currencies begin to issue loans abroad after establishing their own credit. At this point, the issuance of currency is independent and belongs to the autonomous issuance of the domestic currency.

At this time, a foreign central bank that issues a foreign currency cannot be considered the "central bank" of the domestic central bank that reserves the foreign currency, because only the currency issued by the former is being reserved by the latter, and there is no monetary lending relationship between the two. Only when a country's central bank begins to lend to the central banks of other countries will a central bank of central banks emerge.

IV. The Nature and Role of Interests of Currency Issuers

Interest is a concept that we commonly encounter in daily life, and it is also one of the main means for monetary authorities to regulate the money market. Interest is traditionally viewed as the cost of holding money, the cost of borrowing money, and the reward for temporarily losing the right to hold money for the original holder. What is the essence of interest? Is it a usage fee or a service fee? How does interest operate? And how does it affect the economy? The currency issued by the issuer comes from the exercise of the right to issue currency, while the currency held by other market entities comes from exchange or lending. We already know that the currency held by the issuer is fundamentally different from that held by other market participants. So, is the interest charged by the issuer fundamentally different from the interest charged by other market participants?

1. The Value of the Excess Goods Produced by the Borrower Is Owned by Currency Issuer

The coiner in Story 2 did not charge interest to the borrower. Now we adapt the story and call it Story 6. Let's see what happens in Story 6 when the coiner chose to charge the farmer 10% interest per year (the coiner still does not charge interest to the blacksmith and the masseuse). At the end of the year, the farmer pays off the loan and originally has 5 "Z coins" left in the house, but now needs to pay an additional 100 worth to the coiner, so there are only 4 "Z coins" left in the house, while the masseuse still has 5 "Z coins" left unpaid at the coiner's place.

It can be seen that the savings in the market and the debt to the coiners are not equal at this time, and the difference is the interest charged by the coiners themselves. As for how to view this part of interest, we have discussed in detail in the first section "Total Savings Always Equal to Total Liabilities" in Chapter 4 "The Essence and Logic of Credit Currency".

It can be seen that the collection of interest by Currency Issuer will have two effects. First, it requires the borrowers to provide commodities with a total selling price higher than the principal of their loans, which is another driving force for economic growth. Second, the portion of the currency obtained by the borrower from selling commodities is shared with the central bank, resulting in a total savings outside Currency Issuer being less than the total external claims of Currency Issuer. The difference is the accumulated interest collected by Currency Issuer. However, this part of interest is different from the money created out of thin air through lending. The interest is the profit of Currency Issuer, which can be directly used for external exchange of commodities Therefore, it will not affect the total money supply in the trading market.

When commercial banks issue Loan Currency to the outside world, they also charge interest. When borrowers pay off their debts, the principal and interest return to the commercial banks in full. Due to the overcharged interest, the money held by non-commercial banks in the market will also decrease accordingly, but this will not affect the total money supply in the market, as this portion of interest belongs to the profits of commercial banks, which can also act as general currency users to participate in market transactions.

When the issuer of currency collects interest, it results in a reduction of money in the market. If the issuer does not use this portion of money for market transactions, the supply of money in the market will be less than the quantity of tradable commodities. This portion of interest is considered income from services provided by the issuer of currency, not an exercise of Currency Issuance Right. There are corresponding commodities that exist and can be used for exchange in the market. Moreover, this portion of interest should be used for commodity exchange in the market to maintain the balance between the supply of money and the volume of commodities in the market.

2. Borrowers Can Only Reduce Consumption if they Cannot Produce More Commodities

In Story 1, the coiner did not charge interest to the borrower. We also adapt Story 1 and called it Story 7. Let's see how the masseuse would respond if she could not provide more massage time after the coiner chose to charge her 10% interest per year (the coiner still does not charge interest to the farmer and the blacksmith). In this year, the output of the three people on the island remained unchanged, with 1000 kilograms of grain, 100 hours of massage, and 10 spades. The farmer purchased 10 spades and handed over the borrowed 1000 worth to the blacksmith, who purchased 100 hours of massage and handed over the borrowed 1000 worth to the masseuse. However, in this year, the masseuse had to repay the coiner a total of 1100 worth. Therefore, the masseuse had to deduct 100 worth from the 1000 worth collected from selling massage services as interest, leaving only 900 worth for purchasing grain. This meant that the farmer could only sell 900 kilograms of grain to the masseuse and collect 900 worth. At the end of the year, both the masseuse and the blacksmith paid off their loans in full, while the farmer could only repay the coiner 900 worth, leaving a debt of 100 worth. Compared to Story 1, the coiner charged an additional 100 worth in interest, which was different from the principal amount recovered. The coiner could treat this currency as a commodity and use it for commodity trading in the market. At this point, the farmer on the island still had 100 kilograms of grain available for sale. If the coiner was willing, he could use the 100 worth of interest surplus to purchase the remaining grain from the farmer, so that the farmer could use this 100 worth to pay off the remaining debt to the coiner. However, the coiner did not do so.

3. Assume that the Central Bank Issues Loans to Itself as a General Social Entity

If we want to prevent the currency held by non-Currency Issuers in the market from being reduced due to the issuers' interest collection, there is another possible way besides the issuers using all the collected interest for market transactions. This approach is that the issuer considers itself as commodity provider like other social entities, and pre-establish roles as a service provider, a general borrower, and a currency user.

We still use the Z Island model for demonstration, and we adapt story 1 to story 8. In story 8, the coiner still chose to collect an annual interest of 10% from the masseuse. The coiner had predicted that the masseuse's annual output is only 100 hours, which meant the annual output value was 1000. In this case, in order to calculate the amount of loan X that the coiner should give to the masseuse, the coiner had set out an equation $X*(1+10\%) =1000$. After calculation, the masseuse's loan amount X was 909.09. Therefore, in order to facilitated settlement, the coiner and the masseuse agreed to slightly adjust the loan interest rate upward, and the lending amount was determined to be 900. When the masseuse repaid the loan amount of 900 at the end of the year, he paid an interest of 100, which was calculated at an annual interest rate of 11.11%. Therefore, the coiner simultaneously wrote down on the white wallboard: "Masseuse: -900 worth", "Myself: -100 worth", and then handed over 9 pieces of "Z coins" to the masseuse, while also taking one piece of "Z coin" for himself. This year, the production of the three people on the island remained unchanged, with 1000 kilograms of grain, 100 hours of massage, and 10 spades. The farmer purchased 10 spades and handed over the borrowed 1,000 worth to the blacksmith. The blacksmith then bought 100 hours of massage services and passed the borrowed 1,000 worth to the masseuse. The masseur repaid the coiner 1000 as principal and interest. This year, the masseuse only borrowed 900 from the coiner, and only had 900 to purchase grain. This means that the farmer can only sell 900 kilograms of grain to the masseuse and receive 900 in return. At this point, the coiner appeared as a common currency user, and he used the piece of "Z coin" he borrowed from himself to purchase the remaining 100 kilograms of grain from the farmer, and paid the farmer with this 100 worth, this year, the farmer sold a total of 1000 kilograms of grain and earned 1000 worth. At the end of the year, the farmer, the blacksmith, and the masseuse all settled their loans in full. The coiner used the 100 worth of interest returned by the masseur to repay his loan to the himself at the beginning of the year, erasing the mark "Myself: -100 worth" on the white wallboard, and also stored 100 kilograms of grain in his warehouse.

Now, let's summarize story 8. When a Currency Issuer lends money, the difference between the wealth value that the borrower may create during the loan period and the interest on the loan period is the amount of money that the borrower can consume externally, which is also the amount of money that the Currency Issuer should lend. At the same time, the Currency Issuer lends itself the amount of money equivalent to the interest payable during the loan period of the borrower, which we can call "advance interest". This "advance interest" is no longer a production tool for the Currency Issuer itself, but rather a borrowed currency from itself, it is a commodity.

When a Currency Issuer lends money to others, it can use the part of the currency it lends to itself to trade with other market entities in exchange for their products, and pay the corresponding currency to the other market entities. The borrower, with its own production unchanged, saves interest that should be paid to Currency Issuer by reducing consumption, and Currency Issuer repays its debt corresponding to the "advance interest" after receiving this interest, thus completing the cycle of money from nothing to something, and then from something back to nothing. At this point, Currency Issuer's inventory contains the borrower's products exchanged for the "advance interest".

The Currency Issuer is an institution that specializes in lending currency. Generally, it does not directly use currency in exchange. Therefore, under the current monetary system, this practice cannot be implemented, but it does not mean that this method is not worth exploring or will not be implemented in the future.

It is worth mentioning that when the issuer of a currency purchases gold or other currencies with money it has created out of thin air, that portion of money is not its own profit, it is essentially borrowing money from itself and then using the borrowed money. Currency Issuer exercises the right to issue money on the left hand, produces money and hands it over to the right hand. The right hand goes to the market to trade, the money enters the market circulation, and the assets enter the inventory of Currency Issuer. When Currency Issuer needs to withdraw the money one day, the right hand sells the assets and exchanges them for money, then return it to the left hand. Please note that the assets here refer to other assets distinct from creditor's rights, typically referring to tangible assets such as gold and foreign exchange. From the perspective of monetary theory, lending and exchange are two fundamentally different behaviors. Lending to others is issuing, while exchanging to others is buying and selling. Currency Issuers, without making profits, have to borrow money from themselves first if they want to purchase in the market.

V. Difference and Role between Issuance Interest and Rental Interest

The function of money is to meet transactions. Unlike other commodity providers who can only exchange their own goods and service for money, Currency Issuers can directly issue money. Usually, Currency Issuers provide money to others by lending rather than exchanging. Money is not a commodity for Currency Issuers, but a unique production tool for themselves. Generally, it should not be used to exchange other commodities. The money of Currency Issuers comes from the exercise of the right to issue money. For Currency Issuers, it is obtained out of thin air, and the money itself has no cost or price for the Currency Issuer. However, this does not mean that the Currency Issuer does not have a unique position and contribution in the process of Currency Issuance, when issuing money, Currency Issuers should fully consider the credit of borrowers, lend money, and complete the recovery of money. The Currency Issuer pays for the lending service itself, and the cost of the Currency Issuer is reflected in the selection of borrowers and the provision of services for lending and recovering money. The entire lending and recovery service provided by the Currency Issuer itself is the commodity that it can exchange with the market. Correspondingly, the interest collected by the Currency Issuer after recouping the principal amount of money is considered compensation for the issuance services (i.e., the labor of lending and recovery) provided to others. If the market is prosperous in transactions, the demand for money is high, and the stock of money in the market cannot meet the demand for transactions. The market has a strong demand for Currency Issuers to lend money, and the price of lending services is high, with high interest rates. By the same token, if the economy is sluggish, interest rates will be low. This is the law of market supply and demand determining prices.

Unlike Currency Issuers, other socio-economic entities obtain currency either through their own provision of commodities for exchange or through borrowing from Currency Issuers based on their own credit. In either case, they must provide commodities for the market. The difference is that the cost of exchange is past commodities, while the cost of borrowing is future commodities. For non-Currency Issuers, they paid the full cost for the currency, the currency they possess can be used for commodity exchange to meet their own needs. Currency is a commodity for non-Currency Issuers, and it is the consideration for providing goods and service to the outside world. Non-Currency Issuers lending their currencies to others constitutes the transfer of the right to use the commodity. There is no new increase in the supply of currency outside Currency Issuer system, and it does not affect the overall purchasing power of currency. Whether the borrower they choose can provide goods for the society to earn enough money and return it on time or not, it has no essential impact on other market participants. There is a fundamental difference between the currency lending behavior between non-Currency Issuers and the lending behavior between Currency Issuers and market entities. The former is currency leasing, while the latter is Currency Issuance. The core lies in whether the lenders create currency. Therefore, the interest charged by other market entities that are not Currency Issuers for lending out money is essentially rent for the use of the currency, which fundamentally different from the interest charged by Currency Issuers, as the latter is essentially a service fee.

The currency borrowing and lending between market entities that are not Currency Issuers can be called private lending. Private lending activates the stock of currency without bringing new money to the market, improve the efficiency of investment and financing, increase the proportion of direct financing, and can alleviate the pressure of bank savings and investment transformation, effectively making up for the shortage of bank credit funds.

The interest rate of private lending can promote the formation of market-oriented interest rates, further reflect the situation of cash circulation in the market, and thus help form a market equilibrium interest rate.

Based on the essential difference between the interest charged by Currency Issuer and the interest charged by the lender of the private loan, we call the former the issuance interest of the currency and the latter the rent interest of the currency, although both appear to be revenues collected from lending money outwardly.

VI. Principles to be Followed for Issuance Interest and Renting Interest

Based on the essential differences between the two lending behaviors of Currency Issuance and private lending, the principles that should be followed for these two lending behaviors and the corresponding interest should also be different. Currency Issuance is the exercise of public power and the provision of public services. The fee for public services is essentially taxation. As the consideration for providing Currency Issuance services, the interest charged by Currency Issuer to the borrower is the issuance interest, which is the true sense of seigniorage, a reasonable and ethical seigniorage, and even a new type of seigniorage charged by the coiner in the era of Credit Currency.

In the traditional sense, seigniorage is a term used in the era of Material Currency. It is derived from the French word seigneur (feudal lord, monarch, vassal), and is also known as the profit differential resulting from coinage. During the period of metal currency, coiners reduced the precious metal content and purity of the currency, issuing it at a premium, known as "coin edge cutting", in order to gain income from the difference between the face value of currency and its actual value. The American Heritage Dictionary further explains seigniorage as the profit obtained by casting coins, usually referring to the difference between the intrinsic value of the precious metal used and the face value of the coin.

After entering the era of Credit Currency, it usually refers to the part of the face value of currency issued by the issuer that exceeds its issuance and management costs. This increase in wealth is often achieved by the government through means such as issuing additional currency. Due to the extremely low issuance costs of Credit Currency, seigniorage becomes alarming. For example, a $100 banknote may have a printing cost of only $1, but it can purchase goods worth $100. If the person who obtains this $100 does not have to pay any other costs, and uses this $100 to purchase goods of equivalent value, they will profit by $99. This $99 price difference is seigniorage. Usually, the person who enjoys this privilege is Currency Issuer itself or the government that has control over Currency Issuer. Among Nations, the performance of seigniorage is more complex. The currency of reserve currency countries can be accepted by non-reserve currency countries,

CURRENCY 6.0: The Essence, Principles and Reconstruction of Money

so as long as reserve currency countries export their own currency, they can obtain the actual resources and wealth of non-reserve currency countries. After deducting the issuance and management costs of reserve currency countries, these resources and wealth are called international seigniorage.

There is another saying that the seigniorage in the era of Credit Currency refers to the economic phenomenon that after the organization or country has issued the currency and absorbed equivalent wealth, the wealth of the currency holder decreases due to currency devaluation, while the wealth of the issuer increases. For example, in order to achieve its goal of increasing its gold reserves, a government obtains 50 million US dollars of currency from Currency Issuer through a 10-year medium-term treasury bond. At this time, the price of gold is 2,500 US dollars per ounce. The government purchases 20,000 ounces of gold from the market, the person selling the gold held onto the 50 million US dollars. Five years later, when the government's loan matures, the US dollar depreciates by 50%, and the price of gold is 5,000 US dollars per ounce. The government only needs to sell 10,000 ounces of gold to obtain 50 million US dollars to pay off the loan. The government gains a net profit of 10,000 ounces of gold through this round-trip operation. Under the current monetary system, the government is either Currency Issuer itself or has jurisdiction and significant influence over Currency Issuer. The government has a natural advantage position in obtaining benefits through Currency Issuance and currency devaluation.

Credit Currency is borrowed by borrowers based on their own credit. Borrowers promise to provide goods or service to society in the future, thereby earning profits to repay the principal and interest. The price paid by those who borrow money from the coiner and use it is their own credit and their future commodities. However, the beneficiaries of seigniorage merely exploit their privileges and advantages in Currency Issuance to seek their own interests, clearly not intending to repay the principal and interest with sufficient value through honest labor.

Whether in the era of metal currency or Credit Currency, the so-called seigniorage we used to call is not a true national tax, but a special benefit obtained by exercising the Currency Issuance right. In the era of Material Currency, the essence of seigniorage is to cut corners. In the era of Credit Currency, the essence of seigniorage is to abuse credit. Both are essentially theft or fraud, which are unreasonable, illegal, and immoral and should not be accepted by civilized society.

Because the interest charged by Currency Issuers to borrowers is a true and justifiable new type of seigniorage, Currency Issuer should comply with the principle of public welfare when charging interest. Currency Issuer should establish interest rate standards based on the principle of public welfare and strictly identify the borrower credit, which is centered on the borrower's future production capacity. The essence of issuance interest is the "issuing service fee" of Currency Issuer, and the cost of issuing services consists of two parts: one is the operational management cost of Currency Issuer, and the other is the loss of loan principal caused by some borrowers' default. Therefore, the collection of issuance interest is to cover these two costs. At the same time, in order to ensure that the money supply in the market will not be reduced due to the interest charged by Currency Issuer, Currency Issuer should not be profitable. Therefore, the standard for collecting issuance interest should be made to just cover the sum of its own operational costs and the loss of loan principal caused by default, and it should not be More or less. Regarding the formulation of issuance interest rates, we will explain the detailed formula in Section 6 of the last chapter "Ensure the Balance of Payments of Currency Issuers to Maintain the Stability of Currency Value".

Private lending is a market behavior, which is completely determined by the relationship between market supply and demand. Therefore, the lending behavior and rent interest of non-Currency Issuers should comply with the principle of voluntariness. As long as the currency holder is willing, any entity can obtain loans, even direct giving is not inappropriate. As long as the borrower has free will, it is not harmful to society to pay as high an interest as they are willing to pay. Therefore, the interest rate standard of private lending should also be fully competitive marketized to fully reflect the free will of the market and give full play to the flexible role of private lending in resource allocation. Of course, this needs to be implemented under the condition that the public's right to obtain currency from Currency Issuer is fully guaranteed, otherwise it will lead to borrowers being forced to accept usury in a currency shortage environment, which will cause harm to society. If our Currency Issuance work is competent and scientific, those who have the capacity will be able to obtain initial preferential currency from Currency Issuer in a timely and sufficient manner, and we do not need to worry about the negative impact of marketization of private lending interest rates.

Chapter 9: The Logic of Economic Operation

Economy is the contradictory unity of demand and supply. Money is considered to be the blood of the economy, and people usually treat monetary phenomena as economic phenomena directly, believing that the key to economic development and regulation lies in money. Currency was invented merely for the convenience of trade. Is it reasonable to be endowed with such a significant economic responsibility? Where and how should money play its role? What economic problems are beyond the power of money? Where is the underlying logic and fundamental driving force of economic development? Why are some monetary policies effective while others are counterproductive?

I. Economic Growth without Bad Debts Represents Balanced Development across all Sectors of the Economy.

The story 3 above shows that increasing the issuance of currency can stimulate demand, promote transactions, and encourage output, thereby achieving the goal of improving the overall economy. However, due to the unequal income and expenditure of each person, there are liabilities that cannot be settled in the current year and cash reserves that do not need to be repaid anyone.

In story 2, the farmer produced an additional 500 kilograms of grain through labor and the masseuse exchanged the grain for 500 "Z coins" with the borrowed money. At the end of the year, the farmer's drawer had 500 "Z coins" left, while the masseuse had a debt of 500 "Z coins" that she could not pay off to the coiner. It seems that the farmer had a bumper harvest and made a profit this year, while the masseuse did not increase his income and lost money. But let's make an assumption that in the future, the production capacity of Island Z will remain at 100 hours of massage, 1000 kilograms of grain, and 10 spades per year. Then the 500 "Z coins" in the farmer's hand cannot be exchanged for more spades. If the farmer keeps working instead of taking a half-year break, or if the blacksmith suddenly leaves the island one day, there will never be any spades produced on the island, and these 500 "Z coins" will be useless paper. The farmer's needs will not be met more, and the farmer will actually become a victim of interests. For the masseuse, as long as the coiner does not claim the return of his money, he will enjoy 500 kilograms of grain without paying any cost, and the masseuse have occupied the farmer's interests. Therefore, we can say that those who retain currency are future claimants of interests, and at the same time, they are current victims of interests.

The examples in the preceding text are all based on the assumption that the three individuals' debts to the coiner can be deferred. If the coiner demanded repayment at the end of the year or else expelled the debtor from the island, what would happen? This will lead to bad debts or bankruptcy in our daily lives. Without other new entities providing complementary commodities, the economic cycle cannot continue.

To make the problem more intuitive, let's deduce a radical story (Story 9). At the beginning of the year, the masseuse, farmer, and blacksmith received loans of 2000, 1000, and 1000 worth respectively from the coiner. The masseuse paid 2000 worth to the farmer to purchase 2000 kilograms of grain, and the farmer transferred to the blacksmith to order 30 spades. The blacksmith purchased 400 hours of massage from the masseuse. Then the total output value of Island Z soared to 9000 worth. This seems to be a good thing, but at the end of the year, the farmer and the blacksmith each produced 1000 worth of bad debts that could not be settled. Although the masseuse's drawer had 2000 worth of cash remaining, according to the new regulations of the coiner, the farmer and the blacksmith were expelled from Island Z due to their inability to settle their debts. On Island Z, where three people depended on each other, the masseuse could not buy any more grain with 2000 worth, and the economy of Island Z soon felled into collapse.

Therefore, sustainable economic growth is built on the foundation that every borrower ultimately does not generate bad debt. We tell another version of the story (story 10), where the masseuse purchases 2000 kilograms of grain, the farmer purchases 20 spades, and the blacksmith purchases 200 hours of massage. In this year, all three people have no outstanding debts, no one puts "Z coin" in the drawer, and the output of Z Island is 2000 kilograms of grain, 20 spades, and 200 hours of massage. In this situation, all three people on Z Island can have no bad debts and achieve the goal of economic growth.

II. The Underlying Logic of Economic Growth is the Comprehensive Ability Improvement of Various Economic Sectors

In a balanced economy, all sectors are buying and selling, and money is circulating. The amount of money increases with the increase in output and transactions of all sectors, and no bad debts will occur at this time. When bad debts occur, it means that the debtor cannot collect money by selling commodities, and ultimately the person holding the money cannot exchange it for the commodities he need. The amount of bad debts is the excess of money in the market over the amount of commodities. From a static perspective, it is the loss of interest for the holder of the money. The debtor enjoyed the commodities, but cannot provide equivalent commodities. The holder of the money cannot use the money to trade to meet his own needs, which is obviously unfair. Unbalanced economic growth causes bad debts and damage to the overall interests of society.

The purpose of economic growth is to fully meet the diverse needs of all people. Due to the limitations of individual abilities and talents, this kind of demand can only be met through transactions, which are carried out through money. Therefore, allowing people with needs to use money to trade with people who have goods or service is a means to promote economic growth. Allowing people with cash reserves to be willing to spend money, or allowing people without cash reserves to have the ability and willingness to borrow money for consumption, are two situations of this means.

What we pursue is the satisfaction of the needs of all entities, and it is a sustainable satisfaction of needs. This requires that the person who pays for the commodities can purchase the commodities they need after receiving the currency obtained through the transaction. If the person who pays for the currency does not have the output of the commodities, the economy cannot be circular and sustainable. Fortunately, our human society has a large capacity and time is constantly extending. Even if the person who pays for the currency withdraws from the market, there are still others who can produce goods or provide service, which creates a mismatch between enjoyment and contribution.

If the person who pays the currency uses their own retained currency, it is their previous contribution in exchange for their current enjoyment. If the currency paid is borrowed, there are two possible outcomes. One is that their future contribution can provide commodities in exchange for currency to complete the debt settlement. The other is that they will generate bad debts and be eliminated by the market. From the perspective of issuing loans to boost the economy, we should certainly strive for the first outcome, which is to provide loans to those who have the ability to provide commodities needed by society in the future, so that money can not only help commodities complete transactions in space, but also help commodities complete transactions between different entities in time.

If the second outcome occurs, it means that loans are issued to backward production capacity. The occurrence of bad debts is not just a loss on the books of the Currency Issuer, but also results in the person who has paid out goods being unable to exchange the currency they received for sufficient goods. Therefore, issuing loans for future production capacity can promote the comprehensive and sustainable upward spiral of the economy, which is the long-term responsible Currency Issuance for society. Of course, the future production capacity referred to here should accurately refer to the production capacity needed by people who have money in hand. As for how to enhance future production capacity, we believe that it needs to be cultivated from other aspects such as education, scientific research, and the rule of law. This is not the fundamental function of money.

III. The Second-best Option for Maintaining Currency Value is to Add New Production Capacity

The market is a whole with a large enough capacity, and the economy is also constantly developing. The function of money is to trade, which is not a simple one-to-one transaction but a disorderly, cross-space transaction between many parties. this transaction is also a cross-time transaction. Money is widely accepted by the market, even if the borrower does not provide sufficient commodities to the market as scheduled, as long as there are new commodities from other parties being added into the market, the money supply may not necessarily be greater than the amount of commodities, the currency may not necessarily depreciate, and the currency holder may not necessarily lose.

From the perspective of the necessary trend of social development, old production capacity will always be saturated and surplus. If the providers of backward production capacity cannot upgrade and transform in time, they will be eliminated by the market. When the overall balanced development of the market becomes impossible, bad debts will arise. At this time, it has been confirmed that borrowers who cannot adapt to the market will enjoy more consumption of wealth, which is a preliminary unfairness. At this time, we need to strive to maintain the currency's non-depreciation, as currency depreciation will confirm the losses of those who have provided commodities and held the currency. This is a cumulative unfairness.

Therefore, for a society as a whole, In the absence of guarantees that the loans issued by monetary authorities will not be defaulted upon, developing new capacities to compensate for outdated ones is a remedial measure to maintain the purchasing power of currency. It is also fundamental to ensuring economic fairness. New production capacity refers to the production capacity that society needs or will need in the future. Of course, if the person who obtains Initial Currency, that is, the person who borrows money from Currency Issuer, can provide their own production capacity, it will not result in an unfair outcome where they only spend without producing. For the overall interests of society, this is the optimal choice, and having others cover the shortfall is only a second-best economic equilibrium approach.

IV. Demand and Supply are the Double-helix "Economic DNA" Structure that Drives the Improvement of the Economy

Human needs are diverse and complex. Maslow's classic hierarchy of needs theory provides a logical analysis, but the real needs may be far more complex than this theory. Human needs and the supply of commodities together form the double helix structure of economic DNA. Diverse needs and abundant commodities are complementary base pairs located on two long chains, while currencies are the hydrogen bonds that link these base pairs. Money facilitates and drives the continuous extension of the double helix structure of the economic DNA. Demand and supply are the two pillars of the upward ladder of human civilization, and money has paved the steps for humanity to climb up.

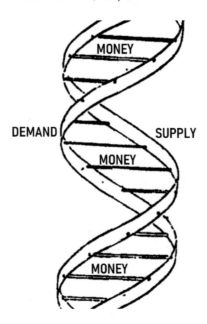

To develop the economy, we need to discovery, recognize, accept, create and meet human needs to the greatest extent. When a demand that was originally considered illegal is officially recognized by the government, people can seek to satisfy this demand through open transactions, and money can be invested in for people to purchase commodities that meet this demand. The provision and purchase of this commodity form an industry, and the transaction volume of this industry can be included in GDP. Extreme examples can be seen in the sex industry in the Netherlands and the legalization of marijuana in some Western countries. When people are free and their needs are released, they will pursue their own needs for satisfaction. The market is also smart enough to capture this demand and create corresponding commodities, which will improve the economy. Of course, things that are prohibited by law or controversial to people's legalization will generally have a negative impact on society. It depends on a country's balanced choice and strengthened management. In any case, freedom is the premise of market transactions, and transactions will bring about the satisfaction of human needs and the improvement of the social economy. Similarly, in a country with freedom of speech, if someone is willing and able to spend money on tickets to listen to a wonderful political speech, then political speech will also create GDP. Waging war may be the most evil way to create demand that we can think of. When war breaks out, security needs and the demand for ammunition will surge. At this time, as long as there is production capacity to match, GDP will grow, but this growth will bring the suffering of chaos to the people. Therefore, we can say that people's happiness lies not in the growth of GDP, but in the content of GDP.

Considering the comprehensive and sustainable development of the economy, in the process of economic growth, what we need to do is to enable those who pay money to buy commodities to have the ability to provide commodities that others need, thus forming more economic DNA and a large and complete economy, promoting a benign internal cycle of the economy. In general, from the perspective of the overall and long-term development of the economy, we should focus on extracting and expanding demand on the one hand, and developing and producing commodities on the other hand. Demand is an objective existence, while goods are subjectively created. For us, the focus is on improving production capacity to manufacture more and better products or provide more and better services. In the contradiction between demand and supply, the production capacity of commodities is the main issue, which fundamentally depends on education and technology. The source of technology is also education, so education is the origin of the economy.

Modern monetary theory advocates that the steering wheel of the economy should be handed over to the financial sector rather than the monetary sector, believing that as long as the government keeps exporting money, the economy will have a steady stream of power. In fact, t This is actually a misunderstanding of the origin of the economy. The origin of the economy is production and education, not finance and currency. To boost the economy, we should focus on education and scientific research. Both the financial sector and the monetary sector are just economic entities, and they possess public welfare characteristics and provide public services. That's all. Neither the financial sector nor the monetary sector is capable of taking on the direct responsibility of economic development.

V. The Quality of Wealth Depends on the Type of Commodities

Generally speaking, the goods or service that can ultimately meet people's needs are wealth, and money is only the intermediary. Therefore, money is only indirect wealth, while goods or service are direct wealth, which are truly effective for human beings. If there are only money in the market without goods or service, money will have no value. The goods or service circulating in the market are collectively referred to as commodities.

As mentioned earlier, people's happiness does not depend on the growth of GDP, but on the types of commodities. War has led to the development of military industry, but it has brought destruction, death, and fear to people. However, airplanes, villas, and bread can meet people's needs in many ways and bring happiness to them.

In this section, we will discuss the accumulation of wealth. The economic strength of an individual or a group is reflected in how much wealth they have accumulated. There are four types of wealth: retained products such as machine tools, aircraft, and atomic bombs; consumable products such as beer, bread, and milk. Of course, milk that can be retained for a long time through measures should be classified as a retained product; retained services such as patented technology, exclusive processes, solutions, etc.; and consumable services such as massage, hairdressing, psychological counseling, etc.

The wealth we can accumulate is in the form of retained goods and retained service. We encourage consumption, which essentially increases the proportion of consumable goods and consumable service in the total economy. Under such circumstances, even if our transaction volume and total economic output increase, our wealth accumulation will not. If our goal is immediate satisfaction, then we should focus on consumption. If our goal is future satisfaction, then we should focus on retention.

For a country, if it wants to achieve national strength, it is not wise to encourage consumption blindly, but to strengthen the production and accumulation of two types of wealth, namely, retained products and retained services, especially those involving national security, key areas construction, and the development of emerging industries.

Chapter 10: The Relationship between Currency and Economy

Economy is essentially the relationship between human needs and commodity supply, and commodities allow humans to exchange what they have for what they need through trade, and money serves as the medium of exchange. At the same time, money is only a link and an element in the economy, and cannot fulfill all economic functions. Correctly positioning and implementing the functions of money is a prerequisite for the normal operation of the economy.

I. The Fundamental Mission of Currency

As a necessary medium for transactions, money is an important factor in economic development. When money is invested in transactions, commodities can be sold and the economy can be improved. At the same time, the borrower's commitment obtained when issuing money drives borrowers to strive to provide commodities for the market, which naturally makes money have the function of promoting production. Therefore, ensuring market transactions, stimulating economic growth, promoting production and creating, and promoting commodity supply are the natural missions of money. These missions can be summarized as promoting economic growth. Money is used for transactions and it facilitates transactions across space and time. Therefore, we intuitively believe that the stability of the purchasing power of money, that is, the stability of the currency value, is an inevitable requirement for ensuring the performance of its functions and maintaining market fairness. However, through our previous analysis, we found that scientific Currency Issuance and management are the prerequisites for maintaining currency value stability, and they are also the methods and means to maintain currency value stability. Therefore, promoting economic growth and ensuring currency value stability are the two major missions of money, the connotation requirement of promoting economic growth should be to promote balanced, equitable, and sustainable growth, rather than neglecting one aspect for another, unfair distribution, or overdrawing future growth. If this connotation requirement is achieved, the currency value can naturally be stabilized. On the contrary, if such high-quality development cannot be achieved, the currency value stability is impossible to achieve, or it can only be achieved at the expense of economic growth. Therefore, promoting economic growth is the primary and fundamental mission, while ensuring currency value stability is the secondary and subsidiary mission. The high-quality Currency Issuance can and should promote economic growth and maintain currency stability at the same time.

Economic growth is the increase in the degree to which human needs are met. Human beings trade based on their needs, so as long as a transaction occurs, that is, money is used once, human demand is met once, and the economy grows once. The details have been described in the chapter 2"The Operation of Contract Currency" through the first law of monetary economics. Based on this, when the economy is sluggish or overheated, money is expected to play a significant role. Countries have introduced monetary policies to stimulate or suppress transactions in order to achieve the goal of regulating the economy.

Article 3 of "The People's Bank of China Law of the People's Republic of China" stipulates that "The goal of monetary policy is to maintain the stability of the currency value and promote economic growth through this." This provision clarifies the two goals of monetary policy, and its meaning is to regard the stability of the currency value as a prerequisite and means to promote economic growth. Many other countries' monetary policies also prioritize maintaining currency stability as their primary goal. The reason for this is that central banks are not direct and primary issuers of currency, they have lost complete control over the issuance of money and can only hope to manage commercial banks through monetary policy, thereby maintaining the stability of the currency they issue.

However, from the perspective of the principle of Currency Issuance, promoting economic growth does not require the stability of the currency value as a prerequisite or means. As long as the currency can be issued and used for transactions, it can promote economic growth. We do not need to establish the stability of the currency value as a prerequisite and constraint condition for promoting economic growth. Of course, this does not mean that the stability of the currency value is not important, but it only shows that promoting economic growth is the first function of currency. As long as the issued currency can be repaid as agreed, it means that the borrower has provided sufficient commodities for society, and the stability of the currency value has a fundamental guarantee.

The original text of the Federal Reserve System Act on the objectives of monetary policy states: "The monetary policy of the United States is conducted by the Board of Governors of the Federal Reserve System with the objective of promoting effectively the goals of maximum employment, stable prices, and moderate long-term interest rates." The United States has set the objectives of monetary policy as "maximum employment, stable prices, and moderate long-term interest rates," without expressing price stability as a prerequisite or means for maximum employment. "Maximum employment" is to fundamentally increase production capacity and provide sufficient commodities to the market, which is consistent with promoting economic growth. "Price stability" is established as an independent second goal, while "moderate long-term interest rates" can encourage businesses and individuals to invest and consume, promoting economic growth. If interest rates are too high, they may inhibit borrowing and investment activities, thereby undermining the first goal, while too low interest rates may lead to inflation and asset bubbles, thereby undermining the second goal. Therefore, the establishment of the third goal is only to ensure the first and second goals, and is essentially a means rather than a goal.

Money is generated through transactions, and its fundamental mission is to ensure transactions. Transactions enable people's needs to be met, and at the same time stimulate production. Therefore, money has become a means to promote economic growth. However, the satisfaction of people's needs and economic growth fundamentally rely on goods or service. The transactions guaranteed by money must be balanced and sustainable, so that the economy can achieve balanced and sustainable development. Therefore, in summary, the fundamental mission of money is to "ensure balanced and sustainable transactions". When money fulfills this mission, the economy will naturally grow, and the value of money will naturally be preserved.

II. Currency Issuance Without a Corresponding Increase in Commodities will lead to inflation

Let's go back to the original model of Island Z and make another hypothetical case (Story 11). As the New Year approaches, the three people again go to the coin maker, who announces that the total loan amount for this year has been expanded by 10 times. In previous years, each person borrowed 10 "Z coins", but this year each person borrows 100. The number on the white wallboard in the coin maker's house is also changed to "-10000 worth", and the three people on Island Z cannot increase their own product output. The production capacity on Island Z remains at 1000 kilograms of grain, 10 spades, and 100 hours of massage. The three people use "Z coins" to exchange as usual, except that now the price of grain is 10 worth per kilogram,

146

the price of massage is 100 worth per hour, and the price of spade is 1000 worth per spade.

The transaction continues and life goes on as usual, but the farmer in Story 2 is not happy. Originally, the remaining 500 in the drawer could be exchanged for 5 spades, but now it can only be exchanged for half a spade. The harvest of that year became a disappointment. The masseuse was extremely happy, she originally had to find a way to provide 50 more hours of service to earn 500 more value, so that he could pay off the coiner's loan at the end of the year. Now she only needs to provide 5 more hours. The miser, who was greatly affected, has only one-tenth of the purchasing power of the 1000 worth in his pocket.

At this time, we believe that the wealth value of 1000 kilograms of grain, 10 spades, and 100 hours of massage has not changed, because the degree to which these commodities meet people's needs has not changed. What has changed is the wealth value of the currency "Z coin". Under the condition that the total value of transactions on Island Z remains unchanged, the amount of currency used for transactions has expanded to ten times its original size. The total value of wealth represented by these ten times the previous amount of currency did not change, and for the first time, inflation appeared on Island Z.

If we want to avoid such inflation, there are three ways. First, increase savings. That is, each person keeps 9000 worth "Z coins" in the drawer, and only uses 1000 of them to trade with others. At the end of the year, the 9000 worth "Z coins" will be collected by the coiner. In real life, attracting money into savings by raising interest rates is a specific application of this way. Second, expand the production of commodities. That is, each person increases their production capacity to 10 times the original level. Third, develop new commodities. That is, someone develops or introduces new products or service with a wealth value of 18,000 worth and put it into circulation on Z Island.

III. The Fundamental Driving Force of Economic Growth is not Currency but Production Capacity

The fundamental function of money is to facilitate transactions, which cannot satisfy any human needs on its own. Money can only generate economic benefits by exchanging commodities through transactions. Therefore, the phenomenon of money is only a representation, and the origin of the economy lies in production capacity and the supply of commodities. When all economic sectors can produce different goods or service to meet the needs of other parts, the economy is balanced. When a certain part only has demand but cannot provide commodities, its own demand cannot be fulfilled, and the corresponding supply department cannot achieve sales, the economy is unbalanced.

As long as the economy is balanced, the more prosperous the transactions are, the more people's needs can be met. This is beneficial and has no drawbacks. Therefore, there is no problem of overheating in the economy, only a problem of imbalance. The so-called economic overheating refers to the situation where the demand in some or most economic sectors exceeds the supply, resulting in rising prices, which indicates that the corresponding supply sector does not have sufficient production capacity, and "insufficient production leads to excess demand". This is a manifestation of the unbalanced development of the economic sectors. Therefore, the so-called economic overheating is essentially a type of economic imbalance, namely "insufficient capacity on the supply side". Another type of economic imbalance is "insufficient capacity on the demand side". When the supply in some or most economic sectors exceeds the demand, resulting in falling prices and even unsalable commodities, we consider the economy to be too cold. This may be due to blind investment in the market, which leads to "excess capacity on the supply side". However, it may also not be a problem on the supply side, but rather a problem on the demand side. Because supply exceeding demand does not necessarily mean that the real demand is really small. It is likely that the real demand is huge, but the demand side cannot produce the commodities needed by the market, thus unable to earn income to support purchases. Therefore, when people's needs are not fully met, the fundamental problem of economic overheating or undercooling lies in insufficient capacity, either "insufficient supply-side capacity" or "insufficient demand-side capacity." These are not monetary issues, but rather issues of capacity. Of course, if we take into account the pressure of resources and environment in terms of whether the economy is overheated, then it is not a question of how to develop, but rather a question of what kind of development is needed.

Products are always purchased with products, and money only plays a mediating role in an instant. The seller gets money in order to use it to purchase other products that are useful to him. Therefore, just as the seller is the supplier of the buyer, he is also the demander of the buyer. As a buyer, he provides demand; as a seller, he provides supply. Money is only a medium of circulation, and it plays a mediating role in the initial moment of exchange. When the exchange finally ends, we will see that a series of exchanges are only product-to-product exchanges[9]

Jean-Baptiste Say's core idea is that "supply creates its own demand." He believed that the production of a product means that the equivalent product has a market at the same time. In other words, he advocated that the supply of the market can automatically create corresponding demand, so there is usually no overproduction in the economy and no widespread overproduction crisis.

---

[9] Jean-Baptiste Say. A Treatise on Political Economy[M]. Beijing: The Commercial Press,1998.

This view is known as "Say's Law" in the history of economics. The positive aspect of "Say's Law" is that it sees the problem of "insufficient capacity on the demand side" and believes that people with demand can obtain income to support their own consumption as long as they have sufficient capacity. At the same time, "Say's Law" ignores the problem of "excess capacity on the supply side." Human economic history proves that "excess capacity on the supply side" is real, Say's "supply automatically creates demand" and "production shortage leads to production surplus" overemphasize the importance of the demand side's payment ability, highlighting the fact that the demand side's production capacity is limited, but ignoring the fact that the demand side's demand is also limited. He was too optimistic in thinking that supply can automatically match demand, thus avoiding overproduction and economic crisis. However, in reality, due to factors such as asymmetric information, uneven resource allocation, and changes in consumer demand, products produced by the "supply side" may not be needed by the "demand side," and the market cannot always effectively achieve a balance between supply and demand, which may lead to excess production of certain products and trigger economic fluctuations and crises. However, Say's theory fully reveals the truth that "the exchange between people is essentially the exchange between products and products," which fully suggests the truth that "all buyers must be sellers." If buyers cannot provide commodities that the market needs on their own, they cannot afford to pay and transactions cannot be carried out.

Every entity in the market is both a demander and a supplier of commodities. Every entity is both a consumer and a producer, and needs to exchange its own produced commodities for those produced by others. For a commodity, the reasons for insufficient supply and excess demand may be insufficient production by producers or strong production by consumers, while the reasons for excess supply or insufficient demand may be strong production by producers or insufficient production by consumers. Taking real estate as an example, the reason for the shortage of supply in the real estate market may be that there are few real estate developers, or that other industries are prosperous. However, as the economic situation changes, the sales offices become empty, which may be due to the fact that the developers have built too many houses and there is no longer a demand for residence, or it could be that people in other industries who had demand have lost their jobs and no longer have an income. If the production capacity of each entity in the market is sufficient to support their own needs, the overall economy will show a prosperous situation of both supply and demand. In the case of insufficient productivity development rather than insufficient natural resources, the fundamental purpose of the economy is to develop productivity and meet human needs. Therefore, the solution to economic problems lies in developing the short-supply commodity sector to enable it to provide commodities needed by society.

In addition, when the cultivation of production capacity is completed and various economic sectors are capable of providing commodities, a free and inclusive trading environment is also an inevitable requirement for trading. The state should provide maximum freedom of trade for its citizens and strengthen the stability and predictability of this freedom through laws. This is a necessary condition for people to maintain their creativity and confidence in the future. "The rule of law" is the most fundamental way to ensure people's freedom, security, and predictability. Therefore, "the rule of law is the best business environment". Public power, as the main body for maintaining social order and public interest, is often considered the biggest threat to private power at the same time. Therefore, the core essence of "the rule of law" is that "public power must abide by the law", which means that " Public power, no action without explicit legal provision", while " Private power, all actions are permissible without explicit legal prohibition". Only in this way can individuals and private units in a weak position have full freedom, sufficient sense of security, and stable expectations for the future.

IV. Composition of the Amount of Money and Commodities in the Market and the Market Transaction Equation

Whether discussing inflation, deflation, or promoting or suppressing the economy, we need to grasp the total money supply and total commodity supply in circulation in the market as a whole. In his book "The Purchasing Power of Money", American economist Fisher proposed the famous Fisher equation, which describes the relationship between the price level, the quantity of money, the velocity of money circulation, and the quantity of commodity transactions. Specifically, the Fisher equation can be expressed as $MV=PT$, where M represents the quantity of money in circulation during a certain period, V represents the velocity of money circulation, P represents the weighted average of various commodity prices (i.e., the price level), and T represents the transaction quantity of various commodities. According to this equation, if the money supply (M) increases while other factors (V, P, T) remain unchanged, then the price level (P) will rise. In the Fisher equation, the money supply (M) is an important variable, but Fisher did not directly provide a calculation method for the money supply. He only generally pointed out that the money supply is usually controlled and determined by the central bank or monetary policy-making institutions. At the same time, the currency quantity M in the Fisher equation is multiplied by the velocity of money circulation V to represent the total amount of currency circulation during a certain period, while the transaction quantity T of commodities is not multiplied by the velocity of commodity circulation. T directly represents the total amount of commodity circulation during a certain period, indicating that T in the equation is equivalent to the product of the quantity and velocity of commodities. The Fisher equation achieves formal neatness at the expense of substantial equivalence.

In order to more accurately grasp the relationship between money and commodities, it is necessary to conduct a more detailed analysis of the supply of money and the supply of commodities. Before this, we must clarify three boundaries. First, the boundary between Currency Issuance and non-Currency Issuance. Under the current monetary system, Currency Issuers not only issue currency through loans, but also exchange currency through other currencies or gold. Since this method of asset exchange is not a true Credit Currency Issuance, we believe that this method is not Currency Issuance, but rather a commodity exchange behavior made by Currency Issuers with other market entities. In legal terms, it is equivalent to Currency Issuance first issuing currency to itself and then exchanging it in the market. We only consider the act of issuing loans by Currency Issuers based on borrower credit as Currency Issuance. Second, the boundary between Currency Issuers and the market. We define Currency Issuers as people who can create currency based on borrower credit, namely central banks and commercial banks. Other non-Currency Issuers in the market who want to obtain currency either provide commodities for exchange in the market or provide credit to borrow from central banks or commercial banks. Third, the boundary between currency and commodities. As discussed earlier, currency belongs to a broad definition of commodities, but when discussing the relationship between currency and commodities, we distinguish between currency and non-currency commodities, Excluding currency, the remaining commodities are narrowly defined as goods or service. Goods include both tangible and intangible products, that are deliverable items, while services refer to human labor.

Now, let's calculate the total money supply (TMS) over a certain period. Firstly, the existing money (EM) amount in the market equals the sum of cash (M0), the Existing Deposit Currency (EDC) (commercial bank certificates based on cash deposits, and the Existing Loans Currency (ELC) (commercial bank certificates obtained based on borrowers' liabilities. Secondly, we add the existing money (EM) amount to the New Loans (NL) issued by the Currency Issuer to market entities and the Interest Paid (IP) from the Currency Issuer to depositors, then subtract the Principal Recovered (PR) and the Interest Recovered (IR) by the money issuer, to obtain a numerical value. Finally, we multiply this value by the Weighted Trading Frequency of Money (WTFM), and the product is the total money supply over a certain period.

$$TMS = (EM+NL+IP-PR-IR) *WTFM$$
$$= (M0+EDC+ELC+NL+IP-PR-IR) *WTFM$$

Let's calculate the total commodity supply (TCS) over a certain period. First, we add the existing products (EP) in the market to new products (NP) and newly provided services (S), then subtract the reduced products (RP) to get a numerical value. Next, we multiply this value by the weighted trading frequency of commodity (WTFC), and the result is the total commodity supply for that period. It should be noted that compared to products, services are instantaneous and cannot be stored. Services are consumed while being provided, so there is no existing stock or loss of stock.

TCS=(EP+NP+S-RP) *WTFC

After fully analyzing the total money supply and total commodity supply, we further introduce the price (P) factor and derive the following equation based on the general principle of Fisher's equation. We call this equation The Market Transaction Equation. Here, the price P does not refer to a single or specific commodity price, but rather refers to the overall price level in the market as a whole.

TMS= TCS*P

That is,

(M0+EDC+ELC+NL+IP-PR-IR) *WTFM
= (EP+NP+S-RP) *WTFC*P

From this, we can see that under the specific conditions of M0, EDC, ELC, and EP, in order to maintain the stability of P, we need to find a balanced development between NL, IP, PR, IR, WTFM on the left side of the equation and NP, S, RP, WTFC on the right side of the equation. Without considering the changes in WTFM and WTFC, we need to maintain NL+IP-PR-IR = NP+S-RP, where NL-PR-IR is the increase or decrease in loan balances, and NP+S-RP is the increase or decrease in commodities (including goods or service). That is to say, without considering the impact of IP, the Currency Issuer needs to ensure that the increase or decrease in loan balances is consistent with the increase or decrease in commodities in the market.

V. Total Factor Analysis and Regulation Methods of Inflation and Deflation

The rise or fall of local or partial commodity prices is called the normal market reaction of the fluctuation of commodity supply and demand relationship. The rise or fall of the overall commodity prices is called inflation or deflation.

Since the emergence of Credit Currency, inflation has become the most common monetary phenomenon, which people have become accustomed to. Some theories even suggest that appropriate inflation is necessary and beneficial for economic growth. This is a self-soothing and self-paralyzing phenomenon when humans do not correctly understand the mechanism of inflation and cannot correctly solve this problem. In fact, since the advent of Credit Currency, inflation has been a constant companion of human society, like a ghost and a disease that has been haunting the economic body, constantly eroding people's labor achievements. Perhaps inflation does benefit some people, but it must be based on the damage to the public. At the same time, the economic depression brought about by economic contraction is also vividly remembered, and those difficult years have left people with lingering fears.

When discussing the causes of inflation or deflation, people usually believe that in a freely traded market, when the overall amount of money is greater than the amount of commodities, inflation will occur, and when the overall amount of money is less than the amount of commodities, deflation will occur. However, this is not the case. Through the above equation, we found that the transaction frequency of money and commodities also plays a crucial role. With the market Transaction Equation, we can further refine the specific factors that cause inflation and deflation.

$$(M0+EDC+ELC+NL+IP-PR-IR) *WTFM$$
$$= (EP+NP+S-RP) *WTFC*P$$

We take the price (P) as the dependent variable, and the other factors in the equation are the independent variables. Under the specific conditions of the stock of money and the stock of goods, the four factors M0, EDC, ELC, and EP are specific. The increase in NL, IP, WTFM, RP and the decrease in PR, IR, NP, S, WTFC will all promote the increase of P, which will cause inflation. In other words, we can solve the problem of deflation through the increase in NL, IP, WTFM, RP and the decrease in PR, IR, NP, S, WTFC. We can expand the loan supply, extend the maturity of loans, reduce the willingness of market entities to deposit by lowering interest rates to increase the frequency of currency transactions, encourage consumption to increase the frequency of currency transactions and increase product consumption, control excess capacity to reduce the supply of new products and services, strengthen material reserves to reduce the frequency of commodity transactions, in order to achieve the purpose of raising prices, boosting the economy, and avoiding deflation.

On the contrary, the reduction NL, IP, WTFM, RP and the increase in PR, IR, NP, S, WTFC will all promote the decline of the commodities prices, which will cause deflation. In other words, we can solve the problem of inflation through the above means. We can reduce the loan supply and raise interest rates to increase the willingness of market entities to deposit, Similar measures also include reducing the frequency of currency transactions, strengthening the recovery of unexpired loans, cracking down on consumption to reduce the frequency of currency transactions and reduce product consumption, expanding production capacity to increase the supply of new products and services, and releasing reserve materials to increase the frequency of commodity transactions. These measures can achieve the purpose of suppressing prices, cooling down the economy, and avoiding inflation. Of course, these regulatory measures also have some side effects, which we will further discuss in Section 8 of this chapter, " Side Effects of Adjusting Economic through Raising and Lowering Interest Rates. ".

VI. Inflation and Deflation are Generated through the Role of People

In the above, we have considered the dual factors of currency and commodities and analyzed the specific factors that cause inflation and deflation in detail. However, how do these factors play a role in specific market transactions? This depends on the most critical subject in the market, namely the people who participate in market transactions. In fact, it is the dual value judgments of commodities and currency by people that determine the market prices of commodities, that is, the subjective price (SP) formed by people on commodities jointly determines the market prices of a commodities. People who are both rational and emotional have sensitive perception of various factors in The Market Transaction Equation. When general commodity prices form general consensus of rise or fall among the general population, inflation or deflation occurs.

We have introduced the concepts of "Value Perception" and "Subjective Wealth Value" of commodities and currencies, and then formulated the internal mechanism of the rise and fall of individual commodity prices. When analyzing the overall price trend, this formula is also applicable as a whole, but the focus of our discussion has expanded from individuals and individual commodities to social groups and all commodities. We will focus on analyzing factors that have a general impact on OWVC, OWVM, VPC, and VPM.

$$SP = SWVC / SWVM$$

$$= (A/B) * (OWVC/OWVM) * (VPC/VPM)$$

Under the influence of democratic politics and financial strength, some developed capitalist countries have seen a decline in the overall spirit of struggle and hardship among their citizens. They have become overly dependent on high-value-added industries such as finance, high technology, and producer services, leading to the phenomenon of industrial hollowing out. The insufficient production capacity of real industries will lead to insufficient supply of goods and service in the market. The low-value-added goods or service that citizens rely on for their daily lives and production mainly come from imports. When foreign low-value-added goods or service cannot enter the domestic market smoothly due to geopolitical and economic frictions, the goods or service needed for citizens' daily life and production will be in short supply, leading to a general increase in the value perception of citizens towards these commodities (VPC), which in turn leads to an increase in the overall subjective price (SP) of the market, driving up the general price of commodities and inducing inflation.

When a Currency Issuer lends money to the outside world, these loans can be divided into consumer loans and production loans based on the currency usage of the borrower. Consumer loans do not generate new commodity supply, but directly increase the money supply, causing a general increase in the national perception of commodity value (VPC) and a decrease in the perception of monetary value (VPM), leading to an overall increase in the subjective price (SP) of the market. Therefore, consumer loans are a positive factor in promoting inflation. While increasing the money supply, production loans also bring investment and production. If the number of newly added commodities invested is greater than the money supply issued by production loans, it will inhibit inflation. If the borrower of production loans fails to invest, they will not be able to recover the money they have invested, resulting in bad debts or non-performing loans. This is the bankruptcy of the credit of the borrower of Credit Currency. If there is a large-scale default on loans, it will lead to the consumption of goods and the increase of money. If there are no other non-debt-producing commodities to supplement, it will cause a general increase in the national perception of commodity value (VPC) and a general decrease in the perception of monetary value (VPM), leading to an overall increase in the subjective price (SP) of the market and promoting inflation.

For Currency Issuers, they issue currency based on the current price level. They generally do not lend out currency at a higher price without any reason, as in story 11, when they know that there are no more commodities for trading. From the perspective of the market, currency is not issued out of thin air, but based on the borrower's commitment and credit to "provide sufficient commodities for the market". No matter how much currency is issued, as long as this commitment is fulfilled, there will be equivalent commodities available in the market, and the overall purchasing power of the market will not decrease. People's willingness to save, consume, invest, and produce is only an influencing factor of currency purchasing power, but not a fundamental decisive factor. The fundamental cause of inflation is that the borrower brings currency to the market without providing corresponding commodities as promised. Therefore, the borrower's breach of trust is the root cause of inflation. For every bad debt of one cent generated by the borrower of Currency Issuer, there is one cent of currency in the market without corresponding commodities. We can call this the third law of monetary economics.

When a country's industrial structure is unbalanced, with overcapacity in labor-intensive industries, and the products and services produced cannot be exported abroad, it will lead to a general surplus of goods and service in the domestic market, a general decline in people's perception of the value of commodities (VPC), and a general decline in the subjective prices of most commodities, resulting in deflation.

It is worth emphasizing that people commonly believe an increase in the money supply leads to a general rise in commodity prices, and a decrease in the money supply leads to a general fall in commodity prices. This may be another huge misconception about economic phenomena. In this market, the key role is always played by humans, not money or commodities. Economic development depends on public sentiment and opinion, not on money. The reality is that people's feelings about the market environment and their expectations for the future determine their value perception of money and commodities. This, in turn, changes their willingness to save, borrow, hold money, or hold other assets, thereby altering various independent variables in The Market Transaction Equation, especially the Weighted Transaction Frequency of Money (WTFM) and the Weighted Transaction Frequency of Commodities (WTFC). These changes ultimately lead to a general rise or fall in commodity prices. The rise and fall of prices also cause the demand for the money supply to increase and decrease. Under the current monetary system, the supply of money has basically achieved market-oriented supply. Like other commodities, money is in a passive position of being chosen by the market, and its decisive role in the market is becoming increasingly unclear. In short, humans are the decisive factor in the market; humans determine prices, and prices determine the money supply, not the other way around.

Citizens living under the spirit of contract possess the strongest sense of stability, the most vitality, and the most significant foresight. The law is the biggest contract between economic entities in a country, especially between citizens and the government. The rule of law not only refers to the compliance of all citizens with the law, but also refers to the strict compliance of public power departments such as the government with the law. The biggest function of the rule of law is to protect individual rights and thus give people full expectations for the future. The rule of law is a stabilizer for society. "No relief, no rights", when illegal and irregular behavior becomes a common phenomenon, especially when public power departments fail to be promptly and effectively corrected and punished for illegal and irregular behavior, The majesty of the law shall yield to the power of an individual, and citizens will lose trust in the rule of law, and cannot make careful plans for the future. At this time, no matter how orderly the social security and management order are, people's hearts are full of insecurity and turbulence. Facing an uncertain future, people will think that the only certainty is the currency they hold in their hands. People's perception of currency value (VPM) generally rises, so business owners dare not invest, families dare not consume, the overall subjective price (SP) of the market declines, production shrinks, unemployment rises, and deflation develops.

VII. Means and Effects of Preventing and Controlling Inflation and Deflation

Maintaining stable prices, that is, maintaining the stability of the currency value, is the main goal of central banks in various countries. The fundamental path is to maintain the stability of the general commodity value perception （VPC） and monetary value perception （VPM） of social groups.

People's value perception is influenced by both external market conditions and internal cognitive conditions. The stability of external market conditions depends on the appropriate supply of goods and service as well as the precise and effective monetary supply. Internal cognitive conditions are closely related to factors such as the perceived legal environment, future production capacity, monetary policy direction, and social trends.

Specific to how to prevent and control inflation, the main path is to ensure that borrowers can provide sufficient capacity, maintain or improve the capacity of existing producers, control the increase in external lending by Currency Issuers, and increase people's willingness to save money. Specific measures and means have been discussed in detail in the section 5 of this chapter " Total Factor Analysis and Regulation Methods of Inflation and Deflation ".

Here, we further explore how common policy measures work. One approach is for the issuer of currency to reduce lending (NL), reducing consumer loans is a direct and effective method. The reduction in consumer loans will decrease transaction volume, thereby affecting economic growth. Reducing production loans also reduces production investment and the possibility of increasing the supply of commodities (NP), which is beneficial for the economy. To avoid these disadvantages, it is necessary to improve the accuracy of production loans and allow those producers who can meet demand of the market to receive loans, while eliminating loans for excess capacity.

Second, reducing the willingness of currency holders to use currency for transactions, that is, increasing the willingness to save money. The usual monetary policy is to raise interest rates. Since people's money usually exists in the form of commercial bank deposits, increasing the willingness to save money will not increase the amount of currency reserves (EDC), but will only reduce the weighted transaction frequency (WTFM), thus reducing the total money supply (TMS) and preventing economic overheating. Increasing the willingness to save money is also divided into suppressing consumption and suppressing investment. Suppressing consumption is directly effective, but suppressing investment will reduce production and also reduce the possibility of increasing the supply of commodities (NP). In the long run, it is not conducive to the fall and stability of commodity prices.

Third, ensuring that borrowers repay on time in all aspects of loan approval, management, and recovery. It will promote borrowers to try their best to provide sufficient goods or service to society. As long as borrowers can repay the principal and interest on time, the amount of money in the market will be recovered due to their repayment behavior, and there will be no excess or surplus of money in the market.

Fourth, non-borrower producers expand production, providing more commodities to society than the currency they use to purchase commodities

157

from society. These additional commodities provided by the non-borrower producers is the part that offsets the excess money in the market, which is generated by borrowers with bad debts. Measures and impacts of preventing deflation can be implemented according to the same logic. We will not repeat them here.

VIII. Side Effects of Adjusting Economic through Raising and Lowering Interest Rates.

When the supply falls short of demand and the amount of money is greater than the amount of commodities, that is, the economy is overheated, the central bank chooses to raise interest rates, which can increase savings, reduce loans, reduce investment, reduce consumption, and reduce the amount of money in circulation. However, not all debtors have the ability to repay loans, and the increase in interest will increase their debt costs and accelerate their formation of overdue, bad debts and bankruptcy, which will reduce social productivity and exacerbate inflation. At the same time, raising interest rates can only attract more money to stay within Currency Issuer system, without changing the ownership and control of the currency. It also allows the currency owner to enjoy higher interest rates and receive more money, which will ultimately be used for transactions.

Reducing investment and consumption will strongly dampen the enthusiasm for investment and production, resulting in further shortages of commodities. Shortages of commodities and bankruptcy of debtors are also contributing to inflation. Therefore, raising interest rates to curb inflation is a short-term contraction of the money supply in the market, but in the long run it increases the money supply in the market. The means of preventing inflation also sow the seeds for more serious inflation. In addition, people who already hold money will deposit it in commercial banks or central banks, which increases savings and the need for commercial banks and central banks to pay their interest. Coupled with shrinking loans, it is easy to cause losses and bankruptcies of commercial banks and central banks. The losses and bankruptcies of Currency Issuers will have a very serious impact on the overall economy.

Next, we will use the market Transaction Equation discussed earlier to conduct a comprehensive analysis of the impact of interest rate hikes on the economy:

$$(M0+EDC+ELC+NL+IP-PR-IR) *WTFM$$
$$= (EP+NP+S-RP) *WTFC*P$$

Interest rate hikes do not affect the total amount of M0+EDC. In the short term, the increase in loan costs promotes loan repayment, increases PR and IR, while reducing borrowers' willingness to borrow, reducing NL and WTFM, and suppressing inflation. At the same time, it reduces investment willingness, reduces NP and S, and reduces RP due to the suppression of consumption. These offset the effect of suppressing inflation. At the same time, in the long run, due to the long-term storage of money in Currency Issuer system, Currency Issuer needs to pay interest to depositors, which will increase IP. The decrease in loan amount will lead to a reduction in interest charged by Currency Issuer, which will reduce IR. This will ultimately lead to an increase in total money supply TMS, creating conditions for future inflation.

When the supply exceeds the demand, the amount of commodities exceeds the amount of money, that is, the economy is too cold, the central bank chooses to cut interest rates, which can reduce savings, increase loans, increase investment, increase consumption, and increase the amount of money in circulation. However, not all debtors have the ability to produce commodities that society needs. The reduction of interest will promote them to invest blindly, which will produce more surplus commodities for society, they will eventually default on loans and generate bad debts, which will lead to inflation. Boosting the economy by promoting consumption is a one-time boost. People use the saved money for consumption instead of investment and reproduction. The goods on the market are digested, and the money remains in the market, but there is no new increase in goods, and there is no further impetus for economic growth. Consumption is a transaction of past production capacity and a confirmation of wealth that has already occurred. It does not generate new social wealth. Regarding the comprehensive analysis of the impact of interest rate cuts on the economy, we can also use the market Transaction Equation to analyze it. Here we will not repeat it.

Whether it is inflation or deflation, prevention and control through monetary policy is only a temporary solution, and the fundamental governance means is to solve the problem from the level of production and supply. Inflation is caused by insufficient commodities and excess money, and the solution should be to increase the supply of commodities or directly withdraw money through taxation. Deflation is caused by excess commodities and insufficient money, and the root cause of insufficient money is insufficient production income of consumers. The corresponding fundamental solution should be to reduce excess capacity, while increasing the production capacity and income of consumers. The secondary distribution through taxation and strengthening the wealth transfer to low-income people are also effective governance means, but this measure is not long-lasting, and it is not fair to get something for nothing.

By raising or lowering interest rates to adjust inflation and deflation, it only adjusts the amount of money between savings and transactions in the short term, without changing the amount of money that social entities can control. Therefore, it can only produce effects in the short term and is a temporary solution without addressing the root cause. It also has obvious side effects, and over time, it will inevitably backfire and disrupt the normal functioning of the economy.

IX. The Impact of Currency Issuers Directly Buying and Selling Commodities

All the above-mentioned money supply behaviors are defined as the issuance of currency by Issuer through lending. In this way, Currency Issuer only has the creditor's rights of the borrower and obtains the commitment to repay the principal and interest of the loan, without obtaining any goods. Under the current monetary system, central banks may directly use their own issued currency to purchase other countries' currencies or gold in the market. Of course, Currency Issuer can also sell these goods to recover the currency. Usually, this behavior is only to enhance their own credit, achieve asset preservation and appreciation, and regulate the money supply. The direct purchase of assets by Currency Issuer from other market entities with their own created currency will lead to an increase in the money supply in the market. Correspondingly, when Currency Issuer sells these assets externally, the money supply in the market will decrease. We regard the behavior of Currency Issuer creating a borrower identity to complete currency creation and recovery as a quasi-issuance behavior of currency. In a narrow sense, Currency Issuance only refers to the behavior of Currency Issuer lending currency to other entities. In a broad sense, it also includes directly creating currency and exchanging it externally. If we follow the aforementioned market Transaction Equation, then the borrower identity created by Currency Issuer can be regarded as a general non-Currency Issuer entity. The increase or decrease in the currency caused by the quasi-issuance behavior of currency includes NL, PR, and IR. Since the goods purchased by Currency Issuer in the quasi-issuance behavior process are not used for their own consumption, Currency Issuer will not produce goods themselves, so the quasi-issuance behavior will not cause an increase or decrease in the quantity of goods.

In order to more clearly analyze the impact of quasi-Currency Issuance on the market's currency volume and commodity circulation, we will analyze the behavior of Currency Issuers using their independently created currency to purchase goods and then sell goods as an independent factor. We still adhere to the boundary between Currency Issuers and the market. When Currency Issuers purchase goods externally, the currency enters the market and the goods exit the market. When Currency Issuers sell goods, the currency exits the market and the goods enter the market. The refined market Transaction Equation has four new independent variables added: the amount of money spent by Currency Issuer to purchase goods (Expenses by the Issuer, EI), the amount of goods purchased by the Currency Issuer (PI), the amount of money recovered by Currency Issuer through the sale of goods (Income of the Currency Issuer, II), goods sold by the Currency Issuer (GI). when the currency issuer is involved in both buying and selling commodities, the market

160

Transaction Equation has evolved to:

$$(M0+EDC+ELC+NL+IP-PR-IR+EI-II) *WTFM$$
$$=(EP+NP+S-RP-PI+GI) *WTFC*P$$

The central bank issues its own currency using foreign exchange as an anchor and buys and sells gold in its own currency, which is a typical external commodity trading behavior of Currency Issuers. Domestic market entities obtain foreign exchange by selling goods or service abroad, and foreign exchange enters the domestic market as a commodity. Usually, the law stipulates that only domestic currency can be used for circulation in the country, and domestic market entities will conduct foreign exchange settlement. At this time, the central bank receives foreign exchange and exchanges its own currency to market entities, increasing the EI. The currency obtained by domestic market entities through foreign exchange settlement enters the domestic market for circulation, and the supply of domestic currency in the market increases. At the same time, the goods provided by domestic market entities when obtaining foreign exchange are no longer available in the country, and foreign exchange is received by the central bank as a commodity, increasing the PI and reducing the supply of goods in the domestic market. With other factors remaining unchanged in the market Transaction Equation, the central bank's issuance of its own currency using foreign exchange as an anchor will drive price increases in the domestic market.

Similarly, when domestic market entities choose to purchase foreign exchange and the central bank sells foreign exchange, II increases, and the supply of domestic currency in the market decreases, the foreign exchange obtained by domestic market entities from purchasing foreign exchange is generally used to purchase foreign goods. Even if there is no import trade, the foreign exchange remains in the market as tradable goods, and GI increases, leading to an increase in goods in the domestic market. In the market Transaction Equation, other factors remain unchanged, and the reduction in the amount of foreign exchange on which the central bank issues currency will drive down prices in the domestic market. The central bank uses domestic currency to purchase and sell gold or other commodities in the market, which can also cause an increase or decrease in the supply of domestic currency, thereby boosting and suppressing prices in the market. As we said earlier, raising interest rates can reduce the velocity of money circulation, but it cannot take back the control of money from the market. In the long run, it will only cause an increase in the supply of money in the market. Cutting interest rates can promote loans, but loans must eventually be repaid. If they cannot promote production, the supply of money in the market cannot be supplemented in the long run. The impact of interest rate hikes and cuts on the recovery and release of money supply is indirect, short-term, and formal. In contrast, the release and recovery of money by Currency Issuers through

161

direct buying and selling of goods is direct, long-term, and substantive.

X. Self-Regulation of Prices in the Market

In the Chinese philosophical system, the idea of "unity of man and nature" occupies a central position. This idea emphasizes the harmonious unity of man and nature, and believes that man and all things in the universe are interdependent and interconnected. Man should conform to the laws of nature and live in harmony with nature. Laozi's "Tao Te Ching" has a specific expression of human behavior norms: "Man follows the earth, the earth follows heaven, heaven follows the Tao, and the Tao follows nature." The market is formed by human natural needs and supply, and all participating parties should abide by their own development laws. Deng Xiaoping, the outstanding leader of China, said in the autobiography of himself: he was not the chief designer of the reform and opening-up, he did not do anything, he merely loosened the people's bonds and lifted some taboos from 1978. Everything was created by the people themselves." Of course, this is a modest remark by Deng Xiaoping, but it clearly reflects his humble, respectful, and open view of the market.

When the borrower's commitment in the process of money creation is fulfilled, the money supply and commodity supply in the market are commensurate. As we have discussed before, when the increase or decrease in the loan balance of the Currency Issuer is consistent with the increase or decrease in the market's commodity supply, the price level will remain generally stable. Now let's take a look at how the price level can achieve self-regulation through interest rates and exchange rates in domestic and international trade.

We have learned from traditional economic theory that the fluctuation of commodity prices is determined by the relationship between supply and demand. When supply is less than demand, prices rise, leading the market to increase supply. When supply exceeds demand, prices fall. This cycle achieves a dynamic balance in commodity prices. Unlike the specific commodity price adjustment mechanisms mentioned above, the overall price level is influenced by the money supply. When the overall price level in the market rises, it means that inflation is occurring. Buying the same amount of goods requires more money, and the market's demand for money increases. As we discussed earlier, Currency Issuance, or the loan service provided by Currency Issuer, is a special form of commodities. The essence of interest is Currency Issuer's service fees. According to general market rules, service prices are adjusted by the relationship between supply and demand, the market's demand for money increases, as a result, Currency Issuer's loan service fees increase. That is to say, according to market rules, when inflation occurs, the central bank's interest rate should increase. As interest rates increase, the willingness of market entities to borrow decreases, and their willingness to deposit increases.

162

The money supply in the market decreases, and prices fall. Conversely, when the overall price level in the market falls, it means that deflation is occurring. Buying the same amount of goods requires less money, and the market's demand for money decreases. Currency Issuer's loan service becomes less scarce. According to general market rules, Currency Issuer's loan service fees decrease. That is to say, according to market rules, when deflation occurs, the central bank's interest rate should decrease. As interest rates decrease, the willingness of market entities to borrow increases, and their willingness to deposit decreases. The money supply in the market increases, which drives prices up.

International trade also has a similar internal adjustment mechanism. When a country's goods are highly welcomed by international importers, the country's exports increase. Regardless of the situation where a specific country's currency is used as the world currency, in general, exporters require importers to pay in the currency of the exporting country, leading to an increase in international demand for the currency of the exporting country and a subsequent rise in exchange rate. This will push up the prices of goods priced in the currency of the importer's country, thereby reducing the willingness to purchase, and the popularity of the exporting country's goods decreases, thus curbing the trade surplus situation.

For hundreds of years, mainstream economics such as the neoclassical economics, Chicago School of Economics, and Austrian Economics have emphasized and defended the role of free markets and opposed intervening in the economy through monetary or fiscal policies. Keynesian economics explicitly criticizes neoclassical economics and advocates that the government intervene in the economy through proactive fiscal and monetary policies to stimulate aggregate demand and achieve full employment and economic growth.

The "Equal Rights Monetary Theory" and "Egalitarian Economics" advocated in this book believe that Currency Issuers and governments are also important participants in the market and should play an active role, but they should do so in accordance with market rules. Compared to other market participants, the uniqueness of currency issuers and governments lies in their position as political rulers with supreme public power, which allows them to utilize state force to enforce their will. In this case, it requires Currency Issuers and governments to be more modest in formulating and implementing monetary and fiscal policies, always keeping in mind that public power is granted by the people and cannot be used to confront market rules or disrupt market order. Instead, they should comply with market requirements and abandon their political power status in economic operations, playing their economic roles as equal market participants.

Public authorities with political power should always be vigilant about their own dual identities and dual roles. Give back to Politics what is Political and to economics what is economic; the dual identities and roles of public authorities must not be confused. Economic measures implemented for political purposes often violate market rules, disrupt normal market supply and demand relationships, and ultimately harm the public. Every market participant, including Currency Issuers and governments, should strive to find and adapt to market rules, focusing on insight into market demand and improving their own supply capacity to seek development. We insist that there is no failed market, only failed market participants.

Chapter 11: Types of Debt, Bad Debts, and Their Effects

Through the analysis of the way of Currency Issuance in the previous article, we found that whether Currency Issuer achieves indirect loans through direct loans or by purchasing bond assets, whether it is for the purpose of lending money or regulating money, and whether its behavior is called "conventional monetary policy tools" or "non-conventional monetary policy and quantitative easing", the work done by Currency Issuer is essentially just lending money to the outside world. Currency Issuance means debt occurrence. How to issue currency and manage currency is essentially how to issue debt and manage debt. Understanding currency cannot be separated from a full analysis of debt. Different types of debt are composed of different creditors and debtors, and each type of debt has different effects on the money supply and economic operation.

I. Types of Creditors of Liabilities and Their Impact on the Money Supply

The so-called liability is that the borrower records the debt on the white wallboard of the lender and takes away the currency. According to the different creditors and debtors of the liability, there are four types: commercial banks' liability to the central bank, non-Currency Issuer entity's liability to the central bank, non-Currency Issuer entity 's liability to the commercial bank, and the liability between non-commercial bank entities,

The first is that commercial banks have liabilities to the central bank. If commercial banks do not lend to non-Currency Issuers, it is equivalent to the central bank not completing the issuance of "Contract Currency" outside of the Currency Issuer. This situation will not result in an increase in the money supply in the market.

The second type of non-Currency Issuer entities directly incurring liabilities to the central bank, whether directly or indirectly, can result in the issuance of "Contract Currency". Due to the highly developed commercial banking system and information system, these "Contract Currency " are generally lent to commercial banks and converted into "deposit currencies" issued by commercial banks. This portion of deposit currencies will further double to produce "Loan Currency ", which means that commercial bank loans will generate a "money multiplier".

The third type of non-Currency Issuer entity directly takes on liabilities to commercial banks. There are two situations: first, the borrower only takes away the commercial deposit certificate, which is the "Loan Currency", so there is only one additional currency in the market, which is equivalent to the commercial bank completing Currency Issuance. Second, the borrower withdraws cash, and according to the second law of money theory expressed earlier, the first deposit in the market has a corresponding liability at the issuer's place. It can be considered that the commercial bank, as an agent of the central bank, has completed the initial issuance of "Contract Currency". In both cases, it will bring corresponding new money supply to the market.

The fourth type is the liability between non-commercial bank entities, regardless of whether the lending object is "Contract Currency" (cash), "Deposit Currency" or "Loan Currency". Because non-Currency Issuer entities do not have the ability to create deposits and issue currency, they will not affect the total amount of currency issued.

II. Types of Debtors and Their Impact on Economic Development

Since the central bank does not engage in external debt, the only debtors are commercial banks and non-commercial bank entities. The function of money is to facilitate transactions between commodity providers, specifically non-commercial bank entities. If money does not circulate in the non-commercial bank market and just stay within commercial banks, it is equivalent to not having completed the issuance. This situation does not have further discussion value. So, we will not discuss the situation of commercial banks' liabilities to the central bank here. We focus on the liabilities of non-commercial banks.

The purpose of Currency Issuance is to promote commodity trading and economic circulation, rather than one-way and one-off purchases by borrowers. Both central banks and commercial banks should provide loans to providers of production capacity that meet the future needs of society, so that the loans can be repaid on schedule, the economy can enter a virtuous cycle, and society can achieve overall improvement. After the debtor receives the loan, there are two payment methods: one is to spend for their own consumption, and the other is to spend for the consumption of others or to give the money to others for free. At the same time, there are two possible outcomes for the loan: one is that the borrower repays on schedule, and the other is that the borrower defaults and does not repay the debt. Based on the above two payment methods and two repayment outcomes, we can classify debtors into four types and further analyze them.

The first type of debtor is to spend for oneself and repay the loan on schedule, which we call the egoistic production debtor. The second type is to spend for oneself but not repay the loan, which we call the egoistic consumption debtor. The third type is to spend for others but repay the loan on schedule, which we call the altruistic production debtor. The fourth type is to pay for others and not repay the loan, which we call the altruistic consumption debtor.

The emergence of egoistic production debtors first meets their own needs, and at the same time their own production capacity increases, providing commodities for the market and meeting the needs of others. The effective circulation of currency release and withdrawal is a virtuous cycle of monetary issuance. As in the situation of Story 3. The farmer, the masseuse, and the blacksmith all use borrowed money to meet their own needs, while also providing more commodities for others. They are all egoistic production debtors.

The emergence of egoistic consumption debtor does not increase their own productivity, but only consumes social wealth. The release of money only transfers the possession of goods. If the person who sold the commodities to them only holds money, then the economy only gets a boost from the use of money by the debtor. As in story 2, The farmer did not make any external purchases, and the island's economy was only boosted once due to the masseuse's lending and spending. If this part of the money is continuously used, the economy will be boosted again until the money is no longer used or there are no commodities available for trade. At the same time, because this type of debt is ultimately not repaid, the money is left in the market and constitutes excess, which will cause damage to the currency devaluation of all those who hold money in the market, and the wealth corresponding to this part of the loss is enjoyed by the egoistic consumption debtor. We have created a new story 12 to specifically analyze egoistic consumption debtors. In story 2, the farmer received 500 worth of "Z coins" borrowed by the masseuse to pay the blacksmith, and purchased 5 more spades. The wealth on Island Z increased by 5 more spades, but the masseuse did not provide more massages and did not plan to repay the 500 worth borrowed. The money was left in the drawer of the blacksmith and could not be exchanged for the massage they needed. The damage to the blacksmith is exactly the enjoyment and consumption of the masseuse. Although the money released cannot be recycled, it still plays a part in promoting the economy. The masseuse in story 12 belongs to egoistic consumption debtors.

We now create a new story 13 to specifically analyze the altruistic production debtor. We adapt story 2, the masseuse borrowed an additional 500 worth, but she did not use it for herself. Instead, she used the 500 worth to purchase 5 spades from the blacksmith and gave them to the farmer for free. This year, the farmer only produced 1000 kilograms of grain and sold it to the masseuse for 1000 worth. At the same time, he also purchased 10 spades from the blacksmith. The blacksmith produced 15 spades and earned

1500 worth. The masseuse increased production capacity and provided 150 hours of massage to the blacksmith, and received 1500 worth from the blacksmith. At the end of the year, the farmer paid off his debt and received 5 spades from the masseuse as a gift. The blacksmith sold 15 spades, purchased 150 hours of massage, and also paid off his debt. The masseuse provided 150 hours of massage but only received 1000 kilograms of grain. However, she fulfilled her full debt obligations. The output value on Island Z still increased by 5 spades and 50 hours of massage compared to story 2, but the altruistic production debtor suffered losses, because the masseuse provided more labor but did not receive corresponding goods. In this story, the farmer is the one who benefited more with less effort, the farmer enjoyed more goods without incurring debt because the masseuse expended more labor without obtaining corresponding goods. It was the masseuse's timely sacrifice that facilitated the farmer's gain without effort.

We set up a new story 14 to specifically analyze the altruistic consumption debtor. We adapt story 2, the masseuse borrowed an additional 500 worth, but she did not use it for herself. Instead, she used the 500 worth to purchase 5 spades from the blacksmith and gave them to the farmer for free. This year, the farmer only produced 1000 kilograms of grain and sold it to the masseuse for 1000 worth. At the same time, he also purchased 10 spades from the blacksmith. The blacksmith produced 15 spades and earned 1500 worth. The masseuse also provided only 100 hours of massage as in the previous year. At the end of the year, the farmer paid off his debt and received 5 spades from the masseuse as a gift. After paying off his debt, the blacksmith had a savings of 500 worth in his hands, although he did not receive more massage. The masseuse received 1000 kilograms of grain and also provided 100 hours of massage. The output value on Island Z still increased by 5 spades compared to story 2, but the blacksmith held the currency and was unable to exchange it for massage and suffered losses. The farmer is the person who enjoyed more and paid less in this story, while the altruistic consumption debtor masseuse did not be able to repay the 500 worth debt.

In a continuously developing society, money has become a unique commodity, and those who hold money can always purchase other commodities they need. Therefore, the damage caused to the market by those who cannot pay off their debts, whether they enjoy consuming social wealth or not, will not be borne entirely by someone who hold money, but will be shared by all market participants through the overall market currency volume exceeding the overall commodity volume. If it is an egoistic consumption debtor like the masseuse in story 12, then this burden is caused by her own enjoyment and consumption. If it is an altruistic consumption debtor like the masseuse in story 14, then this burden is caused by the enjoyment and consumption of others.

III. Bad Debtors and Final Victims of Bad Debts

As mentioned above, due to the "more enjoyment without output" of the debtor itself or others, if no one makes sacrifices as the altruistic production debtor in time, it will lead to unpayable debts, which is a manifestation of the uneven development of various economic sectors. In order to continuously promote economic development, the only way is to continuously expand debt and stimulate consumption. Debts that cannot be repaid are either written off as bad debts or rolled over indefinitely. Essentially, the debts that are rolled over indefinitely are non-performing loans.

When bad debts and non-performing loans occur, in any case, for the borrower, it is impossible to repay, and for the issuer of currency, the currency is produced out of thin air. Therefore, bad debts and non-performing loans do not have any essential harm to Currency Issuer and the debtor. However, in these two cases, the whole society continues to tolerate people who enjoy more consumption with less output. When the production capacity of the whole society is no longer supplemented, the currency holder will not be able to exchange their own needed commodities or exchange commodities with the same amount as before. The currency holder becomes the actual victim, and the excess currency in his hand corresponds to the commodities that were previously enjoyed and consumed by bad debtors.

For the whole society, every increase in bad debts (defined as debts that cannot be settled) or an increase in money supply should be offset by the production of commodities with an equivalent wealth value. In this way, the holders of money will not be damaged and the economy will be able to develop upwards. Bad debts only reflect that some people are benefiting more and producing less, and if the overall output of society cannot be supplemented, there will be currency depreciation and damage to the holders of money.

At the same time, demand is diverse, and a single demand has an upper limit. Capacity saturation means that the corresponding demand has been fully met. Therefore, improving the overall needed capacity of society is the key to economic development. If the newly added capacity is not demanded by society, this new capacity is excess capacity, and the currency will still depreciate, and those who hold the currency will still be the ultimate victims.

IV. Preferred Debtors and the Realization of Balanced Development

A healthy economy refers to one where the output and consumption of various economic sectors are matched, mutually promoting growth, with demand and supply spiraling upwards. The fundamental manifestation is an increase in the amount of money circulated, an increase in the volume of commodities traded, and at the same time, the absence of non-performing loans and bad loans.

When we issue loans, transactions will increase and the economy will grow, but to achieve fairness and soundness, we also need to consider the debtor's ability to repay in the future. This requires that the debtor we choose has the following characteristics: first, there is demand at that time, and after obtaining the currency, they will trade commodities in other people's hands. Second, they have the ability to provide commodities that others need. Third, they have the ability to innovate and upgrade, and can continue to provide commodities that others need in the future. If there are no second and third characteristics, after the currency is put into the market, it can bring short-term and one-sided economic growth, but the debtor's production capacity is lacking, and it needs the relief and supplement of new production capacity from other entities. Some people have bad debts, while others have supplementary ones. It seems that the overall economy is not damaged and the currency remains stable, but if the debtor has no bad debts, the production capacity of other sectors or future new production capacity will require more Currency Issuance, which will also be reflected in future economic growth. Essentially, non-performing loans and bad loans are consumptions of other sectors or overdrafts of future new production capacity.

When we seek growth without identifying the right debtors, we invest money in outdated production capacity, which is either inefficient or excess, resulting in short-term growth and long-term burden. If the debtor can repay normally, then lending is only an overdraft for the debtor himself. If the debtor cannot repay normally, issuing loans is an overdraft for the future overall economy of society.

The direct consequence of bad debts is that money is trapped in the hands of market entities and cannot complete the recycling cycle according to the expected period. At the same time, commodities that should be provided by debtors cannot be provided normally, resulting in excess money compared to the amounts of commodities. Without the addition of other production capacity, the currency will depreciate.

Based on the analysis of the types of debtors mentioned earlier, we found that when the debtor is egoistic production debtor or altruistic production debtor, no bad debts will be incurred and there will be no overdraft in the market. These two types of debtors are our preferred debtors.

V. The Impact of the Currency Type of Debt on the Economy

We have previously discussed the categories of creditors and debtors for debt. Now let's look at the categories of currencies for debt. There are currently three types of currencies: the 4.0 version of "Contract Currency" issued by the central bank, the 5.0 version of "Deposit Currency" and the 6.0 version of "Loan Currency" issued by commercial banks. When the debtor receives "Contract Currency" and "Loan Currency", the debtor borrows money from Currency Issuer, and its normal repayment or bad debt impact is the situation discussed earlier, where all people holding currency in the market share the losses together. However, when the debtor borrows money from non-commercial entities and receives "Contract Currency" or "Deposit Currency", the situation is different. Because deposits represent that the depositor has already paid for commodities, but the depositor has delayed the enjoyment and retained the currency. If the debtor has bad debts, it is a consumption of past wealth accumulation, and the affected party is not the economy of other sectors or the future economy, but rather the creditors who have borrowed money from them.

VI. Government Debt

The government is an independent legal entity, as well as a member of the social and economic entities. Under the current monetary system, the government is often considered to be the Currency Issuer, and there is a high degree of confusion between the Currency Issuer, and the government. We discuss government debt here based on the mutual independence of Currency Issuer and the government. The government provides public services to the people, maintains people's livelihood and fairness, and is generally considered to have a major responsibility to boost the economy. At the same time, the government is also one of the most important economic entities. Under the current monetary system, the government is also designed as the most important participant in the Currency Issuance and currency regulation process.

As an important economic entity, the government continuously borrows money from the central bank or commercial banks to achieve the release of currency to the market. Like other entities that borrow money from commercial banks, the government needs to sell services and products to recover currency and pay off debts. The government's revenue mainly comes from taxes, service fees, and fines, all of which can be understood as the government's fee for selling public services as a commodity.

Compared to Currency Issuers, governments, like other social entities, consume their own resources and provide products or services to society. As a general entity, in order to achieve balanced economic development, governments should also achieve balance of payments and should not incur bad debts or indefinite debts. However, compared to other entities, governments have obvious particularities. The particularity of governments lies in the fact that a large part of the wealth they consume and the services they provide are for public welfare, which cannot be priced according to the laws of market supply and demand. In order to ensure people's livelihood, the government purchases food for free distribution, and in order to improve transportation conditions, the government invests in building roads for people to use for free. These expenditures and costs are all for the needs of other social entities outside the government. Money is paid out but not recovered. Similarly, the government provides a large number of public management services, and a considerable number of people enjoy this service but do not pay for it.

The government's service charges are targeted; those who receive specific and concrete service items pay for them. Various licenses, permits, and management fees are only targeted at the objects who handle specific business. However, taxes are universal fees under the standard stipulated by law, which are the special arrangements designed to compensate for government public welfare. The rich pay high taxes and the poor pay low taxes. Such asymmetric service fee standards can achieve a balance between government revenue and expenditure and social stability.

The inability of the government to pay off its debts means that the sum of the government's own consumption and external welfare expenses is greater than the income from selling its own services. There are three reasons for this: first, excessive consumption, second, excessive external welfare expenses, and third, insufficient income from selling its own services. Consumption refers to the government's own staff occupying and enjoying commodities, while external welfare expenses refer to directly giving money to others or using money to exchange commodities for others to use without compensation (such as building infrastructure). The income from selling government services includes three factors: service quality, quantity, and pricing. The government with excessive consumption is called an enjoyment-oriented government, The government with excessive external welfare expenses is called a welfare-oriented government, the government with low-quality government services is called a inferior government, the government with low-quantity government services is called a lazy government, the government with low-price government services is called a restrained government. There are five factors contributing to the inability of the government to pay off its debts: first, an enjoyment-oriented government with high consumption, second, a welfare-oriented government with high external welfare expenses, third, a inferior government with poor service quality, fourth, a lazy government with low service quantity, and fifth, a restrained government with low service price. A government that benefits the people is clearly a non-enjoyment, non-inferior, non-lazy, welfare-oriented, and restrained government. When government debt continues to expand, we need to analyze the factors in detail to recognize who bears the loss and who benefits.

Chapter 12 International Monetary Relations

A country is a group of market entities within a certain scope. The relationship between countries is essentially the relationship between the groups of entities. Transactions within each group of entities are conducted using a specific currency, while transactions between groups are conducted through currency exchange. When all groups trade with each other using the currency issued by a specific group, that group will enjoy special privileges. If economic integration and fairness are fully achieved, and there are no laws, policies, or forces that deliberately protect the interests of a certain group, and countries engage in equal transactions with each other., then there will be no financial exploitation.

I. The More Other Countries' Reserves of Their Own Currencies, the More Wealth They Possess in Other Countries

The story 15 now is different from the story 2. The output value of Island Z remained at 3000, which meant 100 hours of massage, 1000 kilograms of grain, and 10 spades. The farmer did not produce an additional 500 kilograms of grain. The masseuse still borrowed 500 worth from the coiners, but used this 500 to purchase 500 kilograms of grain from a farmer on another small island called Island Y. The 500 worth "Z coins" were left in the drawer of the farmer on Island Y. The output value of Island Z did not change, but the person on the Island occupied an additional 500 kilograms of grain.

Another example is story 16, which is similar. After story 2, the output value of Island Z remained at 3000 needs, which is 100 hours of massage, 1000 kilograms of grain, and 10 spades. The farmer used the remaining 500 worth "Z coins" to purchase 5 spades from the blacksmith on island Y. The 500 worth "Z coin" remained in the drawer of the blacksmith on island Y. The output value of Island Z did not change, but the person on the Island occupied 5 more spades. Island Y had the foreign exchange reserves of Island Z and was happy about its trade surplus. Island Z occupied more commodities and at the same time, there was an unpayable debt of 500 worth under the name of the masseuse on the white wallboard of the coiner. In the above two stories, the output value of Island Z was 3000 needs, but it occupied 3500 needs of wealth. The extra 500 needs of grain was exchanged for 500 worth of "Z coins".

The currency of each country is guaranteed by law to be used for transactions within the scope of its own national violence. When the purchasing power of the currency, that is, the wealth value of the currency, is stable, the amount of currency used should correspond to the amounts of commodities traded. When a country's currency can be accepted by foreign commodity providers, the central bank of that country can lend more currency than is needed for domestic commodity transactions to its domestic entities, and then the debtor can use the borrowed currency to exchange for foreign commodities and leave the currency abroad. Since the central bank can only lend currency to domestic entities, it can be inferred that the more currency left abroad, the greater the amounts of foreign commodities possessed by domestic entities. At the same time, since each currency left in the market corresponds to a liability that has not been repaid on the central bank's ledger book of domestic entities, it can be understood that leaving more currency abroad means that there is more liability that has not been settled on the domestic side, and there is more asset on the asset side of the currency Issuer's balance sheet. Therefore, the increase in the net value of the country's total debt is the cost of actually occupying the wealth of other countries. Modern monetary theory also believes that from the perspective of resources rather than currency, imports are beneficial, and trade deficits are the net inflow of wealth into the importing country.

Fair economic exchanges domestic and abroad should be reciprocal trade, that is, foreign exchange holders outside the country issuing the foreign exchange should be able to exchange their foreign exchange for commodities from the country issuing the foreign exchange, thus satisfying the demand of the foreign exchange holder and achieving the return of the currency of the country issuing the foreign exchange. Corresponding to the currency exporting country, there is a country that retains foreign currency. If a country holds a large amount of foreign exchange reserves, it indicates that it has exported a corresponding amount of commodities abroad, indicating that the labor achievements of its people have been largely occupied by foreign countries.

II. Exchange Rates and Their Impact on Currencies

The wealth value of a currency lies in its exchangeability, The price of other goods is the ratio between the practical value of these goods and the exchange value of money, while the price of money is the ratio between the exchange values of different currencies. This ratio is known as the exchange rate. In determining the exchange rate of money, the range of use of money and its purchasing power are important factors considered by people. When the issuer of a currency behind it gives people hope and confidence, when a currency can purchase a wide variety of goods and service, and when a currency can be used in a larger range, people are more willing to hold this currency. The popularity of a currency will increase its exchange rate accordingly.

There is a saying that the devaluation of a country's currency is beneficial to the country's exports, so currency devaluation is beneficial. In fact, this statement is inaccurate and one-sided. For the overall benefits and disadvantages of a country, it ultimately depends on how much assets it possesses. The devaluation of a country's currency can indeed bring about an increase in the price competitiveness of its products in the international market and an overall increase in exports.

When the exchange rate of a country's currency falls, to obtain an equivalent amount of foreign currency, this country must sell more domestic assets to foreign countries. However, the acquired foreign currency can only purchase the same quantity of foreign assets. This means that ultimately, more domestic assets are exchanged for fewer foreign assets, which is undoubtedly a loss for the country.

The claim of benefit is only relative to situations where there is an excess production capacity of domestic products that cannot be absorbed within the domestic market. For exporting enterprises, the depreciation of the domestic currency can enhance the purchasing motivation of foreign buyers, leading to increased sales volumes. The foreign currency earned can be brought back to the domestic market to exchange for the domestic currency. This is equivalent to maintaining the price of their products in terms of the domestic currency while significantly increasing sales volume, thereby boosting revenue. The domestic currency obtained through foreign exchange trading within the domestic market allows exporters to fully reap the benefits of increased sales, while the impact of exchange rates on the purchasing power of the domestic currency in the domestic market is shared by all nationals. However, this benefit for exporting enterprises, if considered solely from domestic consumption, is indeed tangible. But such benefits are built upon the overall loss of the domestic populace. Due to the influx of foreign currency, the export volume of domestic commodities has increased. At the same time, this influx of foreign currency has led to an increase in the domestic currency in the local market without a corresponding inflow of commodities, thereby weakening the overall purchasing power of the domestic currency.

III. The Essence of Trade War

The fundamental function of currency is to facilitate transactions. Transactions between countries are international trade. The currency issued by a country is naturally assumed to be obtainable by selling one's own produced commodities to that country. At the same time, people should also can exchange the currency they have earned for the goods they need from that country. This is an inevitable requirement for fair trade. When a country issues a decree prohibiting some other countries from using their own currency to purchase their own goods, it is actually a deprivation of the legal right to use the currency. Whether the reason given is national security or the interests of the people, if it is not a uniform action for all other countries, such a decree is unreasonable and violates the spirit of contract. It is a harm to the interests of the other countries. Other countries use their own produced goods to exchange for the country's currency, but this currency cannot purchase specific goods in this country. This is naked national discrimination, which is equivalent to placing the labor of its own people above that of other people. It is a serious unequal unilateral treaty.

When a country enacts laws to impose tariffs on goods from specific countries, it is also a form of economic discrimination. Taxation is understood as a government public service fee, and tariffs are generally paid by importers, meaning that the importer in the importing country bears the responsibility

174

for paying tariffs. Imposing tariffs means that the same service is charged at a higher service fee to buyers of goods from specific countries. The target of the fee is domestic buyers, which can seriously reduce their willingness to purchase and thus reduce the export of goods from the specific countries.

The export ban issued by a country is to restrict the power of foreign entities to use its currency, while an import tax is a high fee for domestic entities to use their own currencies to purchase goods from other countries. In international relations, there is no coercive force to ensure the principle of fairness or the implementation of international treaties. Countries are still under the law of the jungle, where the strong prey on the weak. It is common for one country to exploit others by taking advantage of its own advantages. Faced with a powerful country, other countries can only strive for equal treatment through their own strength, which includes hard power such as technology and military, as well as soft power such as politics, culture, rule of law.

If we consider the global economy as a whole, the improvement of this whole economy also depends on the balanced development of various economic sectors. High-end industries and low-end industries are interdependent and mutually supply each other, taking what they need respectively. This is a blessing for both sides, but due to political, cultural and other non-economic factors, free trade is undermined by non-market factors, and technological blockade means that products representing high-end industries or advanced production capacity are no longer supplied to some countries. Trade barriers mean that the demand market is no longer open to products representing low-end production capacity. This is a deliberate disruption of supply and demand matching, an interruption of the virtuous cycle of the economy, and an artificial imbalance in the world economy that undermines the global economy as a whole. It should be opposed and resisted by rational economic people.

IV. The Creation and Expansion of the U.S. national debt

The US Treasury bond has been expanding in size and can be considered to have been overdue for many times, but it is maintained by continuously raising the upper limit and borrowing new money to repay old money. So, who benefits and who suffers in this infinite game of currency? How will this game of currency end? Due to the strength and advanced nature of the United States, the US dollar is widely accepted worldwide. The amount of US dollar reserves outside the United States corresponds to the amount of US dollar liabilities within the country. As mentioned in the previous chapter on currency types, there are three types of currency in circulation today: Contract Currency, Deposit Currency, and Loan Currency. If foreign reserves are in the form of US dollar banknotes or Deposit Currency, then this portion of loans is issued by the Federal Reserve System. If it is Loan Currency, then this

CURRENCY 6.0: The Essence, Principles and Reconstruction of Money

portion of loans is issued by commercial banks. Regardless of who issues them, there is a corresponding liability. Since the Federal Reserve System can only lend to domestic entities in the United States, while commercial banks can issue loans to foreign entities, it can be inferred that, aside from foreign currency reserves obtained through loans from foreign entities to commercial banks, the rest of the reserves outside the United States are derived from domestic entities borrowing from the Federal Reserve or commercial banks. The more dollars (including Contract Currency, Deposit Currency, and Loan Currency) are held abroad, the greater the US dollar debt. Even if the foreign reserves are returned to the United States, as long as they are not used to reduce loans from the Federal Reserve System and commercial banks but instead used as deposits, then the US dollar debt will not decrease. Due to the issuance of currency being solely through lending, the dollars obtained by people worldwide in exchange for commodities always correspond to liabilities owed to the Federal Reserve and commercial banks. This fundamentally ensures that there are always entities bearing the expanding US dollar debt. The US government, as a significant domestic user of the dollar, becomes the primary borrower and debtor as the dollar continuously flows outward.

The U.S. national debt is constantly expanding, and Congress has repeatedly raised the debt ceiling to prevent default. Some people simply divide the total amount of national debt by the U.S. population to calculate the average debt per American. This is completely nonsense. National debt is the liability of the U.S. government, and there is no direct legal responsibility between the U.S. government and the American people. Instead, let's analyze the reasons for the continuous expansion of the U.S. government's liabilities. Due to the democratic politics, sound rule of law, and strict supervision in the United States, it can be seen that the U.S. government belongs to the non-enjoyment, welfare-oriented, non-inferior, non-lazy, and restrained type of government. The debt raised by the U.S. federal government is not used for its own enjoyment, but is given to others. Others use the obtained currency to purchase commodities from the international market, and those who receive currency or commodities from the government are the ultimate beneficiaries. According to our previous classification of debtor types, the U.S. government belongs to the altruistic consumption debtor, and its expansion of liabilities represents the expansion of the quantity of commodities enjoyed by the American people, which is beneficial to its own people.

Compared to the US government debt, the debt of some Latin American countries' central governments and local governments at all levels has been increasing, especially the local government debt and the debt of local government platforms, which have reached an unrecoverable level. Some have even defaulted multiple times. The five factors mentioned above that expand government debt are also applicable. In these countries, the common

176

consensus is that government personnel enjoy social resources, government services are of low quality, and government services are highly charged. At the same time, some governments provide a large number of services and infrastructure, which are the main factors that increase government debt. So, these governments can be considered as enjoyment, welfare-oriented, inferior, lazy, and non-restrained type of government. If they want to reduce the scale of debt, they need to reduce public service expenditure, improve service quality, increase service quantity, reduce low-return infrastructure construction, and raise tax and fee standards. These measures are all debtors can refer to.

If the US government does not increase taxes, fees, and fines, its debt will continue to expand and its ceiling will continue to rise, while Americans use the government's borrowed money to purchase and enjoy around the world. There are two ways for the US government to expand its debt: one is to borrow from the Federal Reserve System and commercial banks, which will lead to an increase in the lender's balance sheet and subsequently result in inflation. The other is to borrow from other entities that already hold US dollars, most typically from other governments. These dollars are exchanged for commodities by other countries.

The government of the creditor country exchanges the commodities produced by the hard work of its people for dollars, which initially are borrowed by the US government, enterprises, and individuals with credit from the Federal Reserve System or commercial banks in the United States. The creditor country lends the dollars it has exchanged to the US government, thereby holding US Treasury bonds. It is equivalent to saying that the creditor country exchanges real goods or service for the credit of the United States, and then uses this credit of this country to obtain the credit of the US government once again. It can be seen that Americans have used their credit to the extreme.

V. Development and Endgame of U.S. Treasury Bond

If the debt scale of the US federal government is to be reduced or maintained stable, the United States should increase domestic output value, break trade barriers and technological blockades, and increase government revenue, so that international currencies can complete circulation, international economy can achieve balance, and world trade can achieve fairness. For the U.S. government, in the ways of quickly selling commodities, withdrawing US dollars, and paying off debts, provoking wars and creating demand for arms and high-tech products in other countries may be the fastest way to increase exports. This point should be alarming and resisted by people all over the world.

If the debt scale of the US federal government continues to expand, there may be five possible outcomes. First, the international use of the US dollar continues to expand, and Americans continue to enjoy it. As the world's production capacity continues to increase and people continue to use the US dollar without reducing or even expanding it, the expansion of the US government's debt will not harm the interests of Americans. Americans only exchange printed paper for commodities from the world and then record the debt under the name of the federal government. Second, the US dollar declines and holders of US dollars suffer losses. When the world's production capacity is insufficient or countries reduce or even stop using the US dollar, the US dollar will depreciate and even become worthless. Holders of US dollars will suffer losses, and the US will sell a small amount of commodities to exchange for US dollars after the devaluation of the US dollar and pay off its debts. Third, the federal government declines and the debt is cleared. When Congress no longer allows the government to borrow money, no one will lend money to the government, including the Federal Reserve System and commercial banks. Then the federal government will declare default or even bankruptcy, and the federal government will announce that it will no longer pay off debts to all creditors. Fourth, the federal government declares that it will no longer pay off debts to individual countries or specific creditors through war means or using various excuses. Fifth, it reaches a debt restructuring agreement with various creditors, and each debtor is forced to reduce their claims.

For the Federal Reserve System, the US government, and holders of US government debt, each has their own preferences. The Federal Reserve System and the US government are essentially one and the same, or have a high degree of correlation. They will first choose the first option, then the fourth, followed by the fifth, then the second, and finally the third. Governments or entities holding US government debt will first choose the first option, then the second, followed by the fifth, then the third, and will strive to avoid the fourth option.

VI. The Essence of the IMF's Ordinary and Special Drawing Rights

As we have analyzed in the previous text, the 2.0 version of Receipt Currency issued by banknote merchants and the 5.0 version of Deposit Currency issued by commercial banks are essentially the vouchers of the previous version of currency. Let's review the process of 2.0 version of Receipt Currency and 5.0 version of Deposit Currency. Merchants deposited Material Currency into their own warehouses and issued their own storage vouchers for the providers of Material Currency. Commercial banks deposited the Contract Currency issued by the central bank into their own warehouses and issued their own bank deposit certificates for the providers of cash. People use storage vouchers and deposit certificates to conduct transactions in the market. We can infer that if an international organization across

178

countries deposits gold or currencies issued by various countries into its own warehouses and issues its own vouchers for the governments of countries providing gold and currencies, what would happen? Such vouchers have credit because of the support of gold and currencies issued by various countries, and it is completely logical and reasonable for people to accept and use this voucher for transactions. Therefore, this voucher becomes the international version of 5.0 version of Deposit Currency.

Now, let's analyze the ordinary drawing rights (ODR) of the International Monetary Fund (IMF). When a country joins the International Monetary Fund (IMF), A certain amount of funds must be paid to the organization in accordance with a set quota. According to IMF regulations, 25% of the subscribed quota must be paid in gold or convertible currencies, and the remaining 75% must be paid in domestic currency. When a member country experiences difficulties in its balance of payments, it has the right to apply to the IMF for withdrawing convertible currencies in the form of collateral in domestic currency. The amounts of withdrawals is divided into five tiers, with each tier representing 25%. The application conditions are strictly tiered, with the first tier being the most relaxed, generally allowing withdrawals as long as an application is made. The remaining four tiers are credit withdrawal rights.

The underlying logic is that the IMF receives gold or currency deposits from countries, providing them with " the ordinary drawing rights (ODR)" that can be used to claim currency transactions with other countries and conduct international transactions. Although the "ODR" are not displayed in paper currency, their essence and principles are completely consistent with the 3.0 version of Receipt Currency and the 5.0 version of Deposit Currency we have analyzed. We can regard this "ODR" as a prototype of a new type of 3.0 version Receipt Currency and 5.0 version Deposit Currency. When the use of the "ODR" is within the subscribed gold quota, it is a certificate of gold and essentially a 3.0 version Receipt Currency. When it exceeds the gold quota, it is a certificate of convertible currency or domestic currency and essentially a 5.0 version Deposit Currency. This new type of currency, named "ODR", replaces the gold and currencies provided by countries and can be used for international transactions, it can be regarded as a composite of Receipt Currency and Deposit Currency, but the use of this new currency is strictly constrained.

Let's see if the IMF's Special Drawing Rights (SDR) also fits our logic of the evolution and upgrading of six versions of currencies. Unlike ordinary drawing rights, which are widely available to all IMF member countries, SDR is only available to a select few countries and is more freely used. According to resolutions 6631 and 6708 adopted by the IMF Executive Board in 1980, the SDR basket will be composed of the currencies of the five fund member countries with the highest international export trade and service trade volume as of January 1, 1986. It will be adjusted every five years thereafter, and the five currencies will be designated as freely usable currencies. On May 11, 2022, the IMF Executive Board completed the five-yearly review of the valuation of the SDR, maintaining the current composition of the SDR basket currency unchanged, which is still composed of the US dollar, euro, renminbi, yen, and pound sterling, and increasing the weight of the renminbi from 10.92% to 12.28%. Five specific countries deposit their national currencies into the IMF in accordance with a certain proportion, in exchange for Special Drawing Rights of equivalent value provided by the IMF. This SDR can be applied to the IMF to exchange freely usable foreign exchange with other participating countries, or it can be exchanged for equivalent foreign exchange that is not freely usable by other participating countries through agreements with them. It can also be used for other related financial services between fund member countries and non-member countries upon approval by the IMF, including but not limited to forward trade payments, specific loans, international finance Settlement and international financial business margin, fund interest, dividend payments, grants, etc. If the "ODR" is a prototype of a new 5.0 version of Deposit Currency or a composite of Receipt Currency and Deposit Currency, then the " SDR" is already a complete new 5.0 version of Deposit Currency, which no longer requires any gold quota and is entirely based on "freely usable foreign exchange". However, this new "Deposit Currency" is not called currency and is only used by a few governments.

Along the historical path of currency evolution, we have reason to expect the expansion and optimization of the IMF's "ordinary drawing rights" and "special drawing rights", and also have reason to look forward to the birth of the international version 6.0 Loan Currency, expecting the creation of an international currency that can eliminate the plundering and harvesting between powerful and weak countries through currency. We will discuss this in detail in the chapter "Principles and Reconstruction of the Equal Rights Monetary system".

Chapter 13: The Path of the U.S. as Financial Superpower and Its Weaknesses

The fundamental significance of a country's prosperity lies in the fact that its citizens' needs can be largely satisfied, that is, citizens can obtain sufficient goods or service. Under an equal financial system and international trade system, a country's prosperity lies in its strong production capacity, especially the ability to produce goods or service that other countries cannot produce, in exchange for a large amount of other countries' products and natural resources. Financial power has two meanings. First, financial services benefit the real economy, that is, currency guarantees transactions, allowing the country to increase its production capacity. Second, financial plunder, that is, currency exchanges for commodities, allowing the country to exchange products it needs from other countries through currency issued on credit.

I. The US Dollar Has Become an International Common Commodity, which is the First Wave of Harvesting the World by the United States

As we said before, currency is a commodity within its circulation range. When a country's currency circulates only within the country, no matter how the commodities and currencies circulate among the people, the overall wealth of the country does not increase or decrease due to the currency. However, when the currency is issued only for domestic borrowing and used to purchase commodities, then flows out of the country, is retained by other countries, commodities imported and flowing into the domestic market are purely an increase in wealth.

The United States has established the role of the dollar with its advantages in gold, oil, and strong political, cultural, technological, military, and other strengths. The dollar is widely saved and used by other countries. As long as one more dollar stays outside the United States, it is equivalent to the United States having an extra free possession of foreign commodities worth one dollar. The cost is that the central bank's asset side has one more dollar of claims, and a certain social entity in The United States has one more dollar of debt.

When people around the world no longer doubt the use value of the dollar, the dollar is a commodity, just like gold. The United States has always protested against China's huge trade surplus, but in fact, the country that has actually benefited is crying foul for itself. The real beneficiary is the United States, while China is harmed. What China sends to the United States is goods that can be actually enjoyed, which are the fruits of labor. The retained dollars are just paper issued by the United States based on the credit of domestic social entities. Americans' protests are either due to ignorance or deliberate attempts to mislead.

II. Using Fewer US Dollars to Exchange Assets of Other Countries is the Second Wave of Harvesting the World by the United States

A country's commodities and resources are usually priced in its own currency. When Americans purchase with US dollars, the price first needs to be converted into dollars using the exchange rate between the country's currency and the dollar before the transaction can proceed. When the exchange rate between the dollar and the country's currency remains unchanged, as well as the price of the country's assets denominated in its own currency, an equal amount of dollars can exchange for an unchanged amount of the country's assets. When the dollar exchange rate rises or the price of the country's assets denominated in its own currency decreases, the same amount of dollars can exchange for more assets. The United States has already achieved costless wealth acquisition by exchanging dollars for foreign assets, but it is not satisfied with this, they also want to exchange fewer dollars for more foreign assets. The United States employs every means to strengthen the dollar while creating crises in other countries, causing the price of foreign assets denominated in those countries' currencies to fall. When reaching an extreme, it then buys a large amount of assets with dollars to achieve a greater degree of wealth plundering, which is a disaster for other countries.

The most common human nature is to seek profit and avoid harm. America's monetary plunder perfectly demonstrates the principle from "The Art of War" by Sun Tzu: "To cause the enemy to come of his own accord, offer him advantage; to prevent his coming, show him disadvantage." A common tactic used by the United States is to guide global dollar to flow back to the United States, through interest rate hikes. Since the dollar plays the role of a world currency, countries issue their currencies pegged to the dollar and use dollar reserves as a credit endorsement. When dollars flow back to the United States, the domestic currencies of other countries are repatriated to their issuers' systems through exchanging for dollars, causing liquidity shortages in these countries' markets. Currency becomes precious for market transactions, naturally leading to a significant drop in asset prices. If the United States finds that monetary, economic, and market means are not effective enough, it will utilize cultural, political, and military means to create various destabilizing factors, causing turmoil in target countries and thereby forcing dollars to flee those countries. The strategy of "tempting with benefits, threatening with disasters" has led to a dual suppression of the target country's currency and asset prices, creating a golden opportunity for Americans to harvest more wealth from other countries using the US dollar.

For example, in recent years, the Turkish lira's exchange rate against the dollar has continued to decline, falling by about 44% in 2021, about 30% in 2022, and nearly 50% in 2023. An American multinational company, originally interested in the Turkish market, had not made large-scale investments due to the relatively high cost of investment priced in dollars when the lira's exchange rate was more stable. However, as the lira's exchange rate fell, this American company found that acquiring certain Turkish assets, such as factories, real estate, or corporate equity, with dollars became exceptionally cost-effective. In 2023, the amount of dollars needed to acquire the same assets was only one-fifth of what it was three years ago.

III. The US Government's Borrowing from Foreign Countries is the Third Wave of Harvesting the World by the United States

If we say that the outflow of dollars is the first deprivation by the United States from other countries, namely exchanging dollars for assets, then completing low-cost acquisitions through exchange rate manipulation and undermining the pricing of foreign assets is the second deprivation. The U.S. government's borrowing from other countries constitutes the third deprivation.

As previously mentioned, the endorsement of currency comes from the borrower's promise to obtain loans from the issuer of the currency. People hold currency based on their belief in the issuer's scrutiny and selection of borrowers. People have placed their faith in the currency issuers' confidence in borrowers. In the case of the dollar, the Federal Reserve believes that the U.S. government will be able to provide services in exchange for dollars to repay its debts, thereby purchasing U.S. Treasury bonds and completing the issuance of dollars. Foreign governments and individuals trust the professionalism and responsibility of the Federal Reserve, as well as the U.S. government's commitment to fulfill its promises to provide services and repay debts. Also, given the widespread international acceptance of the dollar, they begin to exchange goods for dollars and accumulate these as foreign exchange reserves, hoping that these reserves can be used to purchase needed commodities from the United States or other countries in the future.

However, the U.S. government does not have the capacity to fully repay all its debts to the Federal Reserve on schedule. Under such circumstances, it can only expand its debt by either continuing to borrow from the Federal Reserve or borrowing from other holders of dollars. When choosing the latter, it essentially amounts to selling its own credit again, promising to repay principal and interest on time in the future.

Those who buy U.S. Treasury bonds also believe that the U.S. government has the ability to earn dollars and repay principal and interest on time. Few people consider that most of the dollars themselves stem from the credit of the United States, or more accurately, from the credit of the debtors of the Federal Reserve, including the U.S. government. Holders of dollars are now lending them back to the U.S. government based on its credit, essentially placing trust in a defaulter once again.

It must be said, this is the ultimate operation of its own credit by the U.S. government, and also a more profound means by which the U.S. government exploits its advantages to deprive the resources of the world.

IV. If the U.S. Government Announces the Abolition of Debt, this will be the Fourth Wave of Harvesting the World by the United States

When the Federal Reserve purchases U.S. Treasury bonds and thereby issues dollars, it hopes that the U.S. government can provide services as expected and repay its debts. This is the first expectation for the U.S. government and the first use of its credit.

When foreign governments conduct foreign exchange reserves, they hope to use these reserves to purchase commodities and resources from the United States in the future. This is the second expectation for the U.S. government, and its credit is amplified and extended. When foreign governments use their own foreign exchange reserves to buy U.S. Treasury bonds, this expectation falls back to the second line, and a third expectation for the U.S. government emerges: that the U.S. government can raise funds on time to pay off its principal and interest, further amplifying and extending its credit for the second time.

When the U.S. government will be truly unable to repay its debts, it can only declare default, and it is highly likely that it will do so against specific creditors. At this point, all three expectations of these individual creditors will be shattered, and the government's credit will be completely dismantled. However, the actual loss still will fall on these creditors, as the U.S. government, through the use of its own credit, has completely deprived these creditors.

This breach of trust will not mean the complete collapse of U.S. credit or the credibility of the dollar. The Americans will utilize their comprehensive advantages in politics, culture, science and technology, and military to proclaim to the world that the reason for this breach of trust lies not with themselves but with the creditors, thus validating the survival of the fittest in a social Darwinist context. Such an outcome may be inevitable or is already advancing, and relevant creditor nations should be sufficiently vigilant.

V. Suppressing the Side Effects of Monetary Policy through Strong Productivity

Whether it is to acquire assets from other countries at low prices or to prevent economic overheating, when the United States raises interest rates, side effects such as reduced loans, increased savings, high debt costs, decreased investment, increased pressure on banks, and reduced consumption will also occur. In general, this means that the economy is suppressed, which can be reflected through indicators such as unemployment rate and per capita income.

However, as mentioned earlier, the root of economic growth lies in production. For the growth of production capacity, money is just one aspect, the growth more depends on non-monetary factors like the rule of law environment, education level, and scientific and technological innovation capabilities. The United States has significant advantages in these areas. It is particularly worth mentioning that the non-debt financing ability of the industrial sector is less affected by interest rate hikes. The United States has a developed capital market, and high-quality enterprises can easily obtain direct financing, effectively avoiding the impact of interest rate hikes on industrial investment.

The United States provides ample momentum for economic growth through advanced productivity, leaving a huge space for monetary policy, allowing it to better harvest other countries through the monetary scissor difference and benefit its own country. This level of proficiency in both industry and finance truly belongs to unique skills, and double-acting play of Americans in industry and finance is not something other countries can easily imitate.

It should be pointed out that the progress of technology is limited and difficult. The support of the United States' advanced productivity for monetary policy is also limited. An uncontrolled predatory monetary policy will inevitably break through the limit of the comprehensive national strength of the United States, eventually causing unavoidable harm to the economy of the United States itself.

VI. New Dilemma and Solutions of the US Dollar

Under the Bretton Woods system, the United States faced the "Triffin dilemma", which meant that the collapse of the Bretton Woods system was only a matter of time. Today, the US dollar is no longer linked to gold, but it faces new challenges. Under the current monetary system, in order to maintain the world currency status of the US dollar, it is necessary to export a large amount of net currency and maintain a long-term international trade deficit in the United States. The currency outflow from the long-term trade deficit is through domestic entities, especially the US government, borrowing from the Federal Reserve System. This will inevitably lead to the continuous expansion of domestic debt, especially the U.S. Government Debt. The continuous expansion of debt is a disguised default. Default will cause damage to the credit of the US government and even the United States. When the US dollar can only be issued through borrowing from the US government and domestic entities, the credit of the US dollar is directly linked to the credit of the US government and the United States. The credit damage of the US government and the United States will lead to the loss of the world currency status of the US dollar. To ensure the credit of the US government, it is necessary to ensure that the US government debt does not default, and it is necessary for the United States to achieve a trade surplus. This will make it impossible for the US dollar to be retained abroad in large quantities and play its role as a world currency. The credit of the US government and the US nation is both the driving force and the pulling force of the US internationalization.

The new dollar dilemma is that the US national credit not being damaged and the internationalization of the US dollar cannot be achieved simultaneously. Specifically, the US cannot achieve both trade surplus and trade deficit at the same time. The new dollar dilemma is a variant of the Triffin Dilemma, which essentially means that the use of the US dollar and the gold content of the US dollar cannot be balanced. It is a contradiction between quantity and quality. In the era of the US dollar pegged to gold, the connotation of the US dollar is gold. The root cause of the Triffin Dilemma lies in the fact that the gold reserves of the United States and even the world

185

are not sufficient to support massive international trade volume. In the era of Credit Currency, credit replaces gold, and people no longer hope to exchange enough gold for the US dollar. Instead, they hope to exchange enough international commodities for the US dollar. The root cause of the new dollar dilemma lies in the fact that the national credit of the United States alone is not sufficient to support massive international trade volume. There are two types of coercive force in the world: one is the internal coercive force of human beings, which is voluntary, and the other is external coercive force, which is violence. The US dollar established a voluntary acceptance and use of the US dollar through its pegging to gold and the production capacity of the United States. Subsequently, multiple means such as military and diplomatic measures are used to maintain the purchasing power of the US dollar for oil and other bulk commodities. However, with the further expansion of international trade volume, the production capacity of the United States alone is not sufficient to support the massive demand for issuing the US dollar. The purchasing power maintained by violence will eventually be abandoned by human beings. If the US dollar does not change its current issuance path and method, its world currency path will inevitably end.

The unnecessary and unreasonable artificial restrictions on the pegging of the US dollar to gold have been removed, but the restrictions on the issuance of US dollars that loans from the Federal Reserve and U.S. commercial banks, that is, the issuance of dollars, primarily target the U.S. government and domestic entities still exists. This is also an unnecessary and unreasonable artificial restriction, and it is also the root cause of the new US dollar dilemma. Since the emergence of credit currencies, the creation of currencies has evolved from being centered on Currency Issuer to being centered on the borrower. The credit of the currency is determined by the credit of the borrower. If the US dollar is to truly assume the responsibility of being the world's currency, it is necessary for the Federal Reserve System and US commercial banks to break the traditional path of only issuing loans to domestic entities, especially the US government, and expand the loan targets to various governments and non-governmental economic entities around the world. At that time, the Federal Reserve System will become a global lender and will also become a global central bank. The US dollar will become a true world currency. For the United States, this move will completely solve the US dollar dilemma and achieve a balance between "the use of US dollars and the gold content of US dollars", at the cost of giving up the privilege of using the US dollars borrowed by domestic entities to "free" exchange for commodities from other countries.

VII. Weaknesses of the U.S. Economy

The combination of real and virtual aspects in American industry and finance, along with its comprehensive strength, forms the foundation of its global dominance. However, the U.S. economy also has its vulnerabilities. Politics is the foundation of the economy, and the root cause of economic weaknesses also lies in politics. The strength of the United States stems from its democratic politics, which brings the country extensive freedom, full people's rights, a prosperous market economy, generous social welfare, and a solid international reputation. It can be said that the root cause of American hegemony lies in democracy. According to the Chinese philosophy of "I Ching" and "Tao Te Ching", for every positive, there is a negative, high democracy enables citizens to enjoy high welfare, leading to excessive enjoyment. In the case of some citizens with low output but high consumption, there are only two ways to maintain it: one is high domestic taxation, which involves the deprivation of citizens with high productivity, but it is limited by its democratic system. The other is to engage in hegemony abroad, which involves depriving foreign people of their output. Apart from war, the only way to deprive foreign people is through the aforementioned financial means. Currently, the issuance of currency is mostly through government borrowing, which leads to the continuous expansion of government debt. This is precisely the reality that the US debt ceiling is constantly being raised.

Under the current monetary system, it is impossible for the US government to achieve a reduction in debt and a virtuous cycle. The continuous expansion is its destiny. This is where the weakness of the U.S. economy lies. The fundamental reason is not the incompetence, inaction or high consumption of the US government. There are two fundamental reasons. First, the internationalized US dollar is stored outside the United States in large quantities, while the issuance of the US dollar mainly faces domestic entities in the United States. The corresponding liabilities are inevitably recorded under the name of domestic entities in the United States. This is the unscientific and uneven nature of the Currency Issuance system. We will explain this in detail in the chapter "Structural Imbalance in Money Supply" of Chapter 15 "Major Issues in Current Currency". Second, the high consumption and low output of American citizens are sheltered by the welfare of the US government, and the resulting debt is ultimately mainly recorded under the name of the US government.

If no institutional reforms are made to the issuance of the dollar, the potential outcomes resulting from this vulnerability in the U.S. economy have already been analyzed in Chapter 12, "International Monetary Relations," Section 5, " Development and Endgame of U.S. Treasury Bond " .For the US dollar system or the United States as a whole, to solve this problem, it is necessary to face the reality that the current monetary system is unfair, unbalanced, and unreasonable in terms of the target of Currency Issuance, and to extend the target of Currency Issuance to all social entities, rather than mainly relying on the central bank to issue currency to the government and commercial banks to issue currency to high-quality customers. This has actually been practiced and verified in the quantitative easing monetary policy implemented by the Federal Reserve System in recent years. However, this practice is merely a passive act of exploration, because there was no solid theoretical foundation and logical reasoning before implementation. The United States also held an exploratory and tentative attitude before implementation. Through our analysis, we found that this is completely appropriate to implement, because it conforms to scientific principles and has achieved great success. As a world currency, the US dollar should also face all foreign entities for Currency Issuance, that is, allowing international economic entities to directly borrow from the Federal Reserve System to obtain US dollars, so as to effectively reduce the debt of domestic entities, especially the US government. On this point, we have already elaborated in detail in the previous section of this chapter, " New Dilemma and Solutions of the US Dollar "

Of course, broad credit does not mean that the creditworthiness of the credit object can be ignored. If the entities that obtain Currency Issuance do not provide production capacity as promised, it will cause monetary excess. This point of view has been analyzed by us through the previous text. For those social groups with insufficient production capacity, from the perspective of fairness and justice, they should not enjoy a too good life at all. Under the American democratic system, the widespread phenomenon of low output and high consumption among the general public is an unreasonable social status quo that should be corrected, otherwise the United States will eventually be undermined by democracy.

For vulnerable groups in society, the government should provide basic public services and livelihood protection, and there is no reason or possibility to require them to provide corresponding productivity. This burden should be solved by the government through taxation, so as to achieve the assistance of those with strong abilities to those with weak abilities. This is a manifestation of human sociality.

For governments outside the United States, if they want to gain an advantage in competition with the United States, they need to focus on attacking its weaknesses before it overcome its own weaknesses. The key to competing financially with the United States lies in formulating and implementing strategies in response to the "four waves of harvesting" by the United States mentioned earlier. These strategies include preventing targeted defaults by the United States, avoiding excessive borrowing from the U.S. government, maintaining domestic asset prices, stabilizing the currency exchange rate, reducing dependence on dollar reserves, and ultimately breaking the universal commodity status of the dollar in the world. Undoubtedly, this is a difficult and lengthy process. Before taking proactive measures, it is essential to avoid one's own failure, as stated in "The Art of

War," "First make yourself invincible and then wait for opportunities to defeat the enemy. Invincibility depends on oneself; victory depends on the enemy." We will discuss this in the section " The State should Ensure Currency Independence and Stability " in the next chapter " Strategies for Various Entities Under the Current Monetary Mechanism ".

Chapter 14: Strategies for Various Entities Under the Current Monetary System

The current monetary system worldwide has evolved through continuous practice by people, based on experience rather than rationality. The products of experience inevitably lead to a pattern of interest competition, where the vested interests have absolute say and meticulously safeguard and strive for maximizing their own interests. However, human civilization is constantly progressing, with more rationality being incorporated into our reform of social systems to improve the inherent flaws of experiential products and avoid the harm that mere interest-driven actions bring to human society. Survival of the fittest, natural selection. For a specific entity, whether it's a nation, a government, or an individual. it should respect history and reality, in imperfect rules and unreasonable systems, people can only survive and develop better by adapting, realizing, and maintaining their interests on the basis of understanding money.

I. The State Should Ensure Currency Independence and Stability

The primary purpose of a nation is to safeguard the interests of all its citizens in international relations. When domestic entities exchange local currency for foreign commodities, foreign entities can also use this currency to purchase commodities from the originating country, establishing equality. If currency is exchanged and remains abroad, it signifies unilateral possession of foreign commodities by the originating country. Therefore, for a sovereign state to maximize its interests, firstly, it must avoid excessive reserves of other countries' currencies and holding too much of their debt, to prevent financial losses caused by the decline in purchasing power of foreign currencies and debt defaults by foreign governments. Secondly, it must avoid dependence of its currency on others, understanding that the value of its currency stems from the supply of domestic commodities, not its peg to stronger currencies. Efforts should be made to promote the circulation of the national currency worldwide and devise strategies to retain it overseas, either as part of other countries' foreign exchange reserves or as a medium for trade between other nations. Of course, achieving this goal would result in a significant increase in the central bank's creditor rights, correspondingly leading to substantial domestic liabilities that may be difficult to repay.

Regarding the stability of currency, establishing a rule of law environment is fundamental. The essence of the rule of law is to prevent any authority from overriding or undermining the law, especially prohibiting illegal acts by powerful entities, including political parties and government departments. A hallmark of the rule of law is providing predictability for the future, under such an environment, currency naturally possesses higher security and stability. The rule of law offers citizens the greatest degree of freedom, with people aware that "what is not explicitly prohibited by law is permissible," while the government adheres to "actions not explicitly authorized by law are forbidden." In a free environment, people are more creative and proactive, and extensive trading freedom ensures comprehensive and deep satisfaction of people's needs, thus providing a vibrant source for the economy. The foundation of law lies in democracy, the rule of law is built upon democratic politics, and implementing broad and scientific democracy is fundamental to a nation's strength.

Building on the foundation of the rule of law, there is a deeper understanding that the essence of the economy lies in production capacity, namely productivity. Through comprehensive measures such as education, scientific research, and venture capital investment, efforts should be made to boost industry, especially emerging industries, ensuring ample purchasing categories and quantities for the national currency. Goods or service represent true wealth and are the concrete support for a nation's strength. While developing emerging industries, a country must also balance the survival and development of traditional industries as well as agriculture, as the circulation of currency is based on balanced development across economic sectors. The decline of traditional industries and agriculture could lead to shortages of basic goods or service needed by citizens and cause economic imbalance and disruption in circulation.

II. The Central Bank Should Control the Amount of Currency Issued

In the current monetary system, the central bank, as an indirect issuer of currency, primarily aims to ensure the stability of the currency's value. Stability of currency value refers to the stability of purchasing power, that is, the synchronization of the amount of currency used and the volume of commodities traded, thereby maintaining price stability.

When there is an excess of currency in the market, it is necessary to withdraw currency back to the issuers, that is, to absorb the currency into the central bank or commercial banks. When there is a shortage of currency in the market, it is necessary to increase external borrowing to complete the Currency Issuance. Increasing the money supply is generally done through lending to market entities, while reducing the money supply is generally done through raising interest rates. The central bank lends to the government or commercial banks, and commercial banks lend to other social entities, increasing the market's money supply. By setting the interbank lending rate, the central bank can absorb currency back into the issuer system. Of course, when the issuer sells bonds, which it already holds, it is equivalent to reducing the amount of loans to other social entities, which is also a major way for the issuer to withdraw currency.

When the central bank directly purchases government bonds from the government, the money in the government's hands is then used for circulation and transactions. When the central bank purchases government bonds from commercial banks, the money obtained by commercial banks can be issued to other social entities. The so-called repurchase, reverse repurchase, and other conventional and unconventional monetary policy tools are, in layman's terms, essentially about buying and selling debt as well as lending and collecting loans. Under the current monetary system, central banks should update their understanding of money and reclassify and manage the circulating currency according to the classification methods described in this book, in order to improve the accuracy and effectiveness of monetary policy. At the same time, central banks can also fully introduce advanced technologies such as artificial intelligence and big data to assist in the research and decision-making of monetary policy, avoiding the "information cocoon" of central banks and the neglect of one aspect for another in monetary policy.

While acting as the issuer of currency, the central bank also plays a more significant role as the administrative department for formulating and implementing public monetary policies. It must fully recognize that under the current monetary system, commercial banks are the main force behind Currency Issuance. As commercial institutions, commercial banks are inherently profit-driven rather than public service-oriented. There is a high likelihood of misunderstandings and misimplementations of central bank policies. Since the central bank cannot directly implement financial services to the real economy, it must make great efforts to strictly enforce the implementation of the central bank's monetary policy by commercial and policy banks.

III. Commercial Banks Should Carefully Select Loan Targets and Strive for a Synergy Between Deposits and Loans

As mentioned earlier, the smooth operation of an economy relies on borrowers' ability to provide commodities as promised and repay their debts. If not, compensation must be sought from the production capacity of others. As members of commercial institutions, commercial banks issue loans generally without considering the overall economic benefits of society, but rather pursue maximization of their own interests, which is to ensure repayment of principal and interest by borrowers. This aligns perfectly with the requirements of economic development. Commercial banks, as profit-oriented corporate entities, while fulfilling government directives, do not need to overly consider fairness and inclusivity. Instead, they should aim for maximizing profits and returns within a given cost investment. Therefore, finding high-quality customers to lend to is the best strategy. What defines high-quality? Large loan amounts, strong willingness to pay interest, and low risk of bad debts are the main characteristics, which is precisely what commercial banks are currently doing.

The profits of commercial banks come partly from service fees but mainly from the interest rate spread between deposits and loans. Under a partial reserve requirement system, after a certain amount of deposits are generated, a portion must be retained as reserves, while the majority can be used for lending, thereby generating interest income. If borrowers keep the borrowed money in the account of the lending bank, or if the payees of the borrowers' payments also have accounts at the same bank, then this money forms deposits again. Based on these deposits, commercial banks can issue more loans. The reserve requirement system limits loans to being less than deposits, but through the method of "lending leading to deposits," the repeated use of deposits can be achieved, thereby expanding interest earnings.

IV. The Government Should Be a Good Coordinator and a Backstop

The government is a representative for all the people. While promoting economic growth, it is also important for the government to maintain fairness, promote public welfare, and achieve balance and sustainability.

The hallmark of economic growth is the amount of money used for commodity transactions. In order to increase this amount, firstly, there must be a sufficient supply of commodities available. This requires the government to vigorously promote education and scientific research, while maximizing the ability of people to provide goods or service for society. Secondly, it is necessary to make those who already hold money willing to hand over their money in exchange for commodities, and encourage those without currency to apply for loans and use them for external transactions. This requires the government to abide by the law and strictly exercise public power under legal norms to ensure the maximization of people's freedom, autonomy, and self-improvement. At the same time, the government should provide sufficient protection in major areas of people's livelihood such as medical care and elderly care, to relieve people's concerns about major uncertainties, enhance their sense of security and stability, and reduce their willingness to save money. We have seen that the stronger the legal system，and the more robust and well-off the social welfare system is, in a country, the stronger the willingness of people to consume. Thirdly, it is necessary to assist and support vulnerable groups in society who have needs but lack the ability. Their necessary satisfaction is also a requirement and manifestation of human sociality. The government transfers the surplus money and purchasing power of the rich to the poor through secondary distribution of social wealth, and the poor use it for transactions to complete consumption or investment, which can also increase the amount of money transactions. At the same time, their needs being met is also part of economic growth.

In addition to being a provider of public policies and services, the government is also the most important economic entity. The government can increase its own debt to expand investment, especially in large-scale, long-term, low-return projects, and increase the use of money to personally directly promote economic growth.

The government can also increase its holdings of foreign exchange, gold, and other important strategic resources, enhancing currency stability through positive interactions with monetary departments such as the central bank.

In summary, what the government should do is to address those matters and tasks that truly meet the needs of its citizens but are unprofitable, unwillingly undertaken, or beyond the capability of other economic entities, serving as a safety net and a backstop for the national economy.

V. Personal Wealth Password

For individuals, the purpose is very singular and clear, which is to increase the amount of money held. In layman's terms, it's about "making more money." Generally speaking, there are two ways to acquire money.

The first way is borrowing, which can be divided into two types based on the lender: one is borrowing from the issuers of currency, namely the central bank and commercial banks. Under the current monetary system, only commercial banks and the government are eligible to borrow from the central bank, ordinary social entities that are neither commercial banks nor government can only borrow from commercial banks. The second type is private lending, borrowing from entities other than the central or commercial banks. Borrowing money is undoubtedly the easiest and least costly way to obtain money, but with borrowing comes repayment, including both principal and interest, which is the burden for the borrower. If the borrowed money is used for direct consumption, it is merely an advance withdrawal of future funds and does not generate more money. Only when borrowed money is used for exchange and investment can more money be obtained.

The second way to acquire money is through exchange, which can be further divided into three types based on the objects of exchange: one is exchanging one's labor, by selling one's goods or service, or in other words, selling one's time and labor. This is a common practice among the general working class, colloquially known as being an employee. The second type is exchanging other people's general commodities, by selling products or services produced by others, commonly referred to as doing business. Regarding the principle of exchanging money for goods, we have already discussed it in Chapter 6 " The Nature of Wealth and the Measurement of Wealth Value " and Chapter 7 " Prices of commodities" of this book. We should strive to find trading counterparts for exchange that have a high

"Value Perception" for our commodities and a low "Value Perception" for money. Of course, if we choose commodities and business models that can generate large-scale sales, earning a huge total profit margin through small unit price differences and massive sales volumes, that is also an effective strategy. The third type is exchanging special financial products or goods with financial attributes, commonly known as investing. Unlike general products and services, in financial markets and capital markets, such as stocks, futures, and other equity products and financial derivatives, as well as real estate, energy, and other special goods with financial attributes, become the optimal options for transaction profits due to their trading scale, price fluctuations, and convenience of transactions.

Under the current monetary system, the secret and password to making money for ordinary social entities is: strive to improve one's credit, borrow as much money as possible at the lowest cost through commercial banks or private lending, use the borrowed money to exchange for commodities and investment products, then use these commodities and investment products to get back more money, and use more money to exchange for more commodities and investment products, thus achieving a cyclical growth of money. After repaying the loan with the money obtained from transactions, the remaining amount completely belongs to oneself, which can be used to satisfy one's real needs regarding clothing, food, housing, transportation, entertainment, etc.

The transitional commodities and investment products in the intermediate link include everything, including other people's products, labor, as well as natural or statutory various physical goods and rights. Of course, this also includes a wide variety of financial products with complex structures. No matter what kind of commodities and investment products are used for operation, the basic requirement is to have an expected price difference, so that more money can be earned by buying low and selling high. This price difference can be achieved by changing a location, waiting for a period, packaging and reselling, or finding wealthy individuals with low demand for money. In layman's terms, it's about holding commodities and investment products that can be sold at a premium. The basic logic of judgment still depends on the supply and demand of commodities and investment products. Of course, if you choose commodities that have a short-selling mechanism, it becomes even more convenient to operate, however, the price difference in this mechanism comes from selling first and buying later, rather than buying first and selling later.

In summary, the key to acquiring money is to have a correct expectation of the future, to hold those commodities that will be in demand in future societies. Then you can exchange them for more money, or borrow those commodities that will drop in price and then sell them, using a small amount of money to buy them back for repayment in the future. When our

194

expectations of price rises and falls are highly successful, we can call it investing, when such expectations have a low success rate, we call it speculating. Earning money through borrowing, exchanging, repaying, and balancing requires an accurate foresight of the future. If you do not possess such ability, then strive to provide goods or service for society! After all, high returns mean high risks. Engaging in business and investing entails the risk of losing one's capital. Being a law-abiding employee is the life choice for most people. Moreover, being an employee does not necessarily mean low income, "employee emperors" are not uncommon across various industries.

If you choose to earn money through labor, this is certainly a method that both the state and society should strongly advocate, because the fundamental source of human wealth is labor. If everyone earns money through trading, there would be no goods or service available for trade in the market. At this point, your way of obtaining money is essentially selling yourself, your own intelligence, time, labor, and even appearance are commodities. According to the price formation system of commodities we discussed earlier, we should first choose industries and employers that have a low "Value Perception" for money and a high "Value Perception" for commodities, that is, those industries and employers that do not care about money but value talent. It's important to know that the same person can receive completely different salaries from different employers and different industries. Meanwhile, you should strive to further enhance your "Objective Value" through learning and training, improve our social reputation and industry recognition to improve employers' "Value Perception" and "Subjective Price" for you. Of course, when you need money for these purposes, you can borrow money first to ensure learning, training, or increasing your own equipment so that you have better service capabilities, making your services more anticipated, thus you can sell your services at a better price and exchange for more money.

We are accustomed to discussing a company's business model to assess its profitability. For ourselves, shouldn't we also plan a life business model based on our own resource endowments to make it easier to acquire money? There is a notion in society that the key to a person's happiness is doing what they love and making money from it. However, if you pursue more money, finding an easier way to make money may be more important than engaging in work you like or are good at. After all, under legal premises, no matter what method you use to earn money, it spends the same way, but different industries and methods of earning money exhibit significant differences in opportunities and efficiency. Commonly, we believe that working for others hardly leads to wealth, while entrepreneurship provides more opportunities and greater possibilities for becoming rich. Merchants who engage in buying low and selling high usually become wealthier than researchers who make outstanding contributions. Those engaged in bulk trade or financial transactions have more opportunities for overnight wealth. Choice is more important than effort, direction is more important than speed, and platform is more important than ability. Regarding making money, we have no reason not to choose a more convenient method.

Chapter 15: Major Issues of Current Currency

The four fundamental duties of an ideal currency are to facilitate transactions, stabilize currency value, promote the economy, and maintain fairness. Since the establishment of modern financial systems, various financial and economic crises have emerged incessantly. Between nations and among different economic entities, inequality and unfair exploitation are carried out through currency. Faced with complex and ever-changing economic phenomena, the economic community is neither able to predict accurately nor effectively respond. The current monetary system, built upon experience, has many inherent flaws.

I. The Overlapping Functions of the Government, Central Bank, and Commercial Banks

In the entire financial system, the primary participants include monetary policymakers, monetary policy regulators, currency issuers, Currency operators, and currency users. These five participants have fundamentally different functions and should be assigned more specialized roles. Separating the powers of monetary policy formulation, currency supervision and accountability, Currency Issuance, currency operation, and currency usage can achieve a separation between referees and athletes as well as the specialization and differentiation of athletes. This is conducive to the scientific, efficient, fair, and public welfare management of national currencies. In the current global monetary systems, there is a widespread phenomenon of unclear division of labor and overlapping functions. The formulation and supervision functions of monetary policy that the government should implement have been largely delegated to the central bank. At the same time, the government also acts as a borrower and currency user, playing an important role in utilizing fiscal policies and participating in market transactions. Central banks, as currency issuers, are endowed with the government functions of formulating monetary policies and supervising policy implementation, possessing the power of currency supervision and accountability. To enhance their own credibility and regulate money supply, central banks also directly engage in foreign exchange and gold trading as currency users. Commercial banks, as profit-oriented commercial institutions, are simultaneously granted direct Currency Issuance rights and currency operation rights.

1. The Functions of Currency Issuers overlap with those of and Currency Operators

The fundamental function of modern central banks is to issue currency and manage the currency created jointly with borrowers. As currency has fully evolved into Credit Currency, the creation of currency relies on the credit of borrowers. Borrowers obtain currency from the central bank for market transactions before creating wealth for society. The creation of currency is an overdraft on the future for borrowers and an investment in the future for central banks. The consumption of borrowers brings demand to the market, and the subsequent wealth creation of borrowers provides supply of goods or service to the market. Therefore, currency creation and recovery are the engine of economic operation. The purpose of Currency Issuance is not to collect interest, but to ensure market transactions, stimulate production potential, and promote economic growth. As long as currency is issued and recovered, the economy is maintained and promoted, and the function of Currency Issuance is completed. The purpose of central banks is not interest income, but "issuing loans and completing recovery" itself. At the same time, currency is circulated nationwide by law, and Currency Issuance is related to the vital interests of all citizens, which requires specialized departments to implement it.

Under the current monetary system, the central bank's Currency Issuance function is not directly performed, but is implemented through commercial banks, which rely on their own interests and independent judgments to select borrowers. The central bank actually loses the power to choose borrowers. If the central bank wants to achieve specific monetary goals or wants to issue currency to specific industries and fields, it can only introduce the currency into commercial banks through monetary policy tools, which are then independently used by commercial banks. The fundamental function of the central bank's Currency Issuance cannot be directly and efficiently implemented, and the responsibility and power of the central bank are not matched, with responsibility exceeding power.

The important thing about banks issuing loans with public money is that the supply of public money is no longer determined by the state or central bank, but by numerous private loans. In capitalist economies with a large banking system, the sovereignty to create money has actually been privatized[10]

In the Bank of England's 2014 quarterly report, there are two articles on the nature of money, "Money Creation in the Modern Economy" and "Money in the Modern Economy: An Introduction", these two articles are quite enlightening for many mainstream economists. The Bank of England economists confirmed that most of the money in the modern economy is created by private banks providing loans. In addition, the Bank of England emphasized that this is "exactly the opposite of the general order described in textbooks". Here we have to make it clear that this is not the failure of a few textbooks, but the failure of almost all economics textbooks. The result is that

---

[10] Mary Mellor. Money: Myths, Truths and Alternatives[M]. Beijing: China Social Sciences Press,2022.

economics students are still being instilled with a false monetary theory[11]

Commercial banks are companies, and their fundamental function should be defined as managing money and operating money rather than issuing it, that is, managing and operating the stock of money. However, in the current reality, commercial banks have taken on the primary function of currency issuance. Under the partial margin system, commercial banks can issue loans without stock money, and the main body that should be managing money actually exercises the power of creation. The power of commercial banks is greater than their responsibility. Meanwhile, "lending to external parties and completing recovery" is a means for commercial banks to profit, not an end in itself, and promoting economic growth is not a function of commercial banks.

The legitimacy of commercial banks' profitability lies in their providing monetary management services for society. When Credit Currency is issued through borrowing and credit, money is no longer physical objects such as gold and silver. Money has evolved from private wealth into public goods, and the issuance of money has evolved from private rights into public power. Using the creation of money to make profits is immoral and even inconsistent with natural law. Aristotle's condemnation 2000 years ago should be taken seriously: "Money was invented for the purpose of exchange, and to increase it through interest is contrary to its nature."

At the same time, commercial banks that aim to make a profit cannot fully fulfill the role of currency issuers.

2. The Functions of Monetary policy Makers and Regulators Overlap with Those of Currency Issuers

The formulation of a country's monetary policy should focus on the balanced development of the overall economy. While ensuring the right to equal access to currency, monetary policy should be tailored to the current state of national economic development, differentiate between key economic sectors for development, predict future economic development trends, and scientifically study and judge the areas, scale, duration, interest rates, and other factors of monetary issuance and withdrawal. It should not solely focus on the performance and interest demands of the currency issuer itself. The power to formulate monetary policy should belong to the highest authority of the state that represents the people in exercising power, so as to ensure that monetary policy is accountable to all people and supervised by all people.

Power should be subject to supervision, and power without supervision will inevitably become a tool for personal gain. Responsibility should also be subject to supervision, and responsibility without supervision will inevitably lead to inaction and disorderly behavior. The supervision power over currency issuance and currency management should belong to the highest authority of

---

[11] Ann Pettifor. THE PRODUCTION OF MOMEY[M]. Beijing: China CITIC Press, 2022.

the state that exercises power on behalf of the people, and at least should be implemented by a government independent of the currency issuer. If the power to formulate monetary policy and supervise is given to the central bank, it is equivalent to allowing the currency issuer to implement self-management and self-supervision, which is inevitably inefficient and low-quality. Under the current monetary system, the responsibility for monetary supervision is held by the central bank, and the responsibility for monetary supervision of the highest authority of the state and the government is bypassed, which seriously weakens the scientific, efficient, fair and public welfare nature of monetary policy.

Under the current monetary system, the central bank, as the issuer of currency, actually exercises the power of monetary policy formulation and monetary policy supervision that should be implemented by the government or the highest authority of the country. In many countries, the central bank is also set up as a branch of the government. This approach of being both a referee and a player makes it impossible for the central bank to concentrate on currency issuance and recycling, and on the other hand, it makes it impossible for the central bank to formulate and implement monetary policies that should be independent of the currency issuer.

3. The Functions of Monetary Policy Makers and Regulators Overlap with Those of currency users

The currency user should exchange their labor results in the market for currency, or borrow currency from the currency issuer with their own credit, and the borrowed currency must be repaid with their future income. The government is also a user of currency, and is an economic entity like other national economic units. Not only that, the government is also the largest and most important economic entity and currency user in a country. To obtain loans from the central bank, the government should also obtain taxes and fees through providing public goods and services to the public, and use them to repay debts. The currency issuer should provide loans to the government in the same way as it does to other economic entities, fully considering the government's service ability and creativity to ensure that it can repay the principal and interest as agreed.

Under the current monetary system, central banks in many countries are subordinate to the central government. Even if the central bank is independent of the central government, the central government usually plays the role of monetary policy maker and regulator. In front of the central government, the independence of the central bank in issuing currency is lost. This brings a natural problem, which is that allowing a specific currency user to actually control a currency issuer may make the currency issuance lose scientific, impartial and public welfare. There are fundamental differences and conflicts in the positions and interests of monetary policy makers and regulators, currency issuers, and currency users. The confusion of the three can easily lead to suspicion of using public tools for private purposes. It may also be to avoid such suspicion that the central bank's currency issuance is subject to layers of restrictions, such as the legal requirement that the central bank shall not directly issue loans to the government. However, the fundamental problem is the overlapping functions, and the wrong means to solve the problem will only make the mistake worse.

4. The Functions of Currency Issuers Overlap with Those of and Currency users

The fundamental function of a currency issuer is to thoroughly and profoundly examine the creditworthiness of borrowers, selecting those who can provide the market with needed goods or services in the future. Based on the specifics of the loan, decisions are made regarding the loan amount, term, and interest rate. Currency users, including the government, should accurately assess societal needs, fully utilize money to integrate resources, and organize production factors for wealth creation. Especially the government, while providing public goods or services to the people, should fully leverage its advantages of large scale, strong credibility, and long lifecycle. It should focus on the national economy's overall situation and play a vital role in major livelihood projects, major infrastructure, and major security sectors that involve huge investments, extremely long cycles, slight returns, and high sensitivity.

Whether it's the government or other economic entities, regardless of the nature of the project being invested in, as long as a loan is obtained from the currency issuer, it should be ensured that repayment can be made in full according to the contract. This is the foundation of currency stability and concerns the interests of all citizens and currency holders. All market entities, including the government, should focus their main efforts on enhancing their own production capacity, which is the source of power to drive economic development. Besides providing currency issuance, currency issuers do not have the capability to produce products or provide other services, currency issuers should concentrate on their primary duties.

As described in Chapter 10 "The Relationship Between Currency and Economy" Section 9 "The Impact of Currency Issuers Directly Buying and Selling Commodities," under the current monetary system, currency issuers usually issue money directly to themselves and use it to purchase some special assets in the market. This oversteps the business scope of currency issuers specializing in lending, easily causing chaos in monetary order and interference with their main business. As discussed in Chapter 4 "The Essence and Logic of Credit Currency" Section 3 "The Essence of Credit Currency and Three Layers of Credit", the essence of a currency issuer's credit is intermediary credit, derived from equal treatment and strict examination of borrowers. The function of a currency issuer is to ensure that those with production capacity can obtain loans and that borrowers can repay both principal and interest.

200

Currency issuers need not reserve assets to enhance their own credit. As for the function of regulating the money supply in the market, it can be completely implemented by government departments, commercial banks or policy banks, while the central bank is only responsible for the release and withdrawal of money to these money borrowers and money users.

II. Structural Imbalance in the Supply of Money

Under the current monetary system, only the government and commercial banks can borrow from the central bank. Although the social entities that borrow from commercial banks are relatively common, the profit-driven nature of commercial banks leads to relatively few entities that can obtain loans from commercial banks. Most entities in the market cannot directly enjoy the benefits of Currency Issuance and must earn money through their own labor. Most social entities do not receive the issued currency, while the government's monetary burden is too heavy, and the debt of governments in all countries continues to expand without exception.

The specificity and limitations of borrowing from Currency Issuers have many adverse effects on the economy. Firstly, it inhibits individuals with creative potential from utilizing currency to leverage their productivity. For example, a young person with legal talent is trapped on a factory assembly line that he is not good at because he has to make money to support his family. If he can borrow from Currency Issuers and secure time for preparing for the judicial examination and internship, he can become an excellent lawyer and provide high-quality legal services to society.

Secondly, the currency that is generally needed by society can only flow into the market through the debt of a few entities and their use. However, the normal operation of the economy requires an adequate supply of currency. Due to the single target of issuance, the currency of the central bank cannot flow into the market efficiently and smoothly, this is the reason why "cash crunches" frequently occur in financial history. For example, a country's economic growth in a certain period mainly depends on real estate, and the Currency Issuance is mainly undertaken by real estate companies. Once the real estate industry shrinks, the supply of money will be hindered, and a large amount of money can only stay within the central bank and commercial banking system. Other small and micro entities in society find it difficult to obtain money for operation, nor can they gain favor from commercial banks, resulting in insufficient momentum for economic development.

Thirdly, economic entities with priority in borrowing can obtain a large amount of funds when their own capacity is insufficient or they do not need funds, causing inefficient issuance of currency and even flooding of currency. For example, the government, as the main economic entity, continuously borrows money from Currency Issuers in order to boost the economy. Due to its own insufficient capacity and insufficient investment returns, the government's debt continues to accumulate and cannot be repaid, ultimately leading to a collapse of government creditworthiness. If other social entities do not have the capacity to supplement the economy, inflation will occur. The debt crisis of the United States government is an example of this happening. Commercial banks have a "scale complex" in their business model and internal assessment, and they issue loans to large-scale enterprises that exceed the effective financing needs of the real economy. Some enterprises use their advantageous position to obtain low-cost loans and use the money to buy wealth management products, save money for fixed-term deposits, or lend it to other enterprises, resulting in inefficient use of funds and money sinking. Some state-owned enterprises and central enterprises obtain a large amount of commercial bank credit funds when they do not need funds to stimulate and enhance their capacity, these funds are either used inefficiently by themselves or lent out to earn interest returns; industries with overcapacity and outdated production capabilities, such as steel and real estate, can still obtain a large amount of loans based on their accumulated size and reputation, but due to their inability to apply for subsequent market demand, they end up with a large number of defaults and bad debts, and Currency Issuers' money cannot be recovered, causing a serious drag on the national economy. These common phenomena have greatly reduced the boosting and stimulating effects of Currency Issuance on the economy, and even endanger the healthy development of the national economy.

The monetary policy of the central bank aims to promote public welfare and strives to provide liquidity support for the real economy. However, the central bank cannot issue currency to the real economy, and can only introduce monetary policies that support inclusive and technological development. Commercial banks are the ones that directly lend money to social and economic entities. However, commercial banks are limited by their profit-making nature as commercial institutions, and inevitably undergo deformation and discounting in implementing the monetary policy of the central bank. This leads to the central bank's monetary policy being unable to exert precise effects, resulting in a situation like scratching an itch from outside the boot or punching cotton.

Rights and obligations are equal. The right to issue currency corresponds to the obligation to invest in the development of the national economy. The currency issuing institution has the obligation to fully issue currency to those with productive capacity to promote production and boost the economy. The first function of Currency Issuer is to discover and activate potential and suppressed productive capacity. Under the current monetary system, the central bank has transferred most of the Currency Issuance work to commercial banks, which have become the main role of Currency Issuance. However, commercial banks are companies, as the famous American comedian Bob Hope jokingly said, "Once you can prove that you don't need money, it will definitely lend you money." The primary purpose of commercial banks is profit rather than promoting social productivity and enhancing social welfare. The social assessment of commercial banks is also conducted from the perspective of profitability. We have no reason to require or expect an institution that aims to maximize its own profit to fully fulfill its obligation to promote the comprehensive development of productivity and promote the overall improvement of the economy. On the contrary, we can fully understand the "loving the rich and scorning the poor" that commercial banks show when choosing loan targets. For Currency Issuance, the primary and only thing to be examined is whether the loan target has potential productive capacity and can sell their commodities as agreed and obtain income, rather than how much interest return can be recovered. The public welfare function of Currency Issuance and the profit-making purpose of commercial banks have caused a functional dislocation in the current monetary system from a mechanism perspective, and are also the institutional and root causes of monetary policy failure.

Under the current monetary system, the 6.0 version of currency, namely Loan Currency issued by commercial banks, has taken the dominant position. However, the profit-oriented nature of commercial banks determines the fate of financial disengagement from the real economy. This is contrary to the fundamental purpose of Currency Issuance, which is to serve the real economy. The real economy refers to the economic entities that produce goods or service. Currency should promote the provision and transaction of goods or service. However, commercial banks, as commercial institutions, do not prioritize serving the real economy. Instead, profit is the fundamental goal. In order to make profits, efficiency must be pursued. Commercial banks will issue a large amount of currency to financial investor or speculators rather than real economic entities. These financial investment institutions or speculators mainly engage in the trading of investment goods and speculative goods to obtain huge profits. Most of these transactions do not produce any goods or service and contribute nothing to society. For example, if commercial banks lend money to housing developers, and the developers build a building, this is serving the real economy. If they lend money to real estate speculators, and after holding the property, they sell it, the house price rises and the speculators earn profits. However, the house remains the same, and social wealth does not really increase. Another example is that commercial banks lend money to financial institutions, and the financial institutions use these currencies to hold equity in listed companies. The companies obtain funds to expand production, which serves the real economy. However, if the financial institutions only trade in the secondary market and earn profits by short selling or long selling, there will be no new goods or service produced, and the overall society will not benefit. Another common scenario is that commercial banks supply money to other banks or non-banking financial institutions, where the currency merely circulates within these financial institutions without entering the real economy sector. Profits are generated from the internal circulation of money within the financial system, giving the appearance of economic development, yet no additional products or services are added to the market. This is called currency idling. In order to make profits, it is necessary to avoid risks and pursue scale. Therefore, another significant tendency of commercial banks is to issue currency to high-quality enterprises or mature businesses that do not need currency. Such behavior can either bring low efficiency or lead to the accumulation of excess capacity. The term of Currency Issuance, namely loan term, should also match the profit cycle of production capacity. For projects with large investment amounts and long return periods, long-term loans should be issued. However, the assessment indicators of commercial banks determine that they can only conduct short-term loans, ranging from one to two years to three to five years. This cannot meet the needs of long-term production capacity development, resulting in the short-sightedness and limitations of Currency Issuance, forcing many high-quality projects that are beneficial to economic development and can meet social needs but take a long time to complete to engage in unnecessary financing activities such as bridge financing, borrowing new money to pay off old debts, and debt swap. Once the situation changes, it is easy to cause default and bankruptcy. The financing of a large number of urban investment companies across China is commonly used for long-term infrastructure investment, which has a positive supporting effect on long-term economic development. However, the funds borrowed are mostly from short-term and medium-term loans. When the central government tightens policies and these companies cannot borrow new money to repay old loans, large-scale defaults are bound to occur, which is caused by the institutional defects of Currency Issuance.

While a wide range of social entities are unable to obtain timely, sufficient, and cyclically matched ending, the government, as the main credit object and Currency Issuance channel, naturally bears the responsibility of undertaking an overloaded monetary mission. The government is only a member of the social entity, and there is no reason to require it to bear excessive responsibility for promoting economic development. The market economy is extensive and deep, and there is no reason to rely on the government's undertaking and use of the required currency. It is this unreasonable monetary system that has caused the "money shortage" in the market and economic contraction, which is also reflected in the continuous expansion of government debt and the diminishing marginal utility of fiscal policy on the economy.

In summary, under the current monetary system, the law allows specific currencies to monopolize transactions, but does not provide smooth access to the original currency for the transaction subjects. Currency is only issued to a limited number of subjects, resulting in institutional injustice. Being able to borrow from Currency Issuer becomes a privilege and benefit, while also preventing the majority of productive social subjects from accessing the original currency, resulting in an imbalance in the supply of currency and causing local money shortages and huge government debts.

III. Unequal Opportunities in the Demand of Money

Under the current credit monetary system, money has been completely separated from practical objects, issued through borrowers' borrowing, and endorsed by borrowers' future production capacity. Therefore, all social entities with transaction needs and future production capacity should have the same right to borrow from the Currency Issuer.

With the prevalence of Credit Currency, the diversity of economic activities, and the continuity of unequal credit policies, people's access to money is more diverse and increasingly unequal than ever before. Some people own huge amounts of money through investment, trade, or intermediary services. They can easily exchange their money for other people's labor, wisdom, products, and even thoughts, health, and life. Most people work hard and earn only a meager salary to support their families throughout their lives. Some people are idle and make a lot of money every day, while others work hard and have no money. The difference in income is not only due to the size of their contribution to society, but also widely affected by factors such as industry, occupation, and region. A few instructions from financial manipulators can earn a Nobel Prize winner's income for decades. Some people exchange time and labor on the assembly line for money, some people borrow money from commercial banks to do business arbitrage, some people put huge sums of money in commercial banks to earn interest, and some people engage in angel investment to obtain excess returns. The unfairness is obvious and seems to be taken for granted.

People are born with differences in talent and background, which is determined by their natural attributes. The social attributes of human beings require us to create a more equitable social environment through institutional settings and human efforts, and equality of opportunity is the most fundamental equality. Under the current monetary system, the most fundamental inequality between people lies in the unequal access to loans, which further leads to differences in how different groups of people acquire money, which brings great injustice and inequality to society. The most significant inequality is manifested in commercial banks adopting different lending standards and interest rates for different social groups based on self-interest rather than public welfare.

As a public good, money should serve the overall interests of society, and be as selfless as sunlight, air, and water that benefit all things. That is, all people with productive capacity should be able to obtain loans, and those who benefit more from borrowing from the issuer of money should pay more interest. However, in reality, banks often issue money at extremely low interest rates to large, high-quality customers for risk control and profitability considerations, while ignoring the legitimate credit needs of small and vulnerable social entities. This can lead to serious polarization and social injustice, resulting in the Matthew effect and social Darwinism in the monetary sense.

IV. The Lack of Effectiveness and Precision in Monetary Policy

The world economy has been highly developed, international and domestic trade is complex, and people's willingness to trade is changing rapidly. The central bank does not have the power and means to comprehensively and accurately measure and evaluate transaction data. In addition, commercial banks independently conduct savings and loans, and it is impossible to judge the amount of money that should be invested based on the balance sheets and deposit and loan data of the central bank and commercial banks. Often, when the economy is in difficulty, a large amount of money is issued, and when prices rise too sharply, the money is contracted. These decisions are made based on experience and speculation. Because there is no scientific measurement and theoretical basis, the effect of monetary policy often goes against expectations.

We are living in a catastrophic monetary era, in which the financial sector has expanded unchecked, and most financiers have little direct relationship with the production of goods and service in the real economy. Producers and creators in the real economy are periodically overwhelmed by "easy-to-obtain but high-interest-rate currencies" and often lack affordable funding.

The monetary policies of central banks and commercial banks involve lending, collecting loans, raising interest rates, and lowering interest rates. Data reveals that the GDP growth generated by newly issued money is diminishing, and the efficiency of the economy is becoming less and less due to the issuance of money. The realization of collecting loans depends on the borrower's repayment ability and willingness, and it is impossible to collect all receivables. Raising interest rates can increase savings and curb loans, but it also suppresses consumption and investment, and makes the cost of using money too high, which will reduce transactions and lower the economy. Lowering interest rates can reduce savings, promote loans, stimulate consumption and investment, and promote economic growth, but people's choice of saving or borrowing is not entirely controlled by interest rate hikes and interest rate cuts, but also affected by other political, legal, public opinion and other factors. The United States has been raising interest rates continuously, and the stock market has repeatedly hit new highs. China has cut interest rates, but private investment has been shrinking. These examples clearly indicate that the effectiveness of monetary policy has been seriously challenged.

V. The Purchasing Power of Currency Continues to Decline

Historical data shows that the purchasing power of currencies is constantly declining even in the fastest growing countries. Since 1913, the purchasing power of the US dollar has also been declining. At that time, one US dollar was defined as 1/20 ounce of gold. When the Bretton Woods system was established, it was 1/35 ounce. Today, one US dollar can only buy 1/1300 ounces. As the consumer price index increases, the purchasing power of the US dollar decreases over time, and the same amount of currency can buy less and less goods. No currency in the world can escape this fate. Mildly, it's normal for a currency to depreciate by half over ten years. Severe inflation is even more astonishing. From 1914 to 1920, the price of Germany increased by 15 times, and the Venezuelan currency bolivar depreciated by 100 trillion times in 13 years.

The management of currencies in both rich and poor countries is not satisfactory. Governments and central banks may know the importance of maintaining price stability, but few of them can actually achieve it. In the 1970s, the price of goods in the United States doubled in 10 years, while in the United Kingdom it took only 5 years. In November 1923, the price of goods in Germany doubled in 4 days, and the annual GDP fell by 15%. Germany's high inflation greatly weakened the power of the Weimar Republic and contributed to the breeding of Nazi totalitarianism. The financial history of the past 150 years can be largely described as a history of attempts to maintain the stability of currency value but always encountering various failures. Governments may have the intention to devalue their currencies, which is an indisputable fact that has been repeatedly verified in historical facts. It can be said that almost all paper currencies, whether intentionally or incompetently, have experienced significant devaluation in different historical periods, including China during the Middle Ages, France during the French Revolution, the United States during the War of Independence and using inland currencies, and the United States during the Civil War and using the Greenback dollar, East Europe after the dissolution of the Soviet Union, as well as Zimbabwe in 2008 and North Korea in 2009. To a lesser extent than these historical cases, many industrialized countries, including the United Kingdom and the United States, have also suffered from the Great Inflation of the 1970s[12]

The purchasing power of currencies worldwide has generally continued to decline, and the public is aware of this and seems to have become accustomed to it. Currency devaluation is a huge infringement on ordinary consumers, as it

---

[12] Mervyn King. The End Of ALCHEMY: MONEY, BANKING AND THE FUTURE OF THE GLOBAL ECONOMY[M]. Beijing: China CITIC Press, 2016.

means that the same amount of savings can be exchanged for less wealth. If you have a five-year fixed deposit of 1 million US dollars in the bank, and when you withdraw it, you find out that someone secretly stole 200,000 US dollars during the five-year period, you will be furious and choose to immediately call the police. Such information is likely to be reported in the newspaper news. Relatively speaking, a cumulative inflation rate of 20% over five years is easily accepted by the public, even if it has the same effect as the former. There is no doubt that inflation is a theft of all currency holders, and the thieves are those who borrowed a large amount of currency at the beginning. They will either repay with depreciated currency, or they will be unable to repay, or they simply do not intend to repay.

In 2023, Argentina's inflation rate reached an astonishing 211.4%, the highest since 1990. In December 2023, the first month of the far-right President Milly's administration, the consumer price index (CPI) climbed to 25.5%, more than twice as high as other months of the year and the highest single-month figure in 30 years. The price increases were mainly concentrated in the food and beverage sector, with a rise of 251.3%, followed by household appliances, with a rise of 231.7%. The same scenario played out in different countries. In the past few years, Turkey's inflation rate once exceeded 60%, reaching a peak of 85% in 2022. Venezuela experienced severe inflation, with its inflation rate reaching as high as 222.3% in April 2022. In the same month, Sudan's inflation rate also reached 220.7%. Behind these exaggerated and cold figures are the blood and tears of tens of millions of families and hundreds of millions of people. Those who hold currency are beating their chests and stamping their feet, while those who are burdened with loans are celebrating.

We should never say with a straight face that "currency devaluation may also bring some positive effects, such as improving the competitiveness of export goods, promoting export growth, and thus driving economic growth. Devaluation can also stimulate domestic production, increase employment opportunities, and improve the self-sufficiency of domestic industries." This is like saying that theft also has positive significance, which can make the victim of theft work harder and create more wealth for society. At the same time, theft also brings wealth to the thief's family and helps them solve problems such as children's schooling and parents' medical care.

VI. Significant Fluctuations in Asset Prices

The price of any asset is a quantitative relationship between assets and currencies, which is the result of people's exchange behavior after measuring currencies and assets, and then forming a dynamic balance. People evaluate assets and currencies based on their own needs. Whether it is assets or currencies, their fundamental value lies in the degree to which they meet people's needs. People's ownership of currencies generally does not suddenly increase or decrease. Therefore, the price of assets should change according to their own quality or scarcity. For example, the price of grain will naturally increase if there is a reduction in production, and major technological breakthroughs in listed companies will also bring about an increase in their own product competitiveness, which will be reflected in the stock price. If people only focus on the fundamental value of assets and currencies, the change in asset prices should be rational and reasonable, that is, the change in price should reflect its satisfaction with people's needs. However, in reality, the fluctuations in the prices of various assets are huge, often unrelated to their own quality changes, and the price changes cannot reflect or serve the satisfaction of people's needs. As mentioned earlier, on April 9, 2024, the share price of China Tianrui Cement in Hong Kong stock market plummeted by 99.04% in 15 minutes. At almost the same time, Haosen Financial Technology (03848) staged a "synchronization drama", with a 90.96% decline in share price within 15 minutes. The share price of Shengneng Group (02459) was cut in half on the same day. Such extreme events reflect the serious deviation between asset prices and asset values, as well as the great instability of using currency as a measure of wealth value.

The sharp fluctuations in asset prices distort their intrinsic true value, causing abnormal interference in the real economy and harming rather than benefiting society as a whole. The reason for the sharp fluctuations in asset prices is speculation, speculation is an act of short-termism, the essence of speculation is to obtain more money in a short period of time through the exchange of money and assets. Money was invented by humans, and its fundamental function is to exchange commodities to meet their respective needs of people. When trading is only for the purpose of obtaining more money, the nature of the transaction has already deviated from people's real needs. Speculators use money to generate money and then exchange it for other people's commodities, but in the process, they do not provide commodities for society, which violates the fundamental function of money.

When speculators use their own money to speculate, this indicates that he has already earned money in the past by providing goods or service to the market. if they make a profit, they are merely pocketing other people's money without increasing or decreasing the overall supply of commodities and money in society. It can only be said that they have earned money through their own efforts and abilities, and there seems to be no unfairness in the monetary system. However, if speculators use borrowed money for speculation, they have not provided any commodities to society throughout the process, but have obtained their own money through the reversal of assets and money, which allows them to directly purchase and enjoy the fruits of labor of other social entities. This is unfairness in the monetary system. In fact, the sharp rise and fall of asset prices are mostly controlled by massive funds, and most of these funds come from credit, which is the issuance of money. In theory, the purpose of Currency Issuance is to promote production, but in reality, it is widely used for speculation, which is the root cause of significant asset price fluctuations. Because only fluctuations can achieve short-term gains, speculators are eager to promote them.

Under a fair system and social environment, asset prices should not have significant fluctuations that are out of line with their own value. Such fluctuations will only result in the plundering of wealth and do not benefit social production and commodity supply. We do not oppose investment, but the real value of investment to society is to allow those with production capacity to own money, thereby integrating resources and turning production capacity into real commodities. Investors enjoy price differences through the improvement of the quality of investment targets, which correspond to newly added commodities or production capacity in the market, rather than monetary plunder under a zero-sum game.

VII. Bank Runs and Economic Crises Cannot be Completely Avoided

Under the current system where commercial banks can issue loans, the bank deposit certificates issued by commercial banks are far greater than their cash on hand. If there is a run on the bank, it will inevitably lead to a bank collapse. The vast difference between the "Cash and Deposits with the Central Bank" and "Deposits Accepted" accounts in the balance sheets of commercial banks represents the amount that commercial banks cannot be run on. In less than 50 years, the proportion of liquid assets held by banks in the UK has dropped from one-third to less than 2% of total assets. In the United States, before the financial crisis in 2008, this proportion dropped below 1%.

There is a theory in society that it is impossible for all savers to withdraw money at the same time, which fuels the public's superstition of financial alchemy. If, after analyzing the behavior of a large number of depositors, banks find that the willingness of savers to make payments or withdraw liquidity is predictable, then the savings balance can be used by banks as long-term operating capital. However, if a significant number of depositors withdraw funds at the same time, then the bank either defaults on its depositors or immediately recalls its loans, and the latter usually leads to borrowers urgently selling their assets, often not enough to repay the bank debt.[13]

Due to the private interests of Currency Issuer and its staff, a large number of loans cannot be recovered, and at the same time, a large number of people who need currency and have production capacity cannot obtain loans, resulting in economic imbalance. Currency and commodities concentrate in

---

[13] Mervyn King. The End Of ALCHEMY: MONEY, BANKING AND THE FUTURE OF THE GLOBAL ECONOMY[M]. Beijing: China CITIC Press, 2016.

the hands of different groups, making it impossible to achieve a virtuous cycle. Employees of coal-producing companies are laid off due to an oversupply of coal that cannot be sold. Without employment, they lack the wages to purchase the coal produced by their own companies, ultimately leading to a situation where they have no coal for heating and are left to suffer in the cold. Employees of milk production enterprises are starving and pouring the unsold milk into the river. This is also a classic picture in economics courses about the period of economic depression. These seem to be jokes, but they are all real. The reason is that other economic sectors do not receive monetary support or have the ability to produce products and earn currency to purchase coal and milk. The local over-issuance, local shortage, and lack of overall planning of currency are important reasons for financial crisis and even economic crisis.

VIII. The Contradiction between Global Economic Integration and the Fragmentation of National Currencies is Becoming Increasingly Prominent

The integration of information, logistics and financial systems has made the global economy interdependent and interconnected, and humans have common interests. However, monetary authorities in various countries often focus only on their own interests when formulating monetary policies, and the factors that affect monetary policies are often placed on domestic employment, inflation and other data, without regard to the impact on other countries. What's worse, strong currencies and strong countries are even more malicious in using their own currency advantages to carry out smokeless wealth plunder abroad through various means. Currency, while facilitating the global economy and benefiting human society, has also become a tool for exploitation and plunder between nations and individuals. The United States, leveraging its control over the globally circulating U.S. dollar, influences global asset pricing through the expansion and contraction of the dollar. It continually harvests from production-oriented and resource-rich countries by buying high and selling low. "Currency has no borders, but monetary policy does" this situation is the root cause of currency plundering.

International financial predators can also cause turmoil by manipulating currencies to plunder huge amounts of wealth. George Soros defeated the Bank of England in 1992 by shorting the pound sterling on a large scale, and in 1997 he shorted the Thai baht, triggering the Asian financial crisis. These operations had brought great pain and profound disasters to the people of other countries. National economic policies can also bring about significant fluctuations in the exchange rate of their own currencies. In May 2021, Turkish President Erdogan won the general election and began to implement the so-called "unorthodox economic policy". The Turkish lira depreciated by 44% in the whole year, and by 19% in the last week, which means that at the end of the year, foreigners can hold almost half of the foreign currencies at the beginning of the year to harvest the labor of the Turkish people.

Before the Russia-Ukraine conflict, on February 16, 2022, the exchange rate of the US dollar against the ruble was 78.83 rubles per dollar. In February 2022, the US and Western countries imposed economic sanctions on Russia, and the ruble depreciated sharply. In March, it hit a record low of 154 rubles per dollar, which was nearly half of the level before the Russia-Ukraine conflict on February 23. Regardless of the justice and legitimacy of the war, the wealth and resource plunder caused by such a significant policy in terms of national wealth alone fully demonstrates the differences and divisions between countries under the current monetary system.

For reserve currency issuing countries, domestic monetary policy objectives often conflict with the requirements of various countries for reserve currencies. Monetary authorities cannot ignore the international functions of their own currencies and simply consider domestic objectives, nor can they simultaneously take into account different domestic and international objectives. They may be unable to fully meet the growing demand of the global economy due to the need to curb domestic inflation, or they may overstimulate domestic demand and lead to a global liquidity glut. In theory, the Triffin dilemma still exists, that is, reserve currency issuing countries cannot provide liquidity for the world while ensuring the stability of the currency value[14]

Chapter 16: Principles and Construction of the Equal Rights Monetary System

In modern social life, transactions are the most common behavior, exchange is the breath of economics. and money, like sunlight, air, and water, is the most common and necessary daily necessities. Currency is a man-made universal object. As the most common form of wealth and the most widely used trading tool, currency should adhere to the principles of "upholding public interest purposes, maintaining stable purchasing power, safeguarding social equity, and promoting economic growth." It should fully exercise its functions as a measure of value, means of circulation, means of storage, means of payment, and world currency, thereby serving the entire society and all humanity. With the advancement of human civilization, political equality has been implemented in an increasingly extensive scope and to a deeper extent. However, economic equality, especially monetary equality, has seen little progress in theory and practice. Globally, the wealth gap is further widening. While money and finance bring overall prosperity to our economy,

---

[14] Zhou Xiaochuan. Thoughts on the Reform of the International Monetary System [OL]. Available at: http://www.pbc.gov.cn/hanglingdao/128697/128719/128772/2847833/index.html.

they also cause increasingly apparent inequality, injustice, and irrationality in our society. The strength of a nation and a society stems primarily from a scientific social system. Just as the British Empire defeated France by establishing the Bank of England and innovating in finance, those who first grasp the principles of currency and establish a comprehensive and efficient monetary system and framework will gain an advantage and higher ground in the competition of modern civilization.

I. Establish the Fourth Political Power "Monetary Power" and Adhere to the Principle of Independent Coinage Power

Exchange is the most widespread social activity in human society. Currency is used as a medium of exchange. It holds unparalleled significance for both nations and their people. Every piece of currency is a direct symbol of wealth, and every citizen has the obligation to deliver goods and services in return. Meanwhile, Credit money is issued based on the credit of the borrower, and all citizens who accept and use the currency should have equal borrower qualifications.

The renowned German economist Georg Friedrich Knapp (1842-1926) established the nationalist school of monetary theory. His work "The State Theory of Money" is a milestone in the history of monetary thought. In his book, he pointed out that money is not merely an economic phenomenon shaped by market forces but is largely a public phenomenon determined by national laws and institutions. The state establishes the legal status and value of a particular form of currency (such as coins or publicly issued banknotes) through legal and administrative means. Money is "a product of law," therefore, the study of the monetary system should be regarded as a branch of political science, not just within the realm of economics.

In Western countries, there is a view that the fourth political power, beyond "executive, legislative, and judicial powers," is the media and public opinion, i.e., the power of public opinion. In fact, even in developed Western countries, there are no specific constitutions, laws, or regulations to explain or establish the fourth power, the so-called "fourth power" has formed naturally. However, whether from a symbolic, practical, functional perspective, or from a professional, important, universal perspective, the influence of money on humanity far exceeds that of public opinion. Former US Secretary of State Kissinger once said: "If you control the money, you control the world." We may encounter many people who do not care about or engage with public opinion, and even those who do not care about or engage with executive, legislative, and judicial matters, but we rarely meet people who do not care about or engage with money. The power of money should naturally become the "fourth power" in human political life. We believe that in the contest for "the fourth power," the power of money will inevitably triumph over the power of public opinion and ultimately be recognized in human concepts and laws. We hereby strongly appeal to governments and peoples worldwide to swiftly establish the power of money as the "fourth political power" beyond executive, legislative, and judicial powers. We refer to the power of currency as "Monetary Power".

Monetary Power includes four aspects: the right to issue currency (legal coinage power), the right to apply for loans from Currency Issuers, the right to use currency, and the right to operate currency. The state should establish the Monetary Power through legislation. The legislation on the right to issue currency should include the establishment, operation, supervision and restriction, and issuance rules of the Currency Issuer. The legislation on the right to apply for currency should include the application conditions, procedures, repayment and relief channels. The legislation on the right to use currency should include interest and bad debt disposal, ensuring the circulation of the entire market, and maintaining the stability of currency value. The legislation on the right to operate currency should include the qualifications of operators, the practice norms of institutions and personnel, etc. Through systematic legislation, the democratization and rule of law of Currency Issuance can be realized, so that people can independently control currency and form sufficient confidence in it. Under Credit Monetary system, the right to issue currency is generated democratically, and the issued currency is shared by the whole people. The whole people should enjoy equal opportunities to obtain Currency Issuance. The idea of "democracy, people's responsibility, and people's enjoyment" of currency should become the mainstream understanding in the world. The right to issue currency should not be a tool or privilege for a few people, especially those in the elite stage.

In order to achieve the function of money, money should have the characteristics of easy identification, trustworthiness, and controllability. Therefore, a country can only have one issuing entity, and this issuing entity should be independent of any entity that uses the currency, to ensure that the currency is used by the entire population, rather than serving any specific entity.

It is particularly important to emphasize that the Monetary Power should be independent of the government that exercises executive power, as the government is also a member of the economic and social body and a user of currency. It should not have special privileges over other social entities in the face of Monetary Power, especially the right to issue currency. The government should also obtain Currency Issuance through its own credit, exchange goods or service for currency and repay debts. The difference between the government and other social entities lies in their public welfare and scale, but this is not a reason for them to interfere with the Monetary Power.

Legislation should clearly define the two core functions of the Currency Issuer: one is to ensure the long-term stability of currency purchasing power, and the other is to promote production and drive economic growth. To achieve long-term stability in currency purchasing power, it is essential to fundamentally prevent the market from having excess currency that has not been backed by corresponding commodities, which we will discuss in detail in chapters six, seven, and eight below. In terms of driving economic growth, it is necessary to emphasize the economic promotion function of the currency issuer, setting assessment indicators for promoting productivity development and introducing policy measures, rather than the current practice of commercial banks using profit as the assessment indicator.

II. Establishing a Special Currency Issuer and Adhering to the Principle of Exclusive Legal Coinage Power

Within the national scope, the right to issue currency is a significant power concerning all citizens. To maintain the centralization and uniformity of currency, the right to issue currency should not spill over. According to legal provisions, a unified central bank should be established nationwide, specifically engaged in currency issuance and management. The currency issuing institution should be produced through democratic procedures. No other institutions should issue currency directly or indirectly without legal authorization or for profit purposes, to uphold the independence, public welfare, and professionalism of currency issuance.

In response to the current situation where commercial banks possess the right to issue currency, a transition period and measures should be established to gradually return commercial banks to their essence as currency operators. The central bank can replace and reclaim the issuance rights by purchasing the "loans and advances" accounts held by commercial banks, thereby abolishing the partial reserve system of commercial banks and confiscating their currency issuance rights.

The proposal to abolish the fractional reserve system was put forward by the most prominent economists in the first half of the 20th century. This was an important spirit of the "Chicago Plan" in 1933, which has been highly praised by economists of all ages. As Irving Fisher, an outstanding American monetary theorist, said, "We can give banks freedom to provide loans in the way they like, but the premise is that banks are no longer allowed to create these currencies for loans... In short: nationalize the currency rather than the banking industry.".

Most of the currencies currently in circulation are created by private sector banks. This is the most dangerous minefield in the management of currency in today's society. In his famous speech entitled "The Golden Cross", William Jennings Bryan eloquently attacked the gold standard -- the needs of the general public should take precedence over the needs of Wall Street. However, the most important content of his speech that has been almost forgotten is: "We believe that the power to coiner and issue currency should be part of the government's functions. We believe that this is part of national sovereignty, just as the state cannot hand over the power of criminal punishment and tax legislation to individuals, this work cannot be handed over to the private sector... Issuing currency is one of the functions of the government, and banks should completely withdraw from the functional space of managing social life. " When he said this, he consciously copied Thomas Jefferson's famous quote from 1809: "The power to issue currency should be withdrawn from banks and returned to the people, after all, the people are the true owners of power."[15]

Some people question the monopoly of currency issuance by bureaucratic institutions, fearing it could lead to economic dictatorship and severely undermine freedom. However, such concerns are unnecessary because the establishment of specialized institutions is based on democratic politics and arises from democratic processes. Monetary authorities are not supreme power organs without restraints, assessments, or remedies, they are merely service institutions exercising specialized functions.

Some people also doubt that the professional knowledge and skills required for risk assessment, providing financing solutions, and managing financing cannot be achieved through a single institution. This is an unfounded concern. Under the central banking system, it is entirely possible to establish multiple levels and different types of subsidiary institutions or branches to carry out comprehensive business operations, and achieve loyal, diligent, rigorous, and professional work standards through training. Since the commercial banking system is considered capable of handling this task, there is no reason to believe that the central banking system cannot do better.

Hayek, a representative of neoliberalism, advocated the decentralization of currency and the free market economy, and believed that the right to issue currency should be a private right rather than a monopoly power of the government. He proposed the solution of "competitive issuance of private currency", which abolished the central bank system and allowed private issuance of currency. He believed that this would end the monopoly of currency and restore the stability of currency. Hayek's view saw that the supply of currency should follow the principles of inclusiveness, fairness, and marketization, but did not see that currency played a role as a value yardstick in the free market, nor did he see that the free market was built on a stable order. If the currency issuers are diversified and the currency types are diverse and complex, it will inevitably lead to uneven value scales and chaotic trading order. The monopoly of coinage rights can achieve fairness, uniformity, and efficiency in market transactions. The exclusive right to coinage is not a government monopoly on currency issuance, but rather a monopoly by

---

[15] Mervyn King. The End Of ALCHEMY: MONEY, BANKING AND THE FUTURE OF THE GLOBAL ECONOMY[M]. Beijing: China CITIC Press, 2016.

specialized institutions independent of the government. Currency issuance is not something that can be accomplished unilaterally by the issuing institutions, it also relies on borrowers. The monopoly on the right to issue currency does not imply a monopoly on money itself. On the contrary, it signifies true "inclusivity, fairness, and marketization." By ensuring that the public enjoys equal Monetary Power, the supply of money can be democratized, marketized, liberalized, and egalitarian. Similar propositions and viewpoints have been mentioned by visionary and idealistic scholars.

The central bank will be responsible for creating new money specifically to support non-inflationary growth. It will directly manage the creation of money, rather than using interest rates to influence banks' borrowing behavior and money creation (This is the current situation.). The decision to create money will be exercised by a newly established money creation committee (or the existing monetary policy committee). The committee will be responsible to the UK Treasury Select Committee, which is composed of cross-party Members of Parliament and is responsible for supervising and reviewing the actions of the Bank of England and the Treasury. The committee will no longer set interest rates, which will be determined by the market. The simplest way to remove the debt created by banks and its growth momentum is to remove the power to create new public money from the banking system or strictly limit it. Banks will be restricted to doing only what is recognized by most people: lending depositors' money to borrowers. The new public money can be issued debt-free by the public monetary authority and directly invested in the economy to meet public demand, rather than being created by issuing debt through banks[16]

III. The Principle of Non-self-interest for Currency Issuers

The right to issue currency comes from the public, and its purpose is also to promote the well-being of the entire population. The Currency Issuer can only complete the issuance of currency by lending with the commitment of the borrower. The value of currency is rooted in the creditworthiness of the borrower, and is determined by the mutual agreement of buyers and sellers in the market. As we have already analyzed in the previous text, the essence of the Currency Issuer is just a credit intermediary.

Currency issuers should not engage in market transactions using the currency they create. This means that the issuance of currency should be accomplished solely through lending to external parties, rather than exchanging goods with social entities for newly created money. This principle ensures the equivalence and reciprocity of market transactions. The value of commodities is assessed based on societal demand, and market entities evaluate the value of commodities during transactions. If currency issuers

---

[16] Ann Pettifor. THE PRODUCTION OF MOMEY[M]. Beijing: China CITIC Press, 2022.

themselves use the currency for transactions, it would disrupt the assessment of commodities' value.

Currency Issuers cannot use their own currency to trade commodities to meet their own needs. Currency issuance is a sacred duty entrusted by law. Since the issuance of currency has almost no cost, if the Currency Issuer can use their own currency to exchange goods and service from other entities, it is like a worker in a banknote printing factory using the printed banknotes to directly purchase goods in the market. This will be absolutely unfair, and the currency will lose its independence, welfare, and fairness. Before the currency is lent to other social entities, it cannot be used for transactions, let alone for the private interests of the Currency Issuer. This will be a serious favoritism and fraud. Currency issuance also should be particularly isolated from the government, and the independence and neutrality of the issuing institution should be upheld.

Currency Issuers should not use Currency issuance to make profits. Currency issuance is a duty, and Currency Issuers and their staff are public servants and workers of the state. They should have a completely public welfare nature, and their operations should not have profit-making purposes. Their work compensation should be limited to labor wages and should be included in the national budget for expenditure. As for the interest charged by the central bank on lending money, it should be renamed "seigniorage" and incorporated into the national tax system through legislation for management. As we discussed earlier, the interest of the central bank is the service fee for monetary lending services of the central bank. However, Currency Issuance Right of the Central Bank comes from the people, and the currency of the central bank is created out of thin air. Issuance services are similar to public services provided by other state organs, and its service fees are legally tax-like and included in tax management.

IV. Optimize the Division of Functions and Improve the Six-level Monetary System

The construction of a monetary system is an important part of national development. It should follow the principles of democracy, equality, independence, professionalism, and checks and balances. A scientifically designed and gradually improved financial system should integrate financial legislation, monetary policy formulation, monetary policy supervision, currency issuance, currency operation, currency usage, and currency circulation.

First level, establish institutions for the formulation and supervision of monetary laws, regulations, and policies. Monetary issues are related to the nation's future destiny and the vital interests of its people. The creation and use of money must be under the supervision of the people. Based on the fact that Monetary Power is a fourth political power independent of legislative,

218

judicial, and executive powers, a special committee should be established within the national highest authority representing all citizens to lead the formulation of monetary laws, build a monetary organizational system, and provide regular organizational guarantees for the formulation and supervision of monetary policy.

Second level, strengthen the administrative supervision and judicial relief functions of government agencies and judicial organs on monetary law and monetary policy. Under the guidance of monetary law and monetary policy, the government should pay full attention to the effective implementation of laws and policies, establish specialized government departments to independently, neutrally, and professionally supervise and account for currency issuers, currency operators, and currency users, in order to ensure the efficient execution of national monetary laws and policies. Judiciary is the last resort for relief. When private rights holders believe that their interests are harmed by currency issuers or relevant government departments, they can initiate lawsuits against their inaction and misconduct. Monetary policy regulators, currency issuers, and currency users can all seek conflict resolution through judicial means.

Third level, recycle and refine the currency issuance rights of the central bank. The creation and issuance of currency are exclusive responsibilities of the central bank. The power of commercial banks to issue Loan Currency should be abolished, as this practice essentially amounts to minting coins, a right that should not be held by profit-driven commercial entities. Furthermore, direct issuance of currency by the central bank can ensure efficient and precise monetary distribution based on its functional needs, achieving a unification of duties and rights for the central bank. The essence of currency creation and issuance is to overdraw the future and invest in the future, and its fundamental function is to promote economic growth. Central banks can strengthen their professional skills and capabilities in issuing currency through establishing branches, public welfare subordinate units, and policy banks. As a provider of public goods and service, central banks should be different from commercial banks, and focus on those basic, long-term, public welfare, low-yield projects in the issuance of currency, and strengthen the key areas of the national economy infrastructure construction, weak links and social undertakings, while deepening credit support for socially vulnerable groups, small and micro enterprises, county regions, and the "agriculture, rural areas, and farmers" sector, while reducing reliance on interest income, will promote production capacity and drive economic growth as its fundamental function, fully embracing the important role of being the "nation's and people's premier investment bank." The central bank should also withdraw from the role of currency use and specialize in currency lending. That is to say, the central bank will no longer borrow money for itself and use the currency it creates to buy and sell goods such as foreign exchange and gold in the market. If it is necessary to conduct credit demonstration or monetary regulation through such means, these operations can be carried out by the government or businesses as users of currency. The central bank lends money to the government and commercial banks as needed, and then the government and commerce complete the buying and selling of gold, foreign exchange, and other assets to achieve monetary regulation. The central bank hands over the formulation and supervision of monetary policy to legislative, administrative, and judicial organs, and recovers the right of currency issuance on its own. At the same time, the right to use currency, that is, the right to participate in market transactions, is transferred to the government. Through the optimal allocation of these functions, the central bank becomes a specialized agency that exercises national Monetary Power by specializing in currency creation, external borrowing, managing claims, and coordinating credit. As a credit inspection and management agency for the nation and government, the central bank does not need to own any assets, and its core value lies in its credit management capabilities and ability to achieve its own balance of payments.

Fourth level, fully leverage the monetary management functions of commercial banks and other licensed financial institutions. The central banking system's retraction of the current commercial banks' disguised right to issue currency does not signify a denial of their professional contributions, nor does it indicate a degradation of their functions. Instead, it requires commercial banks to return to the essence of monetary management and operation, focusing on savings, lending, investment, and settlement. After abolishing the partial deposit reserve requirement of commercial banks, their external loans must be based on real and full deposits. The money in the market will no longer be Loan Currencies that are essentially commercial bank's redemption Commitment but tangible Contract Currency issued by the central bank and deposit currency used by banks as substitutes. This means that banks can still provide loans, but the reserve requirement ratio must reach 100%. The central bank may adopt preferential policies for commercial bank borrowing, indirectly affecting the latter's lending to other social entities through loans to commercial banks. External lending operations of commercial banks proceed as usual, except they no longer have the function of independently creating currency, their source of money is completely controlled by the central bank and depositors. Like other currency users, commercial banks operate independently and bear their own profits and losses, no longer abusing their currency issuance rights due to self-interested motives. Meanwhile, their professional advantages in risk management, financial management, financing management and payment settlement can continue to be leveraged. The essence of monetary management and operation is to optimize wealth allocation and promote civilian cooperation, with the fundamental function being to ensure the free flow of currency. On this basis, the social wealth storage and regulation functions of banks should be enhanced. Commercial banks can directly purchase commodities in the market according to economic development needs for reserves, achieving moderate adjustment of currency and commodity volumes, and playing a supportive role in stabilizing prices and society. Licensed financial institutions such as funds, trusts, insurance, and microloan companies should also act as legally authorized currency operators, fully leveraging their respective professional strengths to facilitate the circulation of currency in different economic sectors in various ways.

Fifth level, establish and improve the private lending system. Under the current partial reserve requirement system, commercial banks rely on depositors' savings to issue loans, earning interest from these loans, which in turn forms the basis for the interest paid to depositors. This is a contribution and sharing based on the interest from commercial bank loans. When the central bank implements favorable borrowing policies for commercial banks, if the latter no longer base their loan issuance on depositors' savings but on their own funds or central bank loan funds, the basis for depositors to earn interest disappears. At this point, it becomes reasonable for depositors to pay for the professional reserve services provided by commercial banks, potentially leading to zero or negative interest rates. To achieve a rational allocation and utilization of social capital, the state should strengthen the development and regulation of private lending. The Chinese people may still be wary of the past P2P debacle, but it must be clarified that those bad debts and crimes were illegal fundraising under the guise of P2P, not genuine P2P. People should not negate the value of P2P due to such misunderstandings, nor should they overlook the significant role of private lending in achieving social resource allocation because of painful experiences. It is worth emphasizing that the interest rate for private lending should adhere to market-oriented principles. The state does not need to restrict it. As long as monetary policies are appropriate, laws are sound, and public security is robust, there is no need to worry about usury or illegal harassment. The marketization of private lending interest rates is conducive to the efficient use of money and the free flow of resources.

The sixth level, expand and strengthen the capital market. People use the money they have accumulated for lending to others to collect interest, which can optimize social resources, help borrowers tap into their production potential to create goods or services for society. However, the monetary allocation based on creditor's rights brings stable returns to lenders, easily fostering a societal habit of reaping benefits without labor and risk-free earnings. The collection of interest is an occupation of the borrower's labor results, regardless of the borrower's output, interest is a fixed burden for the borrower. In contrast, equity investment in the capital market is quite different, where currency holders share risks and futures with future production capacity owners. Through cooperation of manpower and financial resources, they jointly create needed goods or services for society. This is a way of fund utilization that the state should vigorously advocate. A developed capital market can achieve effective use and reproduction of currency, capital enrichment of real industries, national industrial development, and other aspects of mutual benefit and win-win.

V. Adhering to the Principle of Currency Inclusiveness

The fundamental function of currency issuance is to activate social productive forces and promote economic growth. Economic activities stem from all societal entities rather than specific ones. The sole criterion for currency issuance should be whether the issuer possesses potential productivity. Currency should serve the entire populace, not just specific entities. Everyone with productive capabilities should benefit from currency issuance. As an extremely important political power, Monetary Power should be jointly owned by all citizens. Every citizen and private sector, from the day they are established or born, should not only have a legally recognized identity in government departments such as public security and business administration but also hold a dedicated account at the central bank. Through this account, the state ensures the realization of the Monetary Power of all people, providing equal financial accessibility to all citizens. This embodies the fundamental requirements and practical implementation of "People's Money" and "People's Finance."

Traditional central banks only grant loans to specific entities, providing loans to governments or commercial banks by purchasing government bonds, commercial bills, and accepting asset collateral. Commercial banks usually only lend to entities that align with their commercial objectives. This does not match the reality where societal entities generally need currency, and a large amount of capacity awaits activation by currency. Currency is the most valuable public product, and reforming the supply side of currency and finance has become necessary for our era.

Different from the current monetary system where currency issuance is only targeted at specific entities, after understanding the universality of currency and the essence of borrower credit endorsement, central banks should establish their own comprehensive branch networks, leverage the mass base of grassroots governance organizations, and consider "whether the issuer can provide future production capacity and repay principal and interest on time" as the core factor in determining whether to lend, conducting credit assessments and lending to all social entities.

This can achieve fairness and justice in the issuance of currency, so that all citizens have the opportunity to obtain Initial Currency through their own credit, which can be used to enhance their own productivity and develop their careers. Secondly, it can achieve direct and precise delivery of currency. Under the current monetary system, the central bank wants to provide monetary support to specific industries, either by issuing guidance policies and relying on commercial banks to carry out business, or by lending to the government and supporting it through fiscal means. The former cannot produce sufficient and direct effects after commercial banks considering the profitability, resulting in widespread policy failures. The latter overburdens the government, while the relevant supported industry entities do not take their due responsibilities, resulting in an imbalance between rights and obligations. Thirdly, it can comprehensively promote economic growth. The source of economic growth lies in the productivity of various economic units, and the stimulation of productivity requires the mobilization of resources through currency. When Currency Issuance comprehensively covers all potential providers of productivity, the economy will be fully activated. Modern monetary theory advocates increasing employment through unlimited government credit, exchanging currency for employment, and achieving the effect of promoting economic growth. This is the traditional way of driving forward by the locomotive. When Currency Issuance takes into account all economic units, the entire economy is transformed into a high-speed train unit, and all sectors of society can receive appropriate credit and use the resulting currency to organize production factors to create goods or service. Each unit of the high-speed train unit provides the driving force for progress.

The advanced aspect of modern monetary theory is to try to promote a monetary system that truly serves the people and open the door to modern inclusive money. This advanced monetary thinking should be recognized, but it confuses the nature and function of the issuer and the government, mistakenly believing that the government is not a user of money but an issuer of money, making the boundary between the two more blurred, increasing the power of the government, and also increasing the burden on the government. It also weakens the exercise of monetary issuance power and the efficacy of monetary issuance in promoting economic growth.

Modern monetary theory did not propose measures for universal credit after seeing the large demand for money in modern society, but limited itself to providing money supply through traditional government credit, attempting to promote the economy and benefit the people with unlimited government credit. This is a traditional misconception that the credit of money lies in the central bank and the government, without truly understanding that the credit source of modern money lies in the borrower.

Based on the fact that the current currency is the essence of the borrower credit, it can be seen that the current currency has evolved from physical vouchers to credit vouchers, and the currency has shifted from a proof of past wealth to an expectation of future wealth, that is, the expectation that borrowers who obtain currency from Currency Issuer can provide society with equivalent or superior value commodities. Therefore, anyone with credit should have the right to obtain Currency Issuance.

The government, like other market entities, is also a borrower, user, earner, and repayer of currency in front of Currency Issuer. Compared to other economic entities, the government has three special features. First, the government has a large size, a wide range of service areas, and a variety of products provided. Second, the government does not aim for its own profit, but aims to promote the overall development of the national economy and ensure the welfare of the whole people. Third, the government's income sources are tax and service charges, which are monopolistic and compulsory. In addition, the government has no other differences and should not have special privileges. As a huge economic entity, the government can naturally borrow from Currency Issuer, but no matter how huge the loan amount is, it should also comply with the borrower's commitment, that is, to ensure that the principal and interest can be repaid on schedule. Of course, Currency Issuer can determine the loan amount, loan term, and loan interest rate that meet the project construction requirements according to the characteristics of the government loan project. At the same time, the government can determine the price of public services and public products provided by itself according to the legal procedures based on the current situation of national economic development, that is, to promote the formulation of a tax system and fee system that is in line with national conditions. The government's debt should not be unlimited, but should match its own service capacity, product capacity, and income capacity.

The implementation of an inclusive monetary system directly through the central bank has raised concerns that the main body of the original currency obtained through credit cannot repay on schedule, which will result in a large number of bad debts. However, this concern is unnecessary. The current commercial banks are already lending to major social entities. The inclusive monetary system only covers a wider range, targets a more comprehensive group, and provides fairer treatment. To prevent the escalation of loan defaults, the state can also implement systems such as differentiated interest rates, central bank interest offsets for central bank bad debts, special government compensation, and loan insurance to mitigate risks.

The essence of Currency Issuance is to create money with credit. The rights are always equal to the obligations. The central bank enjoys the right to issue currency, and at the same time has the obligation to allow all people with credit to obtain the currency issued by the central bank. This is also the essential requirement of financial accessibility in a civilized society. For social subjects, they have the right to request the central bank to issue currency on the premise of their own production capacity, and the corresponding obligation is to repay the principal and interest as agreed. The implied obligation is to provide goods or service to society. Without relief, there is no right. When the central bank fails to fulfill its obligations, or when there is a dispute between the central bank and the borrower on whether he meet the conditions for borrowing, the borrower should be given the right to file a reconsideration or lawsuit against the central bank's failure to approve the issuance. Because the central bank exercises public power, it should be subject to questioning and supervision, and its inaction or arbitrary action should be subject to legal constraints and norms. Commercial behavior is based on the principle of equality and voluntariness, which can favor the rich over the poor. Public power behavior is based on the principle of public welfare, which should reflect fairness and justice.

VI. Ensure the Balance of Payments of Currency Issuers to Maintain the Stability of Currency Value

Currency, like the water in nature, circulates to facilitate the movement of matter. Maritime transport carries goods across oceans, blood delivers nutrients to every organ in the body, and trees absorb water, which then reaches the branches through transpiration, carrying inorganic salts and minerals. The function of water is predicated on two fundamental principles: circulation and balance. Circulation means that there must be no stagnant water, as it is detrimental to the growth of all things. Similarly, currency should be used for the transaction of commodities and to serve the needs of people's lives and production. When currency remains within the financial system or is used solely for speculative gains, it becomes stagnant. Balance means that there should be neither a shortage nor an excess of water in any given area.

To achieve monetary equilibrium in all sectors of the economy, the first step is to ensure universality in the issuance of currency. This guarantees that there are no local shortages of money, which we have already explained in our fifth opinion earlier in this chapter. So, how do we prevent local accumulation of money? It involves maintaining an appropriate, controllable, and recyclable total amount of money. Since defaults by some borrowers are inevitable, when a borrower defaults, the money remains with the savers, but the commodities are not delivered as agreed, leading to an excess of money. This excess is the fundamental cause of monetary accumulation. Monetary equilibrium requires all issued money to close the loop. For bad debts that cannot be recovered after issuance, they must be filled by public efforts, meaning an equivalent amount of money should be withdrawn from the market through other means. This achieves a balance between the circulating money supply and the volume of commodities in the market, preventing a decline in the overall purchasing power of money due to the portion of bad debts without corresponding commodities.

The central bank should issue currency under the principles of loyalty, diligence, and prudent management, aiming to stimulate borrowers' production capacity, promote economic growth, and achieve balanced development. Currency flows into the market from the currency issuer. If borrowers can repay their debts in full, it means that while consuming commodities with money, they also provide commodities to the market. Even if the money used by borrowers to repay debts is obtained through investment or private lending, these funds are still proceeds from others' wealth creation. As long as the currency issuer can recover the money, the balance between the amount of money and commodities in the market can be maintained, stabilizing the purchasing power of money.

Investment brings risk, and loans bring bad debts. Central banks under the inclusive monetary system lend to borrowers across various industries and social strata. When some borrowers inevitably default, the money left in the market becomes relatively surplus. Reclaiming this surplus from others and returning it to the issuer can achieve a balance between the overall money supply and commodities in the market. We have discussed that money issuance is a political power, a public right, and a national public service, not meant for private gain of the issuer. Through lending, the issuer collects interest, which essentially is a service fee for public authority. The interest, exceeding the principal borrowed by the borrower, corresponds to the price of commodities produced by the borrower exceeding the borrowed amount. At this point, the lender recovers more money from the borrower than initially lent, indicating a reduction in circulating money due to interest recovery. However, not every loan can be fully recovered. The interest collected by the issuer can cover bad debts. From the issuer's accounts, if income and expenditure are balanced, then the market's commodities and money are also balanced.

The financial status of a national currency issuer is an indicator of the overall health of the country's economy. When the issuer spends more than it receives, there is an excess of money over commodities in the market, leading to inflation. Conversely, when the issuer generates a substantial surplus, there is a shortage of money in the market, posing the risk of deflation. Therefore, as a currency issuer, its fundamental role is to ensure transactions, stimulate production capacity, and maintain currency stability. The primary purpose of collecting interest is not for profit but to ensure efficient operations and cover bad debts. The core function of a currency issuer is to maintain a balance of payments while keeping the currency circulation process going. It is important to note that a balanced budget means neither making a loss nor making a profit.

The income of the currency issuer is loan interest, and expenditures are its operational costs and unrecoverable loans. This fundamentally establishes the loan interest rate standard at the time of currency issuance. The interest rate set by the currency issuer should precisely balance operational costs and bad debts. we denote the total amount of loans issued to others (Total Loan) as TL, the interest rate on loans issued to others as r, the principal of loans that cannot be recovered (Bad Debts) as BD, and the cost of establishing and operating its own system (Self Cost) as SC. Therefore, to ensure the stability of the purchasing power of money from the source of the currency issuer, it is required that the interest rate setting conforms to the following equation. Since in this book, we have distinguished between issuance interest and renting interest, we refer to this equation as the issuance interest rate equation.

(TL-BD) *r=BD+SC,

r=(BD+SC)/TL-BD

The currency issuer, as an independent legal entity, is the heart of the financial system and the engine of monetary circulation. Just as a heart cannot function properly if it fails to circulate sufficient blood or accumulates too much blood, the engine in a water circulation system must also ensure that the volume of water pumped out equals the volume of water pumped in. The issuer of currency should also maintain a balance between the output and input of money in circulation

In this equation, we do not consider the interest paid by the currency issuer to currency holders for their deposits as part of the money flowing into the market. This is because the currency issuer's source of funds comes from the exercise of its right to issue currency, eliminating the need to absorb deposits. Under the current monetary system, central banks pay interest on reserves held by commercial banks, and commercial banks pay interest on deposits from savers. The essence of these actions is that of monetary operators, not currency issuers. We argue that there is no necessity for currency issuers to borrow from currency users. If currency users, for various reasons, insist on depositing their money with the currency issuer, they should pay a storage fee, i.e., implement a negative interest rate. At the very least, there is no logical justification for currency issuers to pay interest on the borrowing to the users of the currency.

Under the current monetary system, the central bank and commercial banks, as the issuers of currency, have suffered large-scale losses or even bankruptcy, which directly reflects the large-scale borrower defaults and the interruption of currency circulation, and is the fundamental cause of inflation. Taking the United States as an example, for a long period of time, its government and other domestic economic entities have faced the situation of bad loans and non-performing loans, but have long implemented low interest rates. The ultimate result is inevitably that the Federal Reserve System and various commercial banks, as the issuers of currency, will have insufficient income and huge losses. On March 26, 2024, the Federal Reserve System released its audited financial report for 2023. The report showed that in 2023, the total expenditure of the Federal Reserve System was $114.3 billion higher than its income, which means that the operating loss was $114.3 billion (about RMB 826.2 billion), the highest annual loss on record. At the same time, since

March 2023, Silicon Valley Bank, Signature Bank, and First Republic Bank have closed one after another. The Federal Reserve System report shows that more than 700 banks in the United States are facing "significant safety and solvency" risks due to large floating losses on their balance sheets. The Federal Reserve System and commercial banks in the United States are the issuers of currency in the United States, and the amount of their losses is the excess currency amount that is not matched by commodities in the market, which is also the source of inflation in the United States.

Cases that are the opposite of the situation in the United States are occurring in some other countries where commercial banks are large and profitable, maintaining long-term profitability. The profits generated from the hard work of the real economy are largely monopolized by the commercial banking system. These banks are unable to inject these funds into market circulation, resulting in the real economy not receiving sufficient currency for growth and expansion. This leads to a lack of liquidity in the market and further exacerbates the risk of deflation.

The fundamental cause of inflation is the bankruptcy of borrowers' credit, that is, the newly issued currency does not produce new corresponding commodities. The issuers of currency use interest income to achieve balance of payments, which is the optimal solution to maintain the healthy and sustainable development of the economy and the stability of the currency value. Therefore, the central bank's collection of interest when issuing currency has legal legitimacy and economic necessity. The central bank can even collect differentiated interest according to different factors such as the type of borrower or the borrowing income. This part of interest should be used to offset the bad debts of the central bank first, so as to achieve effective control of the total amount of money and the circulation of commodities under the central bank system.

If the central bank cannot balance its income and expenditure through its own strength, it needs to rely on the strength of the public or the government to repay the claims of Currency Issuer, and effectively eliminate the impact of excess currency through external forces. This can also fundamentally control inflation. If the central bank has difficulties in self-regulation, the government should compensate for bad debts. Under the overall planning of the government, surplus currency in the market should be collected and used to repay the issuer, so as to offset the impact of bad debts of borrowers. The government's currency comes from tax revenue, which we will discuss in the eighth comment in this chapter. Of course, it is also possible to establish a central bank Currency Issuance insurance mechanism, which is jointly insured by all borrowers, to compensate for the losses caused by bad debts or damage of individual borrowers.

The Equal Rights Monetary Theory advocated in this book posits that currency issuance is a fundamental means to fully stimulate social productivity, with the issuers playing a vital role as investors for the public. In pursuit of economic growth, issuers must bear the risk of irrecoverable investments in currency. Excess currency remaining in the market should be absorbed and digested by the central bank, government, or insurance institutions through collective public effort, aligning with the overall national interest. Private lending institutions may incur losses because the loss is of private wealth, merely a transfer among individuals, which does not affect all citizens or endanger the overall economy. However, the central bank cannot afford losses, as this would mean there is more currency than commodities in the market, harming all currency holders and undermining national financial stability.

Following the same logic, if issuers generate profits, these should belong to the state for the service of public interests. The government represents the public interest, therefore, the income from profits of the central bank and other currency issuers should be turned over to the state treasury for the procurement of public goods and services.

Up to this point, we have discussed the principles of preventing currency surplus and shortage from the source of the issuer. However, the reasons for the phenomena of currency pooling and shortage in various economic sectors may not lie in the overall currency supply by the issuer. Instead, it may be due to the reluctance of these sectors to spend the money promptly, as well as their unwillingness to take loans from the issuer when currency is scarce. Human needs are objectively present, and the impulse to develop is inherent. The reluctance to spend, invest, or borrow stems from fear: fear of consumption, fear of investment, and fear of borrowing. This involves issues of overall social security, market expectations, economic confidence, and even political stability. These are not problems that can be solved at the level of the currency issuer but require solutions from the national strategy and planning perspective.

VII. Seriously Deal with the Evasion and Rejection of the Debts Owed to the Central Bank

Credit money is based on a high degree of contractual spirit, which provides people with an efficient and reliable market environment. It can be said that the content of contractual spirit in social activities determines the quality of the economy. After the implementation of the inclusive monetary system, the privilege of special individuals to enjoy monetary issuance benefits has been broken, while bringing about the risk of universal default.

While issuing serious central bank actions and preventing rent-seeking, efforts should be made to address the issue of evading central bank debt, eliminating faults and negligence that lead to bad debts at the central bank. For commercial bank loans or private lending, as their bad debts only cause individual losses to private power entities without endangering the overall economy, they can be resolved within the scope of contract law, allowing the market to self-regulate without the need for special legal regulation.

Through national legislation, the disposal methods for three different types of loans—central bank loans, Licensed Financial Institutions loans, and private lending—should be clearly distinguished. Central bank loans, due to their relationship with overall issues such as the total flow of currency circulation, the spirit of social contracts, inflation, and deflation, should establish a highest-level response mechanism. This mechanism should employ various means such as duty assessments, criminal accountability, and administrative penalties to maximize the protection of the state's authority over coinage.

In the judicial practices of many countries, debts that enter the judicial enforcement stage often face challenges such as difficulty in enforcement, ineffectiveness, selective enforcement, and delayed enforcement. These issues may appear to be judicial problems on the surface, manifesting as insufficient attention from judicial organs to contractual rights and obligations. However, fundamentally, they are economic issues or even political ones. The accumulation of debts in the market erodes the overall spirit of social contracts, reduces social trust, and increases transaction costs in the market. Enforcement is the final link in the judicial chain, representing the last mile for rights holders to reach their destination of power. If enforcement fails, it results in a judicial unfinished building, severely impacting the credibility of the law and undermining social integrity. If the creditor is not a currency issuer, the loss is only borne by the creditor. If the creditor is a currency issuer, since the currency issuer's money comes from the right to issue currency and no cost is incurred for the lent money, there is essentially no loss of the currency issuer. Therefore, unpaid debts directly result in the absence of corresponding commodities for the money borrowed and spent by the debtor in the market. This dilutes the value of the existing money in the market, and the loss is borne by all holders of the currency. This leads to the devaluation of fiat money and the destruction of monetary credibility.

VIII. Establish Special Currency Taxation

The essence of national taxation is the cost of public services provided by the government, characterized by monopoly and compulsoriness. Its purpose is to undertake public construction, assist vulnerable groups, promote social equity, and ensure economic development. The effects of currency issuance vary among social entities, some gain significant assistance after borrowing from the central bank, while others may face bad debts and bankruptcy despite their efforts to create wealth. In a contractual monetary system, bad debts and bankruptcies constitute defaults and damages to the entire society, necessitating collective efforts to remedy.

We have previously discussed the possibility of compensation through government and insurance, which necessitates the establishment of a specific tax category by the government for currency issuance. The interest from the central bank serves as a universal seigniorage tax. Beyond this, a progressive excess earnings tax rate system can be implemented based on the borrowers' profits. The taxes collected by the government due to currency issuance should, like the interest collected by the central bank, be prioritized to offset the debts of borrowers who are unable to repay.

As an independent institution exercising the right to issue currency, central banks should theoretically be able to achieve a balance of payments through their own operations, especially through the scientific setting of issuance interest rates, and should not rely on external forces such as the government to help maintain an appropriate supply of money in the market. However, in practice, various errors can occur, leading to the possibility of losses or surpluses for the central bank. This necessitates a means of relief and remediation. When the central bank makes a profit, the profit should be handed over to the government, which then acts as the user of the currency to inject the excess currency collected from the market by the central bank back into the market. Conversely, when the central bank experiences a loss, the government also has an obligation to subsidize the central bank with fiscal measures to ensure an adequate supply of money in the market.

Such a special tax arrangement can not only ensure the full issuance of money, stimulate social creativity, increase the supply of market commodities, but also share risks among all people, effectively resolve bad debts that inevitably exist, and avoid inflation caused by excess money and insufficient commodities.

In fact, some countries have made explicit legal provisions that the profits of the central bank should be turned over to central government, while the losses should be subsidized by central government. This measure could have fundamentally eliminated the continuous decline in the purchasing power of money, but due to the neglect of the fact that commercial banks are the main issuers of currency under the current monetary system, this provision has not played a stabilizing role in ensuring the purchasing power of money. For example, Article 39 of "People's Bank of China Law" stipulates that "The net profit of the People's Bank of China after deducting its annual expenditures and withdrawing its total reserves in accordance with the proportion approved by the financial department of the State Council shall be turned over to the central finance. The losses of the People's Bank of China shall be made up by the central finance." There are similar provisions in Chapter 7 "Income Distribution" of the "Federal Reserve System Act" of the United States: "Any amounts of the surplus funds of the Federal Reserve System banks that exceed, or would exceed, the limitation under subparagraph (A) shall be transferred to the Board of Governors of the Federal Reserve System for transfer to the Secretary of the Treasury for deposit in the general fund of the

231

Treasury." It is noteworthy that the Federal Reserve Act does not contain explicit legal provisions requiring the U.S. government to compensate the Federal Reserve in the event of losses.

IX. Establishing a Unified Basic Unit of Wealth Value for Humanity

How to measure wealth is a historical puzzle that has plagued humanity, and on such a significant issue, humans have yet to find a unified standard answer. Measurement refers to the standards used to gauge the numerical value or quantity of objects or phenomena, determining their proportions and relationships, with the most crucial characteristic of measurement being its fixity. From ancient times to the present, people have always used currency as the measure of wealth. In the era of Material Currency, it essentially referenced the measurement of weight. Entering the age of fiat money, each country uses its own currency as a measure. However, currency itself does not possess the characteristic of fixity. Even compared to the expedient measure of King Edgar of England, who set the length between his thumb joints as one inch, the fluctuating value of currencies today also fails to provide a more reliable standard. The measure of wealth must find a stable, accurate, and measurable standard, which could be the labor time involved in producing things, or the material energy contained within them. Since the essence of wealth is to satisfy human needs, measuring wealth by "the degree of need satisfaction" might be the most accurate and scientific method, and measuring needs involves researching and understanding humanity itself. Regarding how to construct the eighth basic unit of the International System of Units, we have already discussed this in detail in Sections Four, Five, Six, and Seven of Chapter Six "The Nature of Wealth and the Measurement of Wealth Value." In this field, we are just at the beginning.

X. Creating a World Currency - the World's Version 6.0 Currency and World's Version 4.0 Currency

Under the current monetary system, issuing currency domestically through national legislation for use by local entities, yet having it widely accepted internationally, reveals an inherently flawed setup that can lead to operational mismanagement and biased interests. The varying strengths of currencies worldwide, coupled with the prevalent principle of prioritizing national interests, have allowed countries with strong currencies to extensively engage in financial exploitation of others.

There are two ways to break this unreasonable situation. First, trade between two countries should only use their own currencies, so that commodities and currencies can be exchanged to each other. Even if there is a situation where one country's currency is heavily retained by another country, it only occurs locally and will not lead to significant unfairness and imbalance worldwide. Second, an international currency should be established, and international trade should use this internationally shared currency instead of a specific country's currency, in order to break currency hegemony and currency kidnapping. Economic globalization is a fundamental requirement for human beings to achieve division of labor and exchange, which is in the fundamental interests of people in all countries. Economic globalization urgently needs borderless trade, borderless trade desires borderless currencies, and borderless currencies call for borderless central bank.

Creating an international reserve currency that is decoupled from sovereign states and can maintain long-term stability in currency value, thereby avoiding the inherent flaws of sovereign credit currencies as reserve currencies, is the ideal goal of international monetary system reform. Although the idea of a super-sovereign reserve currency has been around for a long time, there has been no substantive progress to date. In the 1940s, Keynes proposed using 30 representative commodities as the basis for establishing an international monetary unit "Bancor". Unfortunately, it was not implemented, and the subsequent collapse of the Bretton Woods system based on the White Plan showed that Keynes's plan may have been more visionary. As early as the beginning of the exposure of the defects of the Bretton Woods system, the IMF created the Special Drawing Rights (SDR) in 1969 to alleviate the inherent risks of sovereign currencies as reserve currencies. Unfortunately, due to limitations in the distribution mechanism and scope of use, the role of SDR has not been fully utilized to date. However, the existence of SDR provides a glimmer of hope for the reform of the international monetary system. A super-sovereign reserve currency not only overcomes the inherent risks of sovereign credit currencies, but also provides possibilities for regulating global liquidity. An international reserve currency managed by a global institution will make it possible to create and regulate global liquidity. When a country's sovereign currency is no longer used as a yardstick and reference benchmark for global trade, the exchange rate policy of that country will greatly enhance its ability to adjust imbalances. These can greatly reduce the risk of future crises and enhance crisis management capabilities[17]

Due to the lack of a sufficiently powerful force that can maintain the credibility and promotion of international currencies worldwide, international currencies must adopt the form in version 5.0 "Deposit Currency", that is, a special agency established by the United Nations to issue an alternative currency (the international currency), in the form of storing national currencies. Anyone holding the international currency can exchange them

---

[17] Zhou Xiaochuan. Thoughts on the Reform of the International Monetary System [OL]. Available at: http://www.pbc.gov.cn/hanglingdao/128697/128719/128772/2847833/index.html.

back to any national currency they require from the agency. People holding the international currency can also conduct international settlements. Such international currency can be called "standard reserve currency", which are essentially an international upgraded version in version 5.0 "Deposit Currency". As we have discussed earlier, although the current IMF's "Special Drawing Rights" only has a few strong currency players, it already has the characteristics of this new type of currency, and we can expect its further development and implementation.

Let us speculate according to the historical evolution logic of currency forms: Version 2.0 Receipt Currency is a voucher for Version 1.0 Material Currency, Version 3.0 Promise Currency promises to exchange for Version 1.0 Material Currency, while Version 4.0 Contract Currency breaks the promise and issues independently. Version 5.0 Deposit Currency is a voucher for Version 4.0 Contract Currency, and Version 6.0 Loan Currency promises to exchange for Version 4.0 Contract Currency. International Version 5.0 Deposit Currency is a voucher for various countries' Version 4.0 Contract Currencies. The next step will be the creation of an international Version 6.0 Loan Currency, which, in the absence of sufficient reserves of various countries' Contract Currencies, promises to be exchangeable for those Contract Currencies. The step after that would be to break this promise and independently issue an international Version 4.0 Contract Currency.

Only when human civilization has developed to the point where it no longer needs to rely on force to maintain order can we say that humanity has truly matured. A truly civilized human society should be built on the spirit of contract, rather than under violent rule. Only in this way can human wisdom, dignity, and free will be fully reflected. The politics above the spirit of contract is democratic politics, and the economy above the spirit of contract is market economy. Human beings construct society through the formation of contracts. The public contract is the law, and the special contract is the agreement. The law is the public contract issued by the maker, and the agreement is the special law between the signatories. The law and the contract should be the only guidelines for human action.

When the consciousness of a community with a shared future for mankind forms a consensus, and society is built upon the pursuit of common interests, with complete equality among individuals, and rational thinking and the pursuit of ideals become the greatest internal compulsion for people, international specialized institutions can break free from the backing of sovereign state currencies. They can issue loans and release versions 6.0 of "loan currency" and version 4.0 of "contract currency" based on their own assessments of the creditworthiness of economic entities worldwide. At this point, this international specialized institution becomes the central bank of the world's people, independently issuing currency to economic entities worldwide based on the borrower's credit. We can call this money issued by

234

the central bank of the world's people "World Currency."

Under the "World Currency" system, individuals, businesses, and governments from all countries can obtains the issuance of "World Currency" based on their own credit. By providing goods or services to the world through their labor, the currency in people's hands is either obtained by providing goods or services to society or will provide goods or services to society in the future. The exchange between people and between countries returns to the exchange of goods or services. No one can enjoy other people's commodities or possess the wealth of other countries solely by issuing currency. Currency is merely a medium of exchange and no longer a tool for reaping the fruits of labor. The democracy, freedom, fairness, and justice of the human monetary system are realized.

Currency, stripped of its functions of plunder and exploitation, will return to its fundamental role in transactions, eventually being transformed by humanity into a perfect currency, an ideal currency, and a people's currency. The implementation of a "World Currency" will fundamentally eliminate the exploitation and plunder between nations through finance. This requires the evolution of human rationality, wisdom, and civilization. It also necessitates that powerful nations relinquish their own interests for the benefit of all humanity, contributing with their national strength and credit. In a world driven by interests, such a "World Currency" is difficult to achieve in a short time. However, we firmly believe that with the progress of civilization, the maturity of humanity, and the enhancement of productivity, this just, public-spirited, and ideal new category of currency will indeed become a reality.

Epilogue

This book interprets the essence and operation of money through historical analysis and logical reasoning. Comparing traditional and emerging monetary theories that have already been introduced, the views in this book effectively validate many proven theories while critiquing the superficiality and errors of many popular theories. It offers new analyses and solutions to numerous existing economic dilemmas and challenges. The author does not believe that scientific theories must be based on the support or critique of other theories, instead, economics should move away from a foggy, self-amusing status quo to become more practical, accurate, and effective.

In a civilized society, the relationships between individuals, between humans and nature, and between nations are all about rights and obligations under rules or laws. This book reveals the essence of money from the perspective of rights and obligations, explores the principles of the economy, and builds the future of currency. Human history is written by the people, the driving force behind the economy lies in the people, wealth is created by the people, and the purpose of creating wealth is also to meet the needs of the people. This book is based on a rational analysis of money, advocates for the equalization of Monetary Power, and is committed to constructing a brand-new Equal Rights Monetary Theory. This theory posits that within the monetary system, all participants, whether individuals, organizations, or countries, should enjoy equal power. The creation, issuance, management, and use of money should all follow principles of fairness, justice, and transparency, ensuring that everyone's economic rights are equally protected. This book argues that the formulation of monetary policy should be based on public interest rather than the interests of specific interest groups, in order to achieve sustainable economic and social development. As global economic integration deepens, the inequality of Monetary Power has become increasingly prominent, leading to issues such as the wealth gap and financial turmoil becoming more severe. Therefore, promoting the equalization of Monetary Power can help achieve fairness and harmony in the economy and society, making the Equal Rights Monetary Theory significantly relevant in modern economics.

The "Equal Rights Monetary Theory" created in this book is based on the important principles, such as the unity of responsibility, power, and interest; the balance of power; the division of labor; and the freedom of transaction. Based on strict logic and beautiful ideals, it proposes specific and feasible solutions to promote the equal power of all parties involved in the monetary system. By establishing the "fourth political power" status of "monetary power", we can avoid the neglect of "monetary power" by the state and the people, and promote the concretization of monetary power, achieving political equality between "monetary power" and legislative, judicial, and administrative powers. By popularizing the "World Currency", it breaks the plundering of other countries' currencies by powerful countries, and achieves the equality of Monetary Power between countries. By establishing the independent monetary issuance power of the central bank, it makes the central bank independent from public power organs such as the government, avoiding the government's abuse of monetary issuance power for its own interests. It achieves the equality of public power between the central bank and the government. By stripping the central bank of its external transaction functions, it brings the central bank back to the role of a credit operator, a national investment bank, and a professional lender in society, eliminating the central bank's issuance of loans to itself and its use of its own currency for external transactions. It prevents the central bank from acting as both a Currency Issuer and a currency user, achieving the equality of interests between Currency Issuers and the entire society's currency users. By confiscating the central bank's Currency Issuance right and implementing a 100% deposit reserve system, it promotes the return of commercial banks to their original business of currency management and operation, and incorporates commercial bank loans into the management of the franchised business scope of licensed financial institutions, it respects the marketization of private lending interest rates. these measures achieve equal rights to the use of money between commercial banks and other non-bank profit institutions and the private sector. By implementing the principle of universal access to Currency Issuance, expanding, refining, and deepening the central bank's Currency Issuance work, it enables every borrower with production capacity to receive Currency Issuance, achieving the equality of financial accessibility between private sectors. By maintaining the balance of revenue and expenditure of the central bank and ensuring the appropriate supply of currency in the market, it safeguards the purchasing power of currency and achieves the equality of interests between borrowers and currency holders. By legally distinguishing between central bank borrowers, licensed financial institution borrowers, and private lending borrowers, it strictly prevents borrowers from taking advantage of the principle of universal access to Currency Issuance to obtain benefits without working, and undermines the circulation of currency. It achieves the equality of interests between Initial Currency receiver and the general public. These suggestions are unique insights proposed by the "Equal Rights Monetary Theory" to promote the democratization, fairness, marketization, and equality of money.

The author of this book is also the founder, advocate, and promoter of "egalitarian economics", which upholds humanistic thinking and places human needs and satisfaction at the core of the economy. It believes that the quality of human survival and life is the most fundamental value for social development, emphasizing that human needs are the only standard to measure the value of things. It advocates that economic activities should aim at promoting comprehensive human development and social progress, while emphasizing the equality, mutual benefit, and non-predatory nature of all economic entities. By exploring the relationship between money and economic activities, it strives to maximize the satisfaction of human needs through the "Equal Rights Monetary Theory" and the monetary practices. This "egalitarian economics" advocates that countries, classes, industries, and people should treat each other equally in the market economy, complement each other's advantages, exchange what they need, create wealth through honest labor, and share wealth through free exchange. This book imagines a perfect world without ignorance, deception, oppression, or plunder in the economic field.

This book firmly believes that the power of humanity stems from the revelation of truth, the exploration of reason, and the pursuit of sincerity. The " Equal Rights Monetary Theory " based on rational thinking and idealistic pursuit is certain to form a consensus among humans and benefit human society. The author of this book believes that all the qualities needed to build a perfect world are just common sense and conscience of humanity, and a perfect monetary system is not difficult to achieve.

ACKNOWLEDGMENTS

Writing is a laborious task, especially for a practicing lawyer. Over the past few years, I have devoted all my spare time to conceptualizing, writing, and refining this book. Despite many important matters awaiting my attention, completing this book has always been the most meaningful endeavor to me.

I am grateful to my alma mater, Shanghai Advanced Institute of Finance, where my classmates sparked my interest in currency, and the professors provided me with meticulous teaching and guidance.

I thank my family, my wife, Pu Limin, took on an amount of household chores and cared well for our daughter and son, allowing me to focus on writing. Additionally, my daughter, Zhou Meishan, independently manages her studies, which relieves me of worries, while my son, Zhou Dingyuan, is clever and adorable, bringing me endless joy.

I appreciate the team members at my law firm who professionally and diligently worked to alleviate much of my workload. Also, thanks to those friends who encouraged me; your support provided the motivation to complete this book.

Finally, I would like to express my gratitude to those readers who are currently reading this book. Your wise choice has allowed the value of this book to be transmitted and promoted. Your admiration for this book has benefited more people, made more people look forward to changes in currency, and made a more perfect currency possible.

ABOUT THE AUTHOR

Hailin Zhou graduated from the Shanghai Advanced Institute of Finance at Shanghai Jiao Tong University. He is a practicing lawyer and a senior partner at a law firm in Shanghai, China, focusing on financial cases and research in financial law. He formerly served as a commanding officer in the Chinese Navy, with the rank of Captain and as a department manager in large state-owned commercial banks. Zhou has conducted in-depth research and reflection on finance and law, dedicating himself to promoting a social governance environment that is free, equal, fair, and rational. Welcome to contact him through the following email address: hansenattorney@163.com.

Made in the USA
Thornton, CO
09/28/24 11:22:54

a7ba54a5-0073-46ea-a9fc-2de997fa6e39R01